Archibald John Little

Through the Yang-Tse Gorges

Trade And Travel in Western China. Third Edition

Archibald John Little

Through the Yang-Tse Gorges
Trade And Travel in Western China. Third Edition

ISBN/EAN: 9783744753258

Printed in Europe, USA, Canada, Australia, Japan

Cover: Foto ©Andreas Hilbeck / pixelio.de

More available books at **www.hansebooks.com**

THROUGH
THE YANG-TSE GORGES

Travelling House-boat on Upper Yang-tse, the Author in Chinese Dress standing on accompanying "Red, or Life-saving Boat.

Frontispiece.

THROUGH
THE YANG=TSE GORGES

OR

*TRADE AND TRAVEL IN
WESTERN CHINA*

BY

ARCHIBALD JOHN LITTLE, F.R.G.S.

> "Let me journey down
> On the great river, that from town to town,
> Through meadow miles; 'twixt gorges of the hills,
> Sweeps through the land's whole length, and ever fills
> Its widening channel deeper."
> —Yu-Pe-Ya's Lute.

"Good government obtains, when those who are near are made happy, and those who are far off are attracted."—Confucius, "Lun yu," xlii. 16, 2.

THIRD AND REVISED EDITION, WITH MAP AND
ILLUSTRATIONS

LONDON
SAMPSON LOW, MARSTON & COMPANY
LIMITED
St. Dunstan's House
Fetter Lane, Fleet Stree
1898

Low's Popular Library of Travel and Adventure.

Uniform crown 8vo. volumes, fully Illustrated, bound in cloth,
HALF-A-CROWN *each.*

Ten Years' Captivity in the Mahdi's Camp, 1882-1892. From the Original Manuscripts of Father Joseph Ohrwalder. By Colonel F. R. WINGATE, R.A. Also Limited Edition at 6d., just published.

How I Found Livingstone. Including Four Months' Residence with Dr. Livingstone. By HENRY M. STANLEY.

The Cruise of the 'Falcon.' A Voyage to South America in a Thirty-ton Yacht. By E. F. KNIGHT.

The Great Lone Land. A Record of Travel and Adventure in North and West America. By Gen. Sir W. F. BUTLER, K.C.B.

Men, Mines, and Animals in South Africa. By Lord RANDOLPH CHURCHILL.

The River Congo. From the Mouth to Bólóbó. By H. H. JOHNSTON, C.M.G.

Clear Round! Seeds of Story from other Countries; a Chronicle of Links and Rivets in this World's Girdle. By E. A. GORDON.

The Cruise of H.M.S. 'Challenger.' Scenes in Many Lands, Voyages over Many Seas. By W. J. J. SPRY, R.N., F.R.G.S.

Through Masai Land. A Journey of Exploration among the Snow-clad Volcanic Mountains and Strange Tribes of Eastern Equatorial Africa. By JOSEPH THOMSON.

The Wild North Land. By Gen. Sir WM. F. BUTLER, K.C.B.

Coomassie. The Story of the Campaign in Africa, 1873-74. By H. M. STANLEY, M.P.

Magdala. The Story of the Abyssinian Campaign of 1866-67. By H. M. STANLEY, M.P.

Hausaland. By Rev. C. H. ROBINSON, M.A.

Two Kings of Uganda. By Rev. R. P. ASHE, M.A.

Two Roving Englishmen in Greece. By ISABEL J. ARMSTRONG.

How I Shot My Bears; or, Two Years' Camp Life in Kullu and Lahoul. By Mrs. R. H. TYACKE.

On the Indian Hills: Coffee Planting in Southern India. By EDWIN LESTER ARNOLD.

On Horseback through Asia Minor. By Col. FRED BURNABY.

LONDON:
SAMPSON LOW, MARSTON & COMPANY, LIMITED,
ST. DUNSTAN'S HOUSE, FETTER LANE, E.C.

To

MY WIFE,

THE UNTIRING COMPANION OF MY TRAVELS, TO WHOSE SKILL

WITH THE CAMERA I OWE THE VIEWS OF THE

SCENERY, OFTEN TAKEN AMIDST

GREAT DIFFICULTIES,

I Dedicate this Work.

PREFACE TO THE FIRST EDITION

The following pages comprise little more than a transcript of the journal kept by me during a two months' journey from Shanghai, the metropolis of the coast, to Chung-king, the commercial metropolis of Western China. This journal was written up each night, as I travelled along in the native boat, and was despatched home by successive mail for the amusement of my friends in England. I have been induced to publish it in the belief that impressions formed and recorded day by day on the spot, give a better idea of the actual state of things in China than many of the elaborate and carefully compiled books which attempt a more exhaustive description of the country.

So much interest is now felt at home in the "Flowery Land," and such very erroneous conceptions appear to be entertained in regard to China, her wealth, her strength and prowess, and her value as an ally—qualities of which, in my opinion, only the remote potentiality exists at present—that no apology is needed for presenting a literal picture of the country I traversed.

Preface to the First Edition

With the exception of the ubiquitous missionary, the travellers who have ascended the "Great (and sole) Highway" of China to its highest navigable point may be counted on the fingers of one hand. So tedious are the antiquated modes of travel, that of the thousands of European residents at the treaty ports, few have the leisure or inclination to journey outside of the routes covered by our "barbarian" steamers. Of the voyage to Chung-king, up the Yang-tse river, a distance of 1500 miles, 1000 miles are traversed by steamers to Ichang in a week's time. The remaining 500 miles occupy from five to six weeks, a longer time than it takes to go from London to Shanghai. Since the execution of the celebrated "Chefoo Convention" in 1875, the placing of steamers on this upper route has been under discussion, but Chinese obstructiveness has thus far succeeded in staving off the evil day, and nothing but strong pressure on the part of the foreign ministers accredited to the Court of Pekin will bring about this much-needed innovation, an innovation as much desired by the native merchants and traders as it is dreaded by the official and literary classes. Apart from the laudable fear of injury to the livelihood of the existing junk-men, anything that leads to further contact between foreigners and the people at large is deprecated as lessening the influence of the profoundly ignorant ruling class; and thus, notwithstanding the heavy losses in life and property that the present system of navigation entails, this further contemplated invasion of the inner waters of the Empire is strenuously resisted.

In reading this journal, in which I have depicted the existing difficulties of the route, it must be borne in mind that the Yang-tse is not only the main, but the sole road of intercommunication between the east and west of this vast Empire. Roads, properly so called, do not exist in China; narrow footpaths alone connect one town and village with another, and, except by the waterways, nothing can be transported from place to place but on men's backs. In the far north, it is true, cart-tracks exist, and clumsy two-wheeled springless carts are there in use, but in Central and Southern China, land travel is absolutely confined to paths, so narrow that two pedestrians have often a difficulty in passing each other. Traces of magnificent paved roads, of the ancient dynasties, still exist in nearly every province; but they have been destroyed by neglect, and have been disused for centuries past. Since the date of the Mongol invasion (1279), every incentive to progress has come from without, and every foreign well-wisher of the Empire, especially if resident, is impelled to do his utmost to carry on this progress.

The rulers of China should take to heart Bacon's words: "Since things alter for the worst spontaneously, if they be not altered for the better designedly, what end will there be of evil?" Railways have been long talked of, but so far, the short line, built some years ago, which connects the Government coal-mine of Kai-ping with the nearest canal, is the only road in existence. Trunk-lines running north and south are said to have been authorized, but as long as the Government eschews foreign aid they are not likely to be built. A line running east and west presents almost insuperable difficulties, owing to the precipitous mountains and deep gorges into which the whole country west of Ichang is cut up. Hence the necessity of turning the great natural highway of the Yang-tse to the best advantage. Of the great gain to trade, and to British manufacturing interests more especially, which the cheapness of intercommunication between Eastern and Western China would effect, I have spoken more at length in my twelfth chapter.

I must not conclude without paying a tribute of admiration to Captain Blakiston and Dr. Alfred Barton, for their valuable and accurate work, " Five Months on the Yang-tse." These energetic pioneers preceded me over the same ground just twenty years before. Nothing has altered in the interval, and but for the fact that their want of knowledge of the language debarred them from free intercourse with the people, and so cut them off from many interesting social facts, the publication of this journal would have no *raison d'être*.

ARCHIBALD JOHN LITTLE.

ICHANG, *July* 16*th*, 188-.

PREFACE TO THE THIRD EDITION

NOTWITHSTANDING that ten years have elapsed since the last edition of this book was published, the description of the grand Gorges of the Yang-tse remains as true and as fresh as on the day it was written, and little apology is needed for again bringing the scene before the public eye. The outside trade of Szechuan, estimated roughly at about five millions sterling, is still carried on by a fleet of eight to ten thousand junks, whose crews animate the rocks and precipices of the wild scenery, their shouts re-echoing from cliff to cliff as they toil over the broken ground. But during these ten years much has happened in China. The great unwieldy empire has been rudely shaken by the French war in 1885, and by the Japanese war in 1895, which brought about, the latter especially, a cruel exposure of China's weakness. This weakness was well known to residents on the spot, and should have been better appreciated and prepared for by our leading politicians at home. In the following pages of my Diary, written in 1883, it will be seen that I predicted the collapse that was then imminent, and demonstrated the folly of continuing our attempts to conciliate the corrupt camarilla ruling in Peking, and the worthlessness of China as an ally. It was this yielding to the worst features of Chinese conservatism that frustrated my original attempt to open the Upper Yang-tse to steam. Now, at last, thanks to the determination of the Japanese, and to our own Government's fortunate change of front, since the appointment to Peking of our present energetic Minister, Sir Claude Macdonald, a pioneer steamer has ascended to Chung-king, and the account of the voyage is set forth in the last chapter of the book.

ORIENTAL CLUB, LONDON,
October 7th, 1898.

CONTENTS

CHAPTER I.
INTRODUCTORY.

The Government of the Chinese—Revolutions—Trade—Taxes—Our interests in Szechuan—Imports and exports—Comparative trade of all the provinces 1

CHAPTER II.
SHANGHAI TO ICHANG.

Shanghai to Ichang—Hankow—A Yang-tse boat—Shasze—The plains of Hupeh—A Szechuan river-boat—Flooded districts—Approach to the hills—Ichang 15

CHAPTER III.
ICHANG AND ITS ENVIRONS.

The foreign community—Fishing with otters—"Feng Shui"—The conglomerate country—Cave of the Dragon King—Underground Lake—The "Dome"—Startling *coup-d'œil*—Cloud-mist Mountain—Chinese country house—Unexpected hospitality—Master and servant—Auspicious site—Woodcutters—Steep climb—Chinese "Pahs"—Taoist temple—Magnificent prospect—Ascent of the Golden Peak—Chinese candles—A model hotel bill—Plank bridge—Return to Ichang 37

CHAPTER IV.

ABOVE ICHANG.

Start for the gorges—Grand *coup-d'œil*—Tourist's inscriptions—A factory of boulders—Advantages of a light boat—A temple school—A "Feng Shui" problem 50

CHAPTER V.

IN SZECHUAN.

The Customs at Kwei-chow—Transit passes—Their effect on the provincial officials—The drought—Anthracite at Kwei-chow—Visit to a mandarin—A concert—Management of the junks 87

CHAPTER VI.

ON TO CHUNG-KING.

Iron workers—Census taking—Site of old Chung-chow—A rain-bringing opera—Deforesting of the country—Feng-tu—The temple of the Chinese Pluto—Fu-chow—Chang-chow—First sight of Chung-king 107

CHAPTER VII.

CHUNG-KING.

The weather—Morning calls—Visit to a Chinese country house—A fine road—A tedious meal—Personal uncleanliness—The Tung family—"Feng Shui" again—A tough yarn—An inscription 138

CHAPTER VIII.

CHUNG-KING.

Return to town—Catholic and other missions—Visitors—The China Inland Mission—Native post—A Taoist temple—The priests hard-up—Chinese banks—An ephemeral town—Across the river—The Catholic cathedral—Charming surroundings of the city—Filth within—Dull evenings—Chess—Malt liquor—A public garden—The walls—Slow progress of the missionaries 153

Contents

CHAPTER IX.

CHUNG-KING.

Ponies—Silk weaving—Prehistoric caves—A fine country-house—A Catholic chapel—A Buddhist oracle—The coal-workings—Cost of getting and transporting coal—An eviction scrimmage—Ventilation—A huge coalfield—A farmhouse—Opium-smoking—Agile ponies—Return by boat—Fine scenery—Legends—The river rising—Trade guilds—Another country-house—Civility of the Chung-kingese—The women's feet—The Manchus—A pseudo-European dinner 176

CHAPTER X.

THE DOWNWARD VOYAGE.

Adieux—A crowded boat—Change to a salt-junk—A strange manœuvre—A day on the rocks—Sham tea—Equipage of the junk—The gorges once more—Mooring for the night—Delays—Change to a wupan—Pirates—Fêng Tu . . 213

CHAPTER XI.

HANKOW.

Return to Ichang—Hankow—Changes in the river—Lifeboats—Accidents—The "awakening" of China—Pliny on the Chinese 242

CHAPTER XII.

THE PHYSIOGRAPHY OF THE YANG-TSE VALLEY.

ength and fall—Advance of the delta—Direction of river's course—The gorges and rapids—Absence of roads—Coalfields—The flora and fauna—Mineral wealth . . . 253

CHAPTER XIII.

THE NEW "GLORIOUS" RAPID.

The great landslide—Earthquake phenomena—Steps taken to modify the rapid—Need of Admiralty survey . . . 272

CHAPTER XIV.

FIRST ASCENT BY STEAM.

Feasibility of steam navigation in Szechuan—Account of the first ascent of the Yang-tse rapids by steam in 1898—Remarks . 283

APPENDIX.

Address of Welcome from the "Foreign" Residents in Chung-king. 301

Index 303

LIST OF ILLUSTRATIONS

TO FACE PAGE

Travelling House-boat on Upper Yang-tse, the Author in Chinese Dress standing on accompanying " Red," or Life-saving Boat . . . . . (*Frontispiece*)

Buddhist Temple on Summit of Conglomerate Pinnacle 1200 Feet high : on Yang-tse River near Ichang (p. 34)   36

Junks in Ichang, with Masts erected preparatory to starting up Stream (p. 38) 36

View of "The Pyramid," on Opposite Bank, taken from the Promenade on Top of Ichang City Wall. This Natural Pyramid of Sandstone, rising 500 Feet above the River, is almost identical in Size and Shape with the Pyramid of Cheops in Egypt (p. 40) . . . 46

Ferry opposite Ichang City at Mouth of Small River : Sandstone Cliff (p. 50) 46

House-boat in Ichang Gorge ; Dangerous Rock, "the Sleeping Pig" (covered in Summer), in Middle Distance 52

"Pillar of Heaven" in Ichang Gorge ; Limestone Pinnacle rising 1800 Feet above River 54

One of our Crew on Tow-path near Niu-kan Gorge . . 58

Junks waiting their Turn to ascend New Rapid. In Summer Freshets, River rises to Foot of Houses on Right. Shin t'an 62

List of Illustrations

	TO FACE PAGE
Home of Retired "Armateur" at Shin t'an, Mouth of Pingshu Gorge	64
Seven-storied Pagoda below Patung. Note Fluted Rock, about 50 Feet High, on Right Hand, being Ancient "Pot-holes" in the Limestone worn through by the Current	70
Our House-boat, with Cliff, in Wushan Gorge	72
Travelling House-boat, with Tender, moored in Wushan Gorge: Nude Figure in Foreground, Man who swims out to disengage the Tow-lines: Tender is steered by Long Stern-sweep: House-boat with Long Bow-sweep	78
Entrance to Bellows Gorge; Cliffs 3000 and 4000 Feet. In the cliff on the right are cut the Square Holes of Mêng-liang's Ladder	82
Kwei-chow Fu, Five Miles from Upper Entrance to Gorges; Entrance shown in Split Hill on Left, Height 3000 to 4000 Feet	88
Trackers hauling on Bamboo Tow-lines at Entrance to Ping-shu Gorge	94
Chang-fei's Temple, opposite Yünyang, Winter Level. In Summer, Foreground covered to a Depth of 50 Feet.	98
"Full Moon" Pavilion in Garden of Temple dedicated to Changfei, Hero of the Wars of the Three Kingdoms (A.D. 200), opposite City of Yünyang: Wall and Pillars Stone, Roofs Thatch (p. 100)	120
Five-storied Pagoda at Fêng-tu (p. 120)	120
Szechuan Poppy-field in Bloom, in Month of April	118
Free School in Szechuan: Characters "I Shuŏ" (Free Teaching) over Door	130
Cargo-boat rowing down Stream (p. 135)	138

List of Illustrations

TO FACE PAGE

Entrance Gate of Temple outside Walls of Chung-king City; the Chinese Characters are, "Cave of Genii and Spirits" (p. 139)	138
Green and Yellow Tiled Roof of Pavilion (p. 106) . .	158
Graves on Range of Hills opposite Chung-king: the two "Characters" cut in the Limestone indicate that this Mountain is a Reproduction of the Sacred "Mount T'u" in Shantung Province (p. 158)	158
Roof Corner, Guildhall, Chung-king (p. 164) . . .	164
Dinner-party in Chung-king: Guests facing Theatrical Performance; Intervening Courtyard, or "Pit" filled with freely admitted Audience from the Street (p. 200)	164
Hoangko Shu, and *Ficus infectoria* with Shrine as usual round Roots, and my Stallion from Province Kwei-chow, with whom I travelled 1500 Miles . . .	176
Stage Court in Hukwang Guildhall, Chung-king . .	202
Garden in Country-seat of the Yuen Family, outside Chung-king	206
Salt Junk, about 70 Tons, with Screw-oars or "Yuloes" alongside, moored near Entrance to Ichang Gorge: bound down River, Mast lashed alongside . . .	222
Trackers hauling Junk up the Shin t'an, or New Rapid .	238
City of Chung-king, built on Rocky Peninsula at Junction of Kia-ling River, from the North and Yang-tse; View taken from South Bank of Yang-tse	252
Pavilion in Garden of "White Emperor's City," on Cliff at Mouth of Bellows Gorge	282
"We were the First," etc.	288

THE
BRITISH SPHERE OF INFLUENCE

THE British sphere of influence or interest, as it has been indifferently described by our Ministers in Parliament, is defined in the despatch of Sir Claude Macdonald to the Tsung-li-Yamên of the 19th February of this year (1898), as "the Yang-tse region" and the "provinces adjoining the Yang-tse." A more exact definition, and one that we have attempted to embody in the map attached to this work, is the "Yang-tse Basin": the boundaries of this region are naturally and indisputably defined by the crests of the water partings that surround the catchment area; or, in plain English, the area of our so-called sphere comprises the valley of the Yang-tse and the valleys of its tributaries. It is to China what the valley of the Mississippi is to North America, Shanghai's situation at the mouth of the Yang-tse being analogous to that of New Orleans on the Mississippi; and what the valley of the Amazon is to the South American continent, the total area of which is a little greater than that of the Chinese Empire. In each case it is the heart of a continent as represented by the valley of its greatest river. In the case of China, this heart comprises an area of 600,000 square miles, inhabited by about 180,000,000 of the most industrious and peaceable people on the world's surface. It opens out a magnificent prospect for British enterprise, while leaving vast regions in the wide Chinese Empire open to other Powers, should the unfortunate alternative of partition of spheres take the place of equal opportunities for all everywhere, in which case we must accept the Yang-tse basin as a *pis-aller* and lose no more time in securing the region allotted as our sphere by effective occupation.

xxii The British Sphere of Influence

The watershed or catchment area of the Yang-tse basin comprises, outside the Tibetan plateau, the six large provinces of Szechuan, Hupeh, Hunan, Kiangsi, Nganhui and Kiangsu, part of Chekiang, the greater part of Honan, besides the northern drainage area of the provinces of Yunnan and Kweichow; a large order certainly, but in no way incommensurate with our present share in the foreign trade of the Empire. Of this trade British imports and exports amount to fully two-thirds of the whole, while the area in question barely covers two-fifths of China proper, entirely excluding the vast and potentially rich regions of Manchuria, Mongolia, Turkestan and Tibet, all which are still in name subject to the "Son of Heaven." This region, forming the British sphere, extends roughly between the twenty-eighth and thirty-second parallels of north latitude, and between the ninety-eighth and one hundred and eighteenth meridians of east longitude. South of this wide sphere we find the five rich provinces of Fuhkien, Kwangtung, Kwangsi, Kweichow and Yunnan; the last three generally acknowledged as the French sphere, together with the former Chinese dependencies of Annam and Tongking, now definitely annexed to France. Coterminous with our sphere on the north, the boundary line being the crests of the mountain ranges that divide the two basins, lies the great valley-plain (Tiefebene) of the Yellow River, the ancient home of the Chinese race and southern boundary of China until about the beginning of the Christian era.

This Yellow River basin comprises the provinces of Kansu, Shensi, Shansi, Shantung, and the Metropolitan province of Chihli—all provinces with a rich soil and prosperous population, said to be immeasurably rich in minerals. Their climate is temperate, and hence wheat and millet take the place of the rice-fields, the sugar, opium, and cotton of the South. The climate of North China is generally considered one of the finest in the world, and hence, if a partition is to be made, I would gladly take it in exchange for the somewhat more productive but undoubtedly malarious valley of the Yang-tse. To the north of these, again, we have the vast territories of Manchuria and Mongolia—both regions originally pastoral, now invaded by the agricultural settlements of immigrants from China proper. Manchuria is rich in gold, and has a hardy population of some twenty millions; this province, the cradle of the reigning dynasty, has now been overrun by Russia, and the latest telegrams announce the forcible seizure of Newchwang, its one Treaty Port, by the Russians.

In an article in the last September number of the *Contemporary Review* I figured out the present inter-port trade on the Yang-tse River at £30,000,000, and added my opinion that, given a stable and progressive Government, affording encouragement to capitalists, with security for their investments—resulting in improved means of communication and a corresponding development of its natural resources—the Yang-tse valley will increase its trade by leaps and bounds, and the £30,000,000 of to-day will be £300,000,000 to-morrow. I added the grounds upon which I based my expectation of this rapid increase, and wound up by asking, What is our Government going to do in regard to our so-called sphere?

To this question it appears to me that capitalists in this country, and British merchants in China, have a right to demand a definite answer. We were told that the "open door" policy would be upheld even at the cost of war. These were brave words, as spoken by Sir Michael Hicks-Beach in his celebrated Bristol speech, and met a hearty response from Britons on the spot. They have unfortunately not been upheld: if they had been there would have been no war. As things now are, Russia has cancelled a British lien on the railway connecting the Treaty Port of Newchwang with the existing Tientsin line; Germany has warned us off Shantung; France puts a transit duty of ten per cent. on British goods from Hong Kong for the 200 miles distance by the Red River of Tongking to Laokai, on the Yunnan border; at the same time she has compelled the wretched Chinese Government to admit goods over her border for two-thirds of the five per cent. duty collected by the Maritime Customs at the other Chinese ports. This is one instance of many how the object of France and Russia is to steal a revenue from our trade with China rather than the promotion of trade itself. Our ports and the Chinese Treaty Ports are free to all. Our rivals will not grant this reciprocity. Hence, if our Government does not wake up and take hold of the subject seriously, and make the occupation of our sphere effective while there is yet time to do so, we shall learn some fine morning that our rivals have arranged Chinese affairs to suit their own interests exclusively. Then with preferential transit and other tariffs directed against us, we shall have handed over the solid work of three generations of Britons in China to our unscrupulous rivals; or else at last the British people will be aroused, and the Government, *nolens volens*, driven to fight for our tradal existence in the Far East; and this is the course to which we seem helplessly drifting. Two years ago by a firm stand we might have prevented the partition of the venerable Empire whose weakness we have done so much to expose. It is a sad alternative, but to-day there is no other left us but to take our share in the partition now going on, and this no more in our own interest than in that of the people of China.

ORIENTAL CLUB, LONDON,
 October, 1898.

THROUGH THE YANG-TSE GORGES

CHAPTER I.

INTRODUCTORY.

The government of the Chinese—Revolutions—Trade—Taxes—Our interests in Szechuan—Imports and exports—Comparative trade of all the provinces.

THE history of our intercourse with China, from the days of the East India Company until now, is nothing but the record of a continuous struggle to open up and develop trade, with a people who, from the days of Pliny, "ipsis feris persimiles, cœtus reliquorum mortalium fugiunt." There is something pathetic in the honest persistency with which the people and their officials have vainly struggled to keep themselves uncontaminated from the outer world, and it is impossible for any disinterested onlooker not to sympathize heartily with them. An enormous population has here solved, imperfectly, of course, but to a comparatively successful degree, the problem of the greatest happiness of the greatest number. The venality of the officials notwithstanding, the people are, if not well governed, certainly not misgoverned; riches are fairly distributed, and the contrast of grinding poverty with arrogant wealth, the rule in Europe, is the exception here. Taxation is nominal, and such is the innate and universal love of order, that the reserve of force behind the decrees of the magistrate is limited to a few hundred men in a province as large as an European kingdom. Competent investigators compute the total cost of the central and local governments at not more than £40,000,000 a year, say two shillings per head for the whole population. Education is universal and voluntary.

No wonder that such results, due to the universal acceptance of the Confucian Ethics, should make the people look askance at innovations coming from the West, where, as the Chinese say, notwithstanding their marked superiority in applied mechanics, nations live in a permanent condition of armed peace, the monotonous pressure of which is only relieved by the still worse calamity of frequent wars, with their attendant burdens of debt and pauperism.

Revolutions occur at long intervals in China, but the normal state of the Empire is peace. Thus since the last change of dynasty (A.D. 1644), the Chinese have enjoyed the blessings of peace and prosperity uninterruptedly, with the exception of the petty wars of this century with ourselves and the French. Even the terrible Taiping rebellion (1848 to 1864) must be attributed to the unwanted presence of the "foreigner" in the inner land. It was the aggressive zeal of American missionaries in Canton fifty years ago which resulted in the conversion of the fanatical leader, Hung-hsiu-chuen, often cited as the most genuine although misguided convert to Christianity, which the Empire has produced, and who modelled his action on that of the Jewish leaders, his war-cry being "*Sha yao!*" "Slay the idolaters!" And slay he did; it is calculated that over twenty millions of people perished by the swords of the Taipings and the attendant famines. It was the Thirty Years' War over again, re-enacted on another stage. Had it succeeded, China would undoubtedly have been Christian, though possibly differing from us in form. The cruelties practised by the Taipings in their progress alienated public opinion from their cause, and hence we joined our quondam enemies, the Manchus, in suppressing the rebellion, lent Gordon to the Imperialists to train and lead the "Ever-victorious Army" of six thousand disciplined men, and restored Confucianism and countenanced a conservative reaction which, after thirty years' undisputed sway, has now brought the mighty Empire once more to a crisis of dissolution. We have allowed the Chinese mandarins to persist in their *outré* conservatism which will have none of the evil thing called Progress. Instead of actively promoting reforms and innovations, in the way that Sir Harry Parkes, in Tokio, backed up young Japan, even at the cost of civil war, our Government has in China yielded to the corrupt Court at Peking, and, until quite recently, discouraged British enterprise with the pitiful result we see to-day—China ruined by her defeat at the hands of the Japanese, and the resulting exorbitant indemnity; and our trade generally stationary, and in part unfairly excluded from those outlying districts of the Empire already seized by our European rivals.

For, viewing the enormous population, now again estimated at over 400,000,000, the richness of the soil, the genial climate, the inexhaustible mineral wealth, and, above all, the untiring industry of the people, the trade at present carried on is not a tithe of that which we should naturally look for. In the number of Great Britain's foreign customers China proper takes seventeenth rank, being just on a par with Scandinavia. Our exports to the Celestial Empire are not one-fourth of those to the United States, with a population of 60,000,000; just one-sixth of our exports to British India, and not one-tenth of that to our Australian and other Colonies, all, except India, countries fenced in with hostile tariffs ranging from thirty to sixty per cent., while with China, according to treaty, our imports have only to withstand a nominal burden of five per cent. If we include Hong-kong, which is a depôt for many of the surrounding countries as well, we bring up the total figures of British imports to China to £9,000,000, or about one-half of our total exports to the thinly-populated South-American Continent. The great drawbacks, which prevent our trade with China attaining to dimensions on a par with the wealth, civilization, and numbers of its people, are the rudimentary condition of its roads, the discouragement of mining, and the vexatious multiplicity of the inland tax-stations.

These obstacles present themselves in the order named, the first of all being the difficulty of inter-communication. By the compulsory opening to steamers of the Great River as far as Hankow, 600 miles only, the trade of Shanghai was quickly quadrupled. Later on 400 miles additional, up to Ichang, situated at the foot of the first rapid, were reluctantly conceded as part of the indemnity for the murder of Margary in Yunnan, and another great bound took place. But in Ichang we have only a poor mountain town, which derives its importance from being the transhipping point for the rich province of Szechuan, lying in the far west above and beyond the rapids. To reach this, the native merchants have to run the gauntlet of the rapids in frail native craft; the still worse gauntlet of a string of Custom-houses has been partially removed by the opening of Chung-king as a treaty port, but goods are still delayed two or three days for examination at Kwei-kwan. The opening of Chung-king, the commercial metropolis of Szechuan, as a treaty port, should in time, in the words of a late Consular Resident there, create another Shanghai in Western China; such are the ascertained riches of the Great West, of which Chung-king is the key. But Chung-king is nothing without steam communication; now at last, after over twenty years, wrangling with Chinese officialdom, this is about to be established. The difficulty lay with the provincial authorities, whose interests were menaced by the change; but a vigorous minister had only to press the matter home sufficiently upon the Central Government at Pekin, for them to give way, and in their turn plead *force majeure* to the provincials, who then, as in so many other previous instances, promptly, though sulkily acquiesced. The mandarins pleaded for delay, on the ground of the junkmen who would be thrown out of work; but this argument, though good in itself, is dispelled by the experience of other ports opened to steam, where the trade on the subsidiary channels of communication has been so stimulated that more natives are employed in the carrying trade than ever before. Another argument gravely adduced in an official despatch to Sir John Walsham was, that the monkeys in the Gorges would throw down rocks on the passing steamers, and that then the poor Chinese Government would be held responsible!

But in bringing about a radical change like that of steam communication, and at the same time to promote the prosperity of all classes, including those whose vested interests are threatened, what is wanted is permission to the people to avail themselves freely of their almost untouched mineral wealth. It is the studious discouragement of mining enterprise on the part of the authorities that forms the second of the three obstacles to increased trade, which I have just enumerated. It is nothing less than a scandal, that at Ichang, 1000 miles inland, steamers should be driven to burn imported Japanese coal, when Ichang, as Richthofen points out, is situated on the borders of one of the richest coal-fields in the world. The vast carboniferous deposits that underlie the Red Basin of Szechuan, and the outcroppings of which in the gorges of the Yang-tse and its affluents, arrest the attention of all travellers in that region remain a sealed book. When these mines are allowed to be worked by Western appliances, and the coal, the iron, the precious metals, and the petroleum-springs are properly developed, not only will there be such a trade, that junks and steamers together will hardly be able to carry it all; even if the junks be displaced *in toto*, the few thousand trackers thrown out of employment will not suffice to supply one-tenth of the labour required; and in lieu of the miserable pittance they now receive for their arduous and dangerous labours, they will then earn sufficient wages to enable them to live in comparative comfort.

The Chinese Government has a traditional mistrust of all enterprises carried out upon private initiative. There is one steamer company in China, the "China Merchants' Steam Navigation Company," and one coal-mining company, that of Kaiping, to the north of Tientsin, whose operations are large and successful, but they are both worked under Government auspices, the managers being high mandarins, although both employ a large number of European assistants. The capital of both companies is largely recruited from the trading classes, and these non-official shareholders have no voice in the management. So great is the mistrust engendered by the official management of mercantile enterprises, that the trading class, so far, have utterly failed to respond to the recent Government appeals for capital for the proposed railway loans, and it is now clear that the authorities will fail in their endeavour to construct railroads, independently of the foreign aid which has been so lavishly tendered to them by the agents of competing European syndicates.

However, the fact remains, and has to be counted with, that the high Chinese officials are hostile to all trading enterprises in the country, which they do not themselves inaugurate and control. If they ultimately succeed in constructing railroads, and working mines on their own system, employing a few foreigners in subordinate positions only, the expected field for foreign enterprise in China will be materially reduced, and the process of centralization which has been steadily going on of late years will lead to an organic change in the government of the Empire, the result of which it is impossible to foresee. If no disturbing revolution intervene, the prosperity of the people must slowly increase as the latent resources of the country, and consequently their consuming powers, are developed. A few figures, extracted from the foreign Customs return, will show what the present consumption is, how stationary our imports remain, and especially how trifling is now the import of European goods into Western China.

The following table shows the annual value of the foreign trade of all China; the tax upon which, levied by the Imperial Maritime Customs, amounted in 1886 to 15,000,000 Haikwan taels (or, at 5s. per tael, £3,750,000), and in 1897 to 22,742,000 Haikwan taels (or, taking the rate of exchange at 2s. 9d. per tael, £3,032,000). This is exclusive of the internal taxation, which may be estimated at fully as much again.

	1879.	1886.	1897. (Exchange fallen to 2s. 9d. per tael.)
Imports from all countries	£20,557,000	£21,870,000	£25,500,000
Exports to all countries	18,070,000	19,300,000	25,000,000
	£38,627,000	£41,170,000	£50,500,000
	1879.	1886.	1897.
Imports from Great Britain	£5,083,000	£5,508,000	£5,735,000
Exports to Great Britain	6,531,000	4,936,000	1,726,000
	£11,614,000	£10,444,000	£7,461,000

These figures are only approximate. A large portion of the trade with Great Britain passes through Hong-kong, but in the imports thence into China proper the country of origin cannot be distinguished. The apparent falling off in values is due to the fall in silver—nearly fifty per cent.; if quantities be taken, then our export trade to China would show a steady and substantial increase, athough not proportional to that of rival nations. The import trade of Great Britain from China is affected by the decline in the use of Chinese tea, and by the fact that London no longer, as formerly, forms a depôt for Continental Europe.

The following is a complete list of the exports from

Articles.		1897.		1896.	
		Quantity.	Value.	Quantity.	Value.
			£		£
Bristles	Lbs.	823,866	18,611	766,933	21,516
Feathers, duck and fowl	,,	422,800	2,468	367,467	2,306
Fungus	,,	538,266	15,202	502,667	15,764
Hemp	,,	1,805,533	15,445	1,726,133	15,104
Hides, cow and buffalo	,,	284,933	3,226	485,867	5,763
Medicines	Value	...	95,008	...	84,650
Musk	Lbs.	4,383	92,126	4,457	89,707
Lead	,,	2,095,333	11,180	...	...
Nutgalls	,,	1,805,533	31,560	632,667	11,071
Opium—					
Ssŭ-ch'uan	,,	1,252,266	327,153	936,667	234,155
Yünnan	,,	172,533	54,093	138,267	41,507
Dross	,,	22,000	2,707	14,533	2,145
Rhubarb	,,	889,733	17,123	600,533	11,261
Safflower	,,	50,266	2,743	51,867	2,996
Silk, raw—					
Yellow	,,	607,800	155,272	436,133	102,503
White	,,	17,066	4,629	...	...
Wild	,,	124,133	12,205	75,733	7,494
Cocoons	,,	5,433	225	37,067	1,666
,, wild	,,	10,023	192	41,067	1,526
Refuse	,,	77,300	2,311	106,667	3,601
Cocoons, refuse	,,	703,663	20,742	1,033,067	32,314
Spelter	,,	217,721	1,451	...	...
Sugar, brown	,,	86,266	307	1,275,600	4,784
Wax, white	,,	1,300,800	126,515	1,279,333	133,216
Wool, sheep's	,,	3,159,466	27,576	2,930,267	24,175
Other exports	Value	...	27,757	...	23,453
Total		...	1,069,017	...	870,538

The Trade of Szechuan

Chung-king in the year 1897, viz. of those that paid duty at the Imperial Maritime Customs, compared with those of the previous year: Chung-king being the commercial metropolis of West China, to which the Yang-tse Gorges form the approach.

The above figures provide a fair *résumé* of the trade of Szechuan as it stands to-day, but they are incomplete, as it is optional to the Chinese merchant to pass his goods either through the "foreign" or through the native Customs; he, of course, selects the cheaper "squeeze" of the two, according to the quality and destination of his shipment. When the day comes in which all merchandise will be carried by steam, then all will come under the control of the Maritime Customs; but it is to be hoped that in that good time the folly of multiplying Custom-houses all over the interior country will be so universally apparent as to have led to their abolition at the inland ports. Increased "Maritime" dues at the coast ports might be conceded as an equivalent, and the vexatious delays and restrictions of the present mediæval system of collecting the necessary revenue be removed.

Chung-king was formally opened to foreign trade in 1890, and, during the seven years since elapsed, the Imperial Maritime Customs' receipts have advanced in a way most satisfactory to the Central, although less so to the Provincial, Government. The figures for 1897 were as under:—

Total customs revenue at thirty-two treaty ports. Haikwan taels 22,742,000.	Customs revenue on Szechuan trade collected at Chung-king and Ichang. Haikwan taels 813,000.	Proportion of Szechuan collections to whole of China, 3·6 per cent.
Import of cotton piece goods into whole of China: 15,156,074 pieces = £5,723,000.	Import of cotton piece goods into Chung-king: 582,679 pieces = £241,916.	Proportion of Szechuan import, 3·8 per cent.

Import of cotton yarn into whole of China (chiefly Indian): 523,000 bales = £5,230,000.	Import of cotton yarn into Chung-king (chiefly Indian): 56,878 bales = £568,780.	10·87 per cent.
Woollen piece goods imported into all China: 443,894 pieces = £665,841.	Woollen piece goods imported into Chung-king: 27,558 pieces = £41,382.	6·2 per cent.

In 1886 the import of foreign piece goods which passed the Imperial Maritime Customs at that port for transhipment by junk to Chung-king was—(exchange at that date five shillings per Haikwan tael):

Cotton piece goods, value £158,000. Woollen piece goods, £110,000.

Thus the opening of Chung-king as a treaty port has doubled the *quantity* of cotton piece goods imported. Woollens have fallen off, the cheaper wadded clothes, of silk with cotton-wool lining, taking their place. Yarn was imported only in small quantities, paying likin, thirteen years ago.

Of exports from Western China not shown in the above figures, salt from the brine-wells in Szechuan is the principal, to the amount of several thousand tons annually, which further increases the excess in exports. As it is probable that in the long-run the trade balances itself, I presume the balance is effected by the import of yarns and shirtings produced by the Hankow cotton mills, owned by the Viceroy of Hukwang, which do not pass through the "foreign" Customs, by the import of native hand-woven cotton cloths from Shaze in Hupeh and by the import of raw cotton from the same province. Heavy junk-loads of this staple are despatched day after day from Hankow, after the conclusion of the cotton harvest in November, in junks direct to Chung-king, which escape all notice by the foreign Customs.

A peculiar feature in the economy of Western China, and one of great promise to manufacturing interests, once the disabilities that now hamper all intercourse are lightened, is the fact that the country is unsuited to the cultivation of cotton. Hence, with the exception of silk, which is abundantly worn by all classes, the clothing of these vast districts has all to be imported. Yunnan is scantily supplied from Burmah, Kweichow from the two Kwang provinces, and Szechuan from Hupeh (Hankow) and Kiang-su (Shanghai). Raw cotton, as packed by the Chinese, is an exceedingly bulky article; but it is light, easy to handle, and less liable to total loss in the rapids than are heavy bale goods. What the figures of this cotton import attain to, it is impossible to ascertain; but every traveller on the Upper Yang-tse in the winter season is struck by the endless procession of cotton-laden junks struggling up the successive rapids.

It is interesting to compare the proportion of foreign piece goods consumed west of Ichang, with the total import into Shanghai, and also with the relative populations served. Mr. Popoff, late Secretary of the Russian Legation at Peking, has published an estimate of the population of China, based on the recent provincial censuses, which are believed to be fairly accurate, and which I here reproduce.

PROVINCES SUPPLIED FROM SHANGHAI.

	Pop.
1. Eastern and Central:—	
Chili	17,937,000
Shantung	36,546,000
Shansi	10,791,000
Shensi	8,432,000
Kansu	5,411,000

Honan	...	...	...	22,117,000	
Hupeh	...	...	...	33,600,000	
Hunan	...	...	...	21,005,000	
Kiangsi	...	...	...	24,541,000	
Ganhui	...	...	...	20,597,000	
Chekiang	...	...	...	11,685,000	
Kiangsu	...	...	...	21,260,000	
					233,922,000
2. Western :—					
Szechuan	...	...	...	71,074,000	
Yunnan	...	...	...	11,721,000	
Kweichow	...	...	...	7,609,000	
					90,464,000
Leaving (Provinces supplied from Hong-kong) :—					
Kwangtung	...	...	...	29,740,000	
Kwangsi	...	...	...	5,121,000	
Fukien	...	...	...	25,800,000	
					60,661,000
Total population of the eighteen provinces ...					385,047,000

This calculation, which may be taken as approximately correct, shows that thirty per cent. of the population of China, and that the richest and the most in want of foreign piece goods, absorb barely five per cent. of the total imports.

We now come to the third obstacle to the actual increase in our trade, viz. the multiplicity of inland tax stations.

Up to Chung-king, 1500 miles from Shanghai, and the highest treaty port open on the Yang-tse river, the one import duty clears the goods without further charge. Thence onwards to the great consuming districts in the interior of the province, and in the two large neighbouring provinces of Yunnan and Kweichow, and in Tibet, dozens of likin-stations line all the main roads, both by land and water, and have to be visited.

It is true that, under the transit-pass system, an additional payment amounting to half the import duty clears the goods from further tax; but the repeated stoppages of the junks and the vexatious examination of the goods (mitigated to some extent by ample douceurs to the examining officers) have to be endured. One article in demand by the native photographers, who are found in all the chief towns of Szechuan, viz. "dry plates," has been so repeatedly ruined by these examinations, that they are now all smuggled through at a heavy cost. As the real remedy— the total abolition of all inland taxation—although quite practical with good management, is not likely to be applied, the only plan for the present is for "foreigners" to follow their goods in person, and lodge complaints with their Consuls for undue detention until the inland officials give up the harassing of transit-pass goods as a game no longer worth the candle.

To sum up :—In the preceding pages I have endeavoured to show that our trade with China, and especially with the West, is not one-tenth of what, seeing (1) the size of the field, (2) the immense natural resources of the country, (3) the industry of the people, it ought, under proper conditions, to be. The absence of such proper conditions I have shown to be not irremediable, but due to the following artificial obstacles, viz :—

I. The rudimentary condition of communications.

II. The discouragement of mining and other enterprises, which might afford employment to the population, displaced by the introduction of improved methods.

III. The multiplicity of inland tax-stations.

It is to the interest of all concerned in the improvement of our trade, and the prosperity of our manufactures, to do their utmost to bring about an alleviation of these conditions. Trade in China cannot be left to take care of itself as in Western countries. However invidious it may seem, we must admit the fact that past progress has been due to pressure, and that this pressure must be kept up. Our Chambers of Commerce should enlighten and rouse the public, and induce our Government to imitate the Russians in establishing a special ministry for East-Asian affairs, whose duty it should be to watch British interests in the Far East, from Siam to China and Japan, and take care that our rights and privileges are encroached upon neither by the natives themselves, nor by our European rivals in these countries. Our Foreign Office, too much engaged in other quarters, has, of late years, notoriously failed to pay due attention to the Far East; hence the crying need of a special "Far East" department.

The Chinese officials *can* be urged, and should be made, loyally to carry out the obligations to promote trade, which are implied in our various treaties, and the Central Government should be assured of our moral and material support in resisting the preferential demands of our European rivals;[*] but to do this requires an energy that will persevere in the face of the disheartening effects of perpetual procrastination, an art in which the Chinese are admittedly Past Masters—without impatience and without rest—"ohne Hast, ohne Rast."

[*] It does not appear to be generally known that France and Russia have forced the Chinese Government to admit goods from their respective frontiers upon payment of two-thirds only of the treaty tariff, thus handicapping British goods, ocean borne, which have to pay the full duty.

CHAPTER II.

SHANGHAI TO ICHANG.

Shanghai to Ichang—Hankow—A Yang-tse boat—Shasze—The plains of Hupeh—A Szechuan river-boat—Flooded districts—Approach to the Hills—Ichang.

FROM Shanghai to Hankow the voyage is performed by one of the many magnificent steamers of American type which, since the opening of the Yang-tse river to foreign trade in 1860, ply daily between those two ports, a distance of 600 miles. It was on the eve of the Chinese New Year, in the middle of February, when at midnight I rode down in a jinricshaw to Jardine's wharf, and took up my quarters on board the *Tai-Wo* moored alongside, preparatory to starting up-stream the following morning at daylight. But sleep was no easy matter; thousands of fire-crackers were being let off in the streets, alive with countless Chinese lanterns, and the din was deafening. Native passengers were crowding on board, and the coolies carrying their luggage were wrangling over their pay. I at length got to sleep in the early hours of the morning, and woke up to find that we were in the sea of muddy water which forms the lower reaches of the Great River. A thin line of brown, a shade deeper than that of the water, barely visible on the starboard hand, indicated the left bank, while in the opposite direction the muddy waste extended to the horizon. Not a stray junk moving enlivened the desolate prospect; all were in port, keeping the New Year's holidays, and a dull leaden sky completed the gloom of the chill February morning.

Little of interest occurred on the voyage up as we steamed on through four days and nights, picking up and setting down the rare passengers moving at this festal time. We spent an hour upon a sandbank above Kiukiang, ploughing up the muddy bottom in our endeavours to get afloat again. Off Nganking, the capital city of the province of Nganhui, we had the misfortune to collide with a crockery-laden junk, the captain of which quickly ran his vessel ashore, and so saved her from sinking. She was one of the few junks that set sail in the early days of the New Year in order to take advantage of the holidays, during which the Likin or tax stations are closed, and so the junks pass free. Our worthy skipper anchored at once, and put off in a boat to ascertain the extent of the damage. The bales of blue and white rice-bowls of which the cargo consisted, were quickly un-laden and placed on the bank, the hole was patched up and the cargo restored, and the junk taken in tow to Kiukiang, her owner's home. Here the damage was appraised and paid for, and the incident ended. But I could not avoid being impressed with the practical method adopted by the Chinese in the construction of their flimsy-looking junks—in building the hull in compartments, a consequence of which is that, although accidents on the river are frequent, a total loss rarely occurs.

The winter sun, always warm in these latitudes, was shining brightly as we moored alongside the great quay, or "Bund," which extends along the river-front of the British settlement at Hankow. As at Shanghai, a roadway, lined with trees, some eighty yards wide, separates the palatial residences of the merchants from the steep river-shore, which is faced by a magnificent stone embankment. Unlike Shanghai, however, except during the short tea season in early summer, no carriages and but a few pedestrians are seen, and the concession has the lifeless depressing aspect of a seaside watering-place in the off season. The busy crowded quarter in which the Chinese live is entirely cut off from the concession, and the Chinese only resort thither when they have actual business to transact with the few residents who remain in Hankow throughout the winter. After landing from the steamer and ascending the long and wide stone stairs that lead up from the river, I traversed the deserted bund, and making my way to the dirty crowded Chinese city, set about making the necessary preparations for my four months' voyage into the interior. At length, on Saturday, the 24th February, everything was ready for the start, and from this time on, my daily journal, written up each night on the road, tells exactly what I saw, and will not fail, I trust, to convey to the reader, beyond a description of the country traversed, some hitherto undescribed phases of the interesting stationary civilization with which I came in contact.

Sunday, February 25th.—Two boats having been engaged, and all my things sent on board, I hoped, after the endless delays and postponements which had kept me now a week in Hankow, that dinner-time would see me well under way on the mysterious river. To my disgust, my companion, a Shansi merchant, was not forthcoming at the appointed time, but later in the day informed me we should positively start on the following day at ten o'clock. I availed myself of the hospitality of my kind friend, the manager of the Hong-kong and Shanghai Bank, for another night, and on Monday Mr. Chang duly appeared, and we set off together in a sampan from the steps of the bund, a descent of fifty feet from the river's summer level, to join the boats which were to convey us to Shasze, the port at which we are to exchange into the larger boat which takes us up the rapids. The native passenger boats, which ply to Shasze and elsewhere, were moored some distance up the Han river, an affluent which falls into the Yang-tse on its left or western bank, about a mile above the concession limits. Here, after rowing up against the stream past endless tiers of up-country junks, we at length found our boat, which was destined to be my residence during the next fourteen days. This boat had been engaged nearly a week before, but nothing would induce the owner to bring her down-stream, and let me embark in comfort off my host's door. The real reason of his refusal I found to be that each line of boats has its special mooring-ground. The Han river, here about 200 yards wide, and running with a very deep rapid current, was jammed with thousands of junks, large and small, waiting for business. I now thought we were at last off; not at all, my companion had still some business to transact, and the cook was still ashore. I let him go, and waited patiently in the confined cabin six long hours, when, finding it would be impossible to make a start that night, I took a sampan across to the Hanyang shore, and, despite the frightful mud of a Chinese street after a fortnight's snow and rain, stretched my weary legs by a climb up the lofty hill, from which one enjoys a famous and splendid view over the united cities of Wuchang, Hanyang, and Hankow, the scattered mountains, and the vast swampy plain. Returning on board to a cold dinner, I slept as well as I could amidst the unpleasant surroundings of a Chinese junk-fleet at New Year time.

Tuesday, February 27th, at six a.m., found us rowing down the swift current of the Han; when reaching the Yang-tse we turned to the right and made our way painfully up stream, past Hanyang to Siao-ho-kou, thirty li (about seven miles distant), the spot where we quit the main river to ascend another affluent. This thirty li occupied six hours' poling and rowing, the almost continuous line of Hunan timber and bamboo rafts in process of unloading along the banks compelling us to proceed against the full force of the current, which from half a knot, its speed on the day of my arrival in Hankow (14th February), had now increased to about two knots, the river having risen two feet in the interval above its then level, which was the lowest of this winter, and some fifty feet below the height attained in the summer freshets. Little is to be seen in this reach, nearly a mile in width, beyond the outlines of a few distant hills rising above the low horizon, the near view of the country being totally impeded by the lofty mudbanks, in many places absolutely perpendicular, by which the river is now enclosed. The stream we enter at Siao-ho-kou drains one of the numerous chains of shallow lakes which line the central and lower stretches of the Yang-tse's course. These, in summer, form one vast expanse with the river itself—but in winter are separated from it by wide stretches of alluvial land on which is grown winter wheat—and are connected with the river by rapid winding streams, through which the mud-laden Yang-tse flows up in summer, and down which the pellucid lake water, after having deposited its silt, drains off in winter. Into one of these affluents, or as they are called by our own navigators, creeks, we now entered. It was of an even width of about eighty yards, and at the time ten feet deep, and running with a current of five to six knots, against which we were painfully towed, making four miles in as many hours, when, heavy rain coming on, we hitched up to the bank for the night, close to an isolated rocky point round which the creek rushes, called Hwang Sheng Kang; having accomplished in this our first day's journey the very respectable distance of eleven miles. This rocky point is remarkable in standing out isolated from the plain at not more than ten feet above its general level, and large enough only to afford room for a small temple and picturesque two-storied Ting-tze or pavilion, with a lighthouse in the shape of a square paper lantern: a useful beacon to the belated mariner when the waters are out and the floods extend to the horizon.

Wednesday, February 28th.—At daylight a heavy snowstorm rendered progress impossible; the whole country was covered three inches deep, and I lay confined in the dark, owing to all the mats fore and aft covering the boat. At length, at ten o'clock, the weather cleared, although the clouds hung ominously low on the neighbouring hills. The stream here widens out to about 200 yards, and the current slackened to about two knots, rendering progress by coolies tracking along shore comparatively easy as compared with yesterday. Notwithstanding we only made twenty li, say six miles, in four hours; after which we again came to a halt at a place called P'u-tan, sixty li from Hankow, say seventeen miles. This place turned out to be the home of our "Lao-ta" (old-great) or captain, and this necessitated his spending the night ashore. We did not, however, lose much, as, after sundry hailstorms, heavy rain set in at four o'clock, and continued throughout the night. The country through which we passed to-day forms in summer the bed of a vast lake, out of which rise, like islands, isolated barren sandstone hills of from ten to 200 feet high. On one of the former is built the village of P'ut-an, at the height of the summer floods. It has an untidy, dilapidated look, like a place that has recently been under water, the stone bunding with which the banks of the hillock are partially protected being, like everything else in the land, in a ruinous, tumble-down condition.

During the next ten days we tracked, poled and sailed through a dreary country of alternate shallow lakes and embanked watercourses, the home of immense flocks of wild-fowl which are snared by the amphibious inhabitants of this wild region, the greater part of which formed a vast lake in the preceding summer, owing to a break in the embankment. The lakes or lagoons are filled with aquatic plants, chiefly "Kao-tsao," which shelter innumerable fish who yield a fine prey to the many devices of the ingenious Chinese fishermen. In one lake were crowds of small boats fishing in company: after clustering together they suddenly separate, forming a large circle; then, hammering with all their might with two flat bamboos on the forward deck, they all draw in suddenly to the centre, driving the fish before them. The noise was great, and heard a long way off before the boats came in sight. Great expanses of muddy land, fertilized by a fresh layer deposited in last year's floods, had been sown with wheat, now just sprouting, to be reaped in May. We fared poorly, there being no good food purchasable at the miserable collections of reed-and-plaster huts, termed villages, alongside which we usually tied up for the night. We once secured a fine carp, five pounds for fivepence, upon which I hoped to make a good dinner; but the cook, whom I remonstrated with for not killing the fish before scaling him, let the poor thing jump overboard with half his scales scraped off him. The fact that his cruelty reacted upon the perpetrator afforded me little compensation.

The reeds which cover the marshy banks and extensive flats bordering the Great River, from its mouth to where it issues from the mountains below Ichang, are a notable product of, and peculiar to, the Yang-tse valley. They grow to a height of fifteen to twenty feet, and form the building material and fuel of a vast population. At some villages were four-wheeled wooden trucks, the primeval model of the modern railway truck whose method of construction they closely foreshadow, the wheels solid and below and within the frame of the truck, the axles revolving with the wheels. In the lower parts of the plain sledges are employed to convey produce over the marshy ground, much as the Samoyedes drive their sleighs across the Siberian tundras in the short Arctic summer. All alike are loaded with reed bundles, some are pushed by men, others drawn by the patient water-buffalo across the flats. Arrived at the water's edge, these reeds are placed upon pairs of flat-boats, of which we meet many descending the stream, looking like floating haystacks. All one morning immense flocks of wild-fowl passed overhead on their flight to the north; this being the first fine day, they seem to be all starting for their summer quarters. They rose from the lake on our right, and in a minute were out of sight.

In Shansi there is a city called Yen men Kwan (Wild-goose Gate Barrier), so named because the wild-fowl pass over and through the town in which this gate is situated, and when the gates are shut the wild geese settle and wait for them to be opened before passing. This occurs both on their northward flight in the spring and on their southward flight in the autumn. For this reason, and their supposed conjugal fidelity, the Chinese will not kill or eat them, their intelligence being almost human. This story, my companion, a native of the place, insists upon being literally true. He is confirmed by our cook, also a Shansi man, who neglects his cooking to reassure my unbelief.

On the banks of the night mooring-stations the whole extent of water frontage is occupied by ornamental *cabinets d'aisance* placed by the truly scientific agriculturists of this country, to allure all possible contributions from the travelling public, and prevent the pollution of the streams— a defect characteristic of Europe from which China is happily free.

I passed much time on this dull journey in conversation with my Shansi friend, who told me his history. He had been ten years employed by a large Shansi firm in different parts of the empire and latterly in Western Szechuan, on the Thibetan border, buying musk which is his speciality; until two years ago he left for home, the possessor of 500 taels, to bury his family, nine persons including his wife, the whole of whom had perished in the famine of 1877-8. He then married another wife, whom he left at home, and to whom he allows ten taels a year (£2 10s.) for food. She can exist a year on a picul of wheat (133 lbs.), which here costs one tael (5s.), while during the famine the price in Shansi was 30 taels (£7 10s.); and yet nothing but forcible persuasion will induce the governors of this misguided country to allow railways to be built for them. Wheat and millet, eaten mostly in the form of dumplings, but without any fat in their composition, form the staple diet in the north and west, rice being there the luxury of the rich. These our Shansi cook is, of course, an adept in; but I find them rather heavy and sour to the taste, the flour being coarse and of a dirty colour.

At last, on the eleventh day out from Hankow, the second stage of my journey came to an end as the town of Shasze loomed up on the high embankment between us and the Great River. We passed a handsome and extensive building, the Shansi guild-house, and the town with its commanding pagoda, appeared to rise up before us. We are approaching Shasze from behind, the front proper being to the Yang-tse, on and in the rear of the embanking dyke on which the town is erected. This dyke is twenty-five feet above the level of the country, which is here all below the level of the Yang-tse waters both in winter and summer. As in Hankow, to which in its situation and in its trade Shasze is in many respects analogous, the business and bustle is along the river-front, and the country-side is dull and lifeless. The total distance from Hankow by this inland, partly canalized, route is 220 miles, the distance by the river being 300. This channel is called by the Chinese the "Pien Hŏ," or accommodation river, the common term for a short cut on water. We moored alongside the bank just below a stone bridge, 100 yards long, but with only two small arches in it, being on the inside of the dyke slope, which was covered with graves sheltered by a few fir-trees. I went for a short stroll, but the mob was so troublesome that I could see nothing, so returned to my boat, and shut myself up in the cabin (all my people were ashore arranging for a boat to take us on to Chung-king); but a rain of mud and stones, the latter fortunately scarce in this alluvial plain, summoned me to show myself. My people arrived at length, and expostulated with the crowd, which, however, did not disperse till after dark.

Sunday, March 11th.—"Under Heaven"—*i.e.* "in all the world," by which is understood, the Empire of China—Shasze is the Chen (trading-place), Hankow the Kou (river's mouth or port); and Shanghai the Hsien (district city) *par excellence.* Shashe, or, as it is usually spelt, Sha sze, means, literally translated, "Sand-market," which probably designates the origin of the place. The "Market on the Sands" probably sprang up on one of the numerous sandbanks which block the river-channel hereabouts, possibly before the dyke was built; at this time it would exist in winter only, and be built of reed huts, removable in the summer floods, like many of the mushroom towns one now meets with, adjacent to the junk anchorages. Shasze is thus reputed the most important Chen or mart in the empire; Hankow, the most important Kow or mouth; and Shanghai, the most important Hsien or district city. Of Fu, or prefectural cities, the most celebrated "under Heaven" are Su-chow and Hangchow (Chow meaning divisional city), of which the old proverb says :—

"Above is Heaven's hall (Paradise),
Below are the cities of Su and Hang."

At daylight set out to cross the dyke, on and behind which the town is built, and up to which the canal by which we came runs. Lying in the main river, and moored to the opposite slope of the dyke, lay the Szechuan boat that my man had hired to take us to Chung-king; the distance across the dyke and through the town being about one mile. I started thus early so as to avoid being mobbed in the streets; these were in the abominably filthy condition common to all Chinese cities. At length reached the river-bank, down which I clambered a distance of thirty feet, and entered the boat. Here I waited alone from 7 a.m. till 1 p.m., for the men with our luggage. The cook engaged for the trip did not turn up at all, and, alone in the boat, I had to content myself with a meal of dry bread, fourteen days old, the last remnant of my Hankow provisions. Eventually, after dark, the cook turned up, bringing with him an enormous sack, weighing 133 pounds, and containing dried shrimps, his little private spec. for the Szechuan market. Not wishing to raise more trouble and cause further delay, I forebore to pitch the unsavoury package into the river, as I should have liked to do, especially as he had not brought the supplies, thus preventing our starting to-morrow at daylight, as I had intended, and making the time occupied in the transfer of boats extend to the third day—such is travel in China.

Shasze has a noble stone embankment facing south and south-west, built up in three tiers, each about twelve feet high, with a fine promenade or bund on the top. This was built up in the time of China's greatness. Imagine the Thames Embankment built on the banks of a river with an annual instead of a daily tide, and that a degenerate people have gradually encroached on the roadway until at places a sedan-chair can hardly pass. In other parts, and wherever there is room, beggar huts crowd the traffic to the very edge of the bank, the ancient stone balustrade being intact only in a very few isolated spots; over this edge all the rubbish and filth of a big city are thrown until the stone river-wall is hidden for more than half its extent, and over these muck-heaps lead steep steps up from the tiers of junks, about two thousand in number, and averaging thirty tons burthen, which are moored the whole length of the city, their bows to the bank. In these mud-heaps, which I watched during the six weary hours I was waiting for my luggage, a mixed filthy assemblage of half-starved dogs, pigs, chiffonniers and chiffonneuses, these latter with the stumped feet which in North China rich and poor alike affect, were grubbing assiduously: a good specimen of China in her decline, decay, and dirt. Fine stone stairs, crowned by archways, are let into the embankment at regular intervals; but these are in such a filthy condition of black slime that the steep paths in the muck-mounds are generally preferred.

King-chow and its Pagoda

Two miles inland, and above Shasze, lies the prefectural city of King-chow, the seat of a Taotai, whose jurisdiction extends westwards as far as Ichang, a walled city of which Shasze forms the trading suburb. This portion of the Great River, called throughout its whole course by Westerns the Yang-tse, is known locally as the King River or River of King-chow. The Yang-tse is known to the Chinese indifferently as the Ta-kiang (Great River) or Chang-kiang (Long River); if spoken of as the Yang-tse, it would be totally unrecognizable to the natives of the land. But the term Ta-kiang or Chang-kiang applies generally to the main stream which takes its origin in the nine streams flowing into the great Tung-ting Lake, whence the main volume of its waters are derived. The river we are now on is an affluent which flows into the Ta-kiang a few miles below the Tung-ting Lake, and at right angles to its course, at a village called King ho kou, literally, King River mouth— the terms Ho and Kiang being analogous to the *Fluss* and *Strom* of the Germans. The name King-ho, however, only applies to the distance covered by the stream as far as it flows through the district of " King " or King-chow; above Ichang, where it passes out of the district of King, it is commonly called the Chuan Ho or River of Szechuan. The western extremity of Shasze is marked by a very ancient pagoda of seven stories, up which I mounted, followed by a noisy rabble, which the entrance fee of two cash (half a farthing) did not deter. This pagoda adjoins a monastery which is built behind and below the embankment, so that the lowest story of the pagoda is entirely hidden from the river. On the outside, each story contains a recess on each side of its eight faces, and in each recess is a stone Buddha. The interior is adorned with tiles, on which are embossed Buddhas in various positions, some squatting on the usual lotus-leaf, others with wings. The entrance and window staircase, which is built in the wall, is pitch dark, and so narrow that my shoulders touched both walls as I cautiously groped my way up the broken steps. From the four narrow windows in the topmost story I looked north over the flooded country through which we had just passed on our way from Hankow, south over the low land and paddy fields on the opposite bank, east over the picturesque (as, owing to the highly finished roofs, all Chinese towns are from a distance) town of Shasze, and west over the waste of sandbanks through which at this winter season our to-morrow's course lay. I had to share my binocular with the rabble who accompanied me, and by whom I was nearly suffocated in the descent.—A fine spring day, 60° Fahrenheit in the cabin.

Monday, March 12th.—Owing to fresh delays on the part of my Shansi friend, we did not get away till the afternoon, and then again, at the last moment, we had to wait for my special aversion, the cook, who had gone ashore again to buy tea and probably to take a parting pipe in some opium den, which he much preferred to the boat, in which he could only enjoy his pipe in solitude; and at length, at two p.m., with a fair wind, we got under way for Ichang. I had thus ample time, while trying to control my impatience at the needless delay, on this the third day at Shasze, to examine the buildings on the embankment, the bulk of which were of wood, from which the varnish had disappeared years since, of two stories, and more or less upright, as befits architecture founded on the tent of the Nomad. A few brick houses, sadly in want of a fresh coating of whitewash, were interspersed along the quay—analogous to the Café-Restaurant of the French; one immediately opposite or rather almost immediately overhead, rejoicing in the name of Ching-hsing-lo Cha-kwan, or the Star-view Tower Tea-shop and Eating-house. From the rickety balustrade of its low upper story some two dozen tipplers (of tea) gazed uninterruptedly down on the barbarian hired boat on the chance of the occupant exhibiting himself. The level of this house, like that of most others, was, in view probably of the summer floods overtopping the embankment, raised some four feet above the quay, a flight of stone steps leading up to its front door. Shasze, like Chung-king, has now (1898) been converted by the energy of the Japanese from a nominal to a real port of call for foreign steamers; its formal opening with Consuls and Customs took place last year. In May of this year I happened to be passing down river as the foreign settlement was burning, and assisted at the rescue of Mr. Neumann, the Commissioner of the Imperial Maritime Customs, and of the members of the China Inland Mission, who had been driven out by the mob, but had fortunately escaped in boats down river. In this, the tenth riot in the Yang-tse Valley, the new Customs' buildings, the Japanese Consulate, with the hulks of the British Consul and of the China Merchants' Steam Navigation Co., were totally destroyed. The cause of the riot was attributed to the forcible removal of the junks from their old anchorage off the foreign settlement, and to the transfer of the Likin collection to the foreign Custom-house.

Our boat is quite different to anything I had expected. Being built specially for the passage of the rapids, these boats never descend below Shasze, where their freight and passengers are exchanged into the Hunan boats in which the traffic of the lower river is carried on. We have hired a small boat as more expeditious; it is called a Shen Potse, or Wife of Shen (the town of Hunan where they are built); is about forty feet long and three deep; carries down-stream

10,000 catties (six tons) and up-stream 4000 catties (two and a half tons). It is now laden with about one ton of luggage and stores, including several piculs of rice for the crew, numbering six in all, besides five passengers who form our party—making the draft just fourteen inches; but the peculiarity of the boat is her lightness of build, resembling in that respect the rapid boats of Japan: built of oak planking, she has no timbers, no flooring, and, except forward, no deck; but she is held together by five bulkheads which divide the central portion of the boat into four holds, besides the tapering bow and stern, in the former of which are the crew's quarters and galley, and in the latter reside our cook, with his portable earthenware stove, and the helmsman. We in the centre are thus literally between two fires, and get the benefit of the acrid wood-smoke from whichever side the wind comes. The planking is one inch only, and as the place of the flooring is taken by a sort of light bamboo platform at the bottom of each hold, upon which the cargo rests, the whole has great elasticity, and three men run her along at three to four miles an hour against a two-knot current with the greatest ease; besides, she is unharmed by the continual bumping to which she is subjected in her longshore voyaging. The forward deck is a foot below the top of the bulkheads which enclose the hold proper, and when the vessel is fully laden is almost awash. Upon this, in reaches where tracking is impracticable, stand the crew, rowing with their faces to the bow, Chinese fashion, when they use their long oars with a quick jerky stroke, keeping strict time. The mast is about twenty feet high, and on it is a small lug-sail, eight feet by fifteen, only used when the wind is dead aft or on the quarter. The only part covered is the central hold in which we live; the covering is of arched bamboo matting, and being open at either end, a fine draught is always blowing through. Having heard much from the few Europeans who have travelled there, of the superiority of the Szechuan people, as possessing an approach to that manliness and good breeding which is so markedly deficient in the Chinese with whom we come in contact in the coast provinces, I examined our crew, the first specimens of the "Four Streams" (Szechuan meaning Four Streams) province I had yet met, with some interest. The Lao-ta and his brother, the former of whom steered while the latter stood all day in the bow helping, with a long iron-shod bamboo pole, were both tall, fair-skinned, with pleasant voice and quiet manner when giving their orders, which were obeyed by the crew with an alacrity and silence that formed a great contrast to the frightful noise and confusion with which any manœuvre is carried out in China generally, on board boats or elsewhere. The men jump out with the tow-line, and set off with a swinging step, wade through the water and jump on board, and are off again in a fresh spot with scarcely a sound. They tow from dawn to dark, only coming on board for meals three times a day, at which times, unless the wind is strong and fair, we moor to a stake driven into the bank, the boat not being weighted with anchor or chain. The most important part of the gear are the tow-lines, and these are of plaited bamboo, almost indestructible but for the jagged rocks against which in the upper portion of the river's course they are gradually frayed out. We proceeded up the river, which is here about three-quarters of a mile wide, past the walled city of King-chow Fu, which, however, lies hidden behind the embankment, until seven miles above Shasze, we passed the Tai-ping ho (River of Peace), a "cut off" a quarter of a mile wide, with high artificial banks, about 100 miles long, through which the junks sail in summer to the

Tung-ting Lake, avoiding the numerous bends and dangerous sandbanks of the river proper. It is now a vast expanse of sand, being entirely dry. At length, at seven p.m., after making sixty li, say fifteen geographical miles, in five hours, we moored for the night in a small channel between sandbanks, at a place called Shih Tao Tse, or Stone Headland.

Tuesday, March 13th.—Off at six a.m., the trackers proceeding gaily along the top of the high bank, here almost perpendicular. The river narrowed perceptibly after passing Chiang-kow (River's Mouth), a large straggling village on the left bank, and with its clear shallow water forming a marked contrast to the turbid whirling stream off Shasze. The banks were covered with villages and fine trees, but the plain behind is evidently still flooded in summer, the great breach in the dyke, made by the gigantic flood of 1870, being still unrepaired. At length, on reaching a small town called Yung-tse, we caught the first sight of the Western mountains, and were glad to realize that the dismal plain of Hu-Peh was at last coming to an end. A vertical section of the bank, here cut by the river, showed the first departure from the alluvial mud through which the river, with the exception of its passage through the range above Kiukiang, makes its way from here down to the sea, a distance of 800 miles. This section showed a stratum of two feet of gravel beneath six feet of mud. Above Yung-tse and below the big island of Pa-chow, or, as Blakiston has named it, Spring Island, I noticed a junk's mast sticking out above the surface in the middle of the stream, and I found that a large Hunan junk, bound down from Ichang, and laden with Szechuan produce, had run on to a bank here two days ago, and that two women of our Lao-ta's family had been drowned in her. The survivors were encamped in some of the wreckage on the adjacent bank. It is very uncomfortable on board, owing to the arched mats, which cover the central portion of the boat, and which form a tunnel about twenty-two feet long, under which we squat, producing a most cutting draught, which I have not yet found means effectually to exclude. Fortunately we are enjoying a continuance of bright spring weather; in fact, we have jumped suddenly from winter into summer. Distance: 120 li—thirty geographical miles; in all from Shasze, forty-five.

Wednesday, March 14th.—Off at six a.m., tracking in a dead calm, with a bright warm sunshine. The river has at length entirely lost its monotonous alluvial scenery, and the reach we now passed through was bounded on either side with low wooded hills, the gentle slopes to the water's edge at their feet being bright with the young spring wheat. The reach had the appearance of a placid lake, from which the warm sun was fast displacing the morning mist. We entered a new climate—Shui-tu (Water-earth), as it is called by the Chinese—bright clear water and a rich red soil, the former, for the first time after leaving Shanghai, sweet and drinkable without filtering. This water comes mainly from Szechuan, there being no affluent of importance between this and Fu-chow, 400 miles higher up. A week back the field sown with wheat showed nothing but the black alluvial soil; here, the plant is already six inches above the ground. In May, when the river rises, the clear colour disappears and much of this lower land is flooded, at times too early to allow of the wheat harvest all being reaped. We passed the walled district city of I-tu, situated upon a small affluent called the Ching Chiang, or Clear River, which takes its rise in the province of Hu-Nan to the south. The small river is a true affluent, its waters flowing constantly into the Yang-tse, although there was no preceptible current as we passed its mouth. The high land of Ichang now appeared, but was immediately hidden in a thunderstorm which here burst upon us. The point we were now rounding, known as Opossum Point, was covered with large loose boulders, the first seen, a foretaste of the mountains to come. Below this spot the points consisted of true sand; higher up the boulders seemed to have consolidated into conglomerate or pudding-stone, large masses of which, recently undermined by the water, formed dangerous rocks for boats approaching too near the bank. This conglomerate ledge, here three feet thick, lies between two strata of hard sandstone. Porpoises have kept us company all the way from Shasze, but they do not ascend above Ichang, being arrested by the first rapid, which is situated just below. There is little or no current to-day, which explains the pellucidity of the water; in summer the water here varies from pea-soup to chocolate. Brought up at Matung Chi (the "race" of Matung), having made 100 li, say twenty-five miles; in all from Shasze seventy miles.

Thursday, March 15th.—Off at daylight, in thick mist increased by heavy dust-storm, which rendered the scenery of the Tiger Teeth Gorge (Hu-ya hsia), through which we now passed on our way to Ichang, quite invisible. This gorge forms a break in the last of the cross ranges, athwart which the Yang-tse breaks its way from the Szechuan plateau to the great Hu-peh plain. This range, precipitous on its north and west flank, rises to a height of 2600 feet on the right bank, one of its wall-sided peaks being crowned by an apparently inaccessible Buddhist temple; and falls away to about 300 feet where it crosses the river bed. The gorge is 600 to 800 yards wide, and about two miles long, and is situated just ten miles below Ichang. The perpendicular cliffs consist of a moderately coarse conglomerate like all the country hereabout, and, as towing is impossible, our crew had to row with might and main to make any headway against the two-knot current. In summer this gorge cannot be attempted by junks except with a strong fair wind, which, however, by a kind provision of nature, seems to blow here pretty steadily all the year round from noon till sunset. As it was calm when we passed, in the forenoon, we crept through with no little difficulty, taking advantage of the eddies, and brought to a standstill at every projecting point of the rock, round which the current rushed vehemently. Half-way between the gorge and Ichang stands a conspicuous pagoda, enclosed in a walled garden planted with firs, the whole in an unusually good state of preservation. Ichang itself stands on a conglomerate cliff, rising only just above the summer level, and overhanging a long, low, level sand-spit, which in winter occupies nearly one-third of the river's width. Above this sandbank, and opposite the walled city, lies moored a large fleet of Szechuan junks; below the city is the suburb which stretches along the river-bank, and here is situated the temporary Customs' pontoon moored in the river channel. This suburb is nothing but a long narrow Chinese street, ruinous at its lower end, straggling along the bank, and composed of third-class native shops. Behind, the country covered with grave-mounds as far as the eye can reach, rises gradually into low brown gravel hills, inter-mingled with boulders, and interspersed with a few small vegetable gardens; in the bottoms are rows of terraced paddy fields with roomy farmhouses of mud and wattle. The view of the opposite bank facing Ichang is bold and picturesque. Pyramid-shaped hills, with vertical cliffs along the river front, 500 to 600 feet high, backed by ranges of lofty mountains extending to the distant horizon, neat villages and temples in groves of willow and bamboo, form a delightful contrast to the squalid surroundings of the so-called foreign settlement. Under the conglomerate ledges of this, the left bank, which have been partially undermined by the river, house innumerable beggars, whose fires, made for preparing their evening rice, give a weird aspect to the scene as viewed in the darkness from the sandbank beneath. These snug nooks are not, however, free from danger, for last winter a large slab of conglomerate toppled over, crushing eight unfortunates beneath it.

I landed at four p.m., having made seventy li since daybreak, say eighteen miles, making eighty-eight from Shasze in three days—a fast boat passage.*

* August, 1898.—In 1893, when I made this journey, no steamer had attempted to run between Hankow and Ichang in winter, and hence I had to spend seventeen days over a journey which is now accomplished in three days. In 1894 I put a small 200-ton twin-screw boat on the line, "Y-ling," which ran regularly, winter and summer, between the two ports until crowded out by the four large vessels of American type which now control the trade.

Buddhist Temple on Summit of Conglomerate Pinnacle 1200 Feet high: on Yang-tse River near Ichang (p. 34).

Junks in Ichang, with Masts erected preparatory to starting up Stream (p. 38).

To face p. 36.

CHAPTER III.

ICHANG AND ITS ENVIRONS.

The foreign community—Fishing with otters—" Feng Shui "—The conglomerate country—Cave of the Dragon King—Underground lake—The "Dome"—Startling *coup-d'œil*—Cloud-mist Mountain—Chinese country house—Unexpected hospitality—Master and servant—Auspicious site—Woodcutters—Steep climb—Chinese " Pahs "—Taoist temple—Magnificent prospect—Ascent of the Golden Peak—Chinese candles—A model hotel bill—Plank bridge—Return to Ichang.

THE foreign community of Ichang, in 1883, comprised a Commissioner of Customs with an indoor assistant, who combined medical with clerical duties, and two outdoor examiners. These, with the missionaries—one Scotch Presbyterian and his wife, and two Roman Catholics—then formed the whole resident foreign population. The British Consul appointed to the port resided, at the time of my visit, at Hankow. I was much pleased at finding a medico here, as, shortly before landing, while walking along the river-bank, following the boat, a dog had rushed out of the wheat, and bitten me in the calf of the leg through my knickerbocker stocking, and I now let myself be thoroughly cauterized. These dogs in China are the bane of one's existence; they have a mad antipathy to the barbarian, that the longest acquaintance fails to modify; the scent, appearance, or sound of his movements seems to infuriate them to madness; they rush out violently barking, and as a rule stop short of biting, but to any one with sensitive nerves there is no enjoyment in a walk outside the police-guarded roads of the larger "settlements." In the present instance I was attacked by a dog who did not bark, and I had no stick ready for him; but such instances are rare.

Now, in 1898, the "foreign" community has increased to twelve Europeans employed in the Impérial Maritime Customs and thirty missionaries. The mercantile community is represented alone by the agents of the three steamer companies running to Hankow, and by the agent of the Chung-king Transport Company, Limited, all of whom are Chinese. The trade of Ichang is almost exclusively a transit trade. The town is situated in the midst of a poor, mountainous country, whose people, unlike the Szechuanese, have little money to spend upon foreign luxuries. Ichang is the capital of a prefecture, the *Fu* or Prefect having numerous *Hsien*, or districts, under his jurisdiction. The trade is a busy retail one, but there are no large banks and wealthy wholesale merchants such as congregate in the plain *Chên*, or mart, of Shasze, eighty miles lower down.

Friday, March 16th.—A calm, mild, sunny morning, the sky still obscured by the otherwise invisible dust. These dust-storms, which the nor'-west gales of winter bring from the Mongolian deserts, carry the fine sand particles to an incredible distance. On one occasion I was on board a steamer in the Inland Sea of Japan, also in the month of March, when, in midday, the captain was compelled to bring the vessel to an anchor, as though in a North-Sea fog. By means of these dust-storms, the plains of North-Western China are supposed by geologists to have been raised, in the course of ages, several hundred feet.

After tiffin, I crossed the river with the Shuiwu Sze (Commissioner of Customs) to inspect the otter fisheries peculiar to this place. The opposite shore rises in pyramidal cliffs, separated by steep narrow valleys which just admit of a landing on the rocks, the conglomerate formation observed lower down shading off here into hard sandstone. Attached to the rocky shore, in a small bay, sheltered somewhat from the violence of the current, the fishermen have their otter station. From the bank, and overhanging the water, depend small bamboos, like fishing-rods, to the extremity of each of which is attached an otter by an iron chain fixed to leather thongs crossed round the animal's chest and immediately behind the shoulders. Some of the animals were playing in the water, swimming as far as the length of their tether would allow them; others had hung themselves across their bamboos, resting, doubled up, and looking for all the world like otter skins hung up to dry in the sun. When required for use, the fisherman, after casting his net, which is heavily loaded all round the foot, draws up its long neck to the water level, and inserts the otter through the central aperture; the otter then routs out the fish from the muddy bottom and rocky crevices, in which they hide. Fish, otter, and net are then all hauled on board together, the otter is released and rewarded, and a fresh cast is made.

We then ascended the steep valley, at the extremity of which we had landed, and, walking to the other end, mounted a steep narrow sandstone ridge with an equally steep descent on each side. After so many years spent in the plains, I was quite blown when we reached the hilltop, but the ascent from thence up one of the lower peaks was less steep. From the top was one of the finest and most characteristic views I have ever enjoyed in China, unless it be that from the Kushan monastery in Foochow, which it in some respects resembles. On the right and at our feet was the placid Yang-tse with the spreading city and suburb of Ichang, its crenelated walls winding over the undulating ground, which rises into a low range of hills at its rear, 200 to 250 feet in height. Before us, to the west and north, rise range upon range of steep mountains, from 1000 to 6000 feet, amidst which the great river disappears immediately beyond the city. On our left and behind, to the south and east, rise cone upon cone of pyramid-shaped hills, from 600 to 2500 feet high, through which winds a clear stream, seven-eighths of its sandy bed now dry.

Saturday, March 17th.—I rose early—a lovely summer's morning—sat under an orange tree in the garden and read the *China Express* of the 19th January, containing Hosie's reports of the trade of Chung-king, and of the feasibility of running steamers through the gorges and rapids to connect Ichang with that port, and so open up its trade by direct communication. I also read Consul Spence's report, and that of the Commissioner, my host. These are all most interesting, and I have now to go and form my own opinion. After tiffin, walked to a temple built on the crest of the hills in rear of the town, to which the Chinese are erecting an addition in the shape of a pavilion of three stories, to be seventy feet high, and to cost 30,000 taels (£5,000). This most conspicuous structure is to face and to counteract the pyramidal hill on the opposite side of the river, to the evil influence of which is due the ill-success of the Ichang candidates at the triennial examinations. The native trading community likewise suffers from its tendency to throw the profits of the business into the hands of strangers to the place. This unfortunate pyramid is situated due

Excursion to the White-cliff Mountains 41

south of the town, and hence the Feng-shui is ruined, and needs "puhing," or supplementing by artificial means. For the sake of the foreigners about to settle in Ichang, let us hope the new departure will prove ineffectual. This universal prevalence of the belief in Feng-shui or Geomancy gives interest to every step in Chinese travel.

Upon one of the bright, cloudless, calm days, which compose the monotonously beautiful Ichang winter, I once set out with two chair-coolies carrying my chair—an open wicker-work, or rather rattan, mountain sedan-chair—in which were packed my bed and a change of clothes, also one hired coolie carrying food. We crossed the Yang-tse, and landed in a break in the cliffs, which line the right bank, at the mouth of a narrow valley, which we ascended, following the course of the stream which falls into the Great River on its right bank, opposite the walled city of Ichang.

After walking six or seven miles on an almost level plain, crossing and recrossing the clear stream continually on stepping-stones, the valley, hitherto half a mile wide, narrowed to a ravine, on the left being the steep precipices of the "Pai ai Shan" (White-cliff Mountains), and on the right the conical, or rather pyramidal, hills, which are the characteristic of Ichang scenery. The latter are limestone, the former conglomerate, their varied outlines, the result of erosion, dependent upon the toughness of the material.

We then left the narrow patches of beans and wheat, and the pine woods and bamboo groves sloping down the talus, and entered upon a ravine choked with conglomerate blocks, that have tumbled down from the overhanging peaks (1500 feet high), until we reached a side valley on the right, bounded by precipices on both sides, with the smallest patches of cultivation here and there in apparently inaccessible spots; our path led along a ledge about half-way up, with the dry river-bed of smooth pebbles below, a desolate and romantic scene. My followers having lagged behind, I wandered on, wondering when I should come to the rock temple, in which I intended to pass the night, the valley getting even more desolate as I advanced, as if I were coming to the end of all things. The sun had already set behind the mountains on my left, but the tops of those on my right were still brilliantly illuminated. Suddenly, a sharp turn discloses another steep valley, ending in a wall of conglomerate, below which is a fine wood of evergreen trees. The narrow path winds round and leads to the wood, through which ascends a fine stone staircase, announcing the approach to a temple. At length, a deep wide cave, which the trickling water has slowly excavated out of the mountain behind the wood, becomes visible, and I toiled up the steep flight as the vesper bell sounds through the still twilight. Very rich and full sound the deep-toned strokes of the ancient single bell, such as all these Buddhist temples possess. A gate leads into a paved courtyard, whence another flight of steps ascends to a terrace, which runs in front of three spacious temples, all built under shelter of the huge overhanging cavern. A stone basin rises from the terrace, filled by the perpetual dripping from the roof of the cavern, some sixty feet above, which, as one sits in the guest-room, and looks out through it on to the wood, has all the appearance of a shower of rain. The cave, called "Lung Wang Tung" or Dragon King Cavern, is about 100 yards across the opening, and extends inwards almost the same distance. At the back of it is a lake, which the priests say extends inwards an unknown distance; only one man has ever tried to explore it, and he never came back again. They objected to my launching their boat upon it, as this is never done but in times of drought, when they go upon the lake to solicit the dragon prince to turn himself round and produce rain. Were the dragon to come out at this opening and escape out of the country, according to Chinese superstition, there would be another Biblical deluge. Hence the three temples to shut him in safely.

The whole scene was so weirdly romantic that I longed to explore it more thoroughly, and next morning I started early, and walked four or five miles up another ravine, fuller of precipices than anything I had seen yet, with again a dreary dry river-bed, a special feature of the conglomerate country, and a waterfall, now almost dried up, which seemed, as far as I could judge, to make one leap of over 1000 feet. In this region the valleys, bordered by precipices with bulging sides, mostly end not in winding narrowing glens, but in precipices abruptly shutting them in. A steep climb brought me to the top of a ridge, whence the inaccessible-looking " Wên Fo Shan" suddenly burst upon my astonished view like a *coup de théâtre*. At my feet a yawning gulf separated me from the conical " Wên Fo," or as the few Europeans who have visited it call it, the Dome, which was only connected with the ridge—upon which I was sitting, to prevent being blown off—by a narrow causeway, from four to ten feet wide, and with vertical walls some hundreds of feet deep. Opposite, reaching two-thirds up the Dome, a perpendicular wall of rock stretched for a thousand feet downwards, looking almost as if it had been planed, so smooth was it. And these startling features were framed in what by itself would be a glorious amphitheatrical view of range beyond range of mountains. Crossing the causeway, looking neither to the right hand nor to the left, I was confronted by the steep cone, up which a scrambling path leads to a narrow platform at the top, upon which is built a small temple. After spending an hour gazing on the jagged peaks all round, I got back to the causeway, not without some difficulty, and retraced my steps to the Dragon King's cavern, where I spent a second night. A fourteen miles' walk brought me back to Ichang next day, through a lovely little village, the prettiest feature in the view from Ichang. The bright morning air, following on a frosty night, gave this return walk a special charm.

On another occasion I arranged a more distant trip to the "Yun wu Shan," or Cloud-mist Mountain. Having slept in my boat, I landed at seven a.m. at the mouth of the Ichang Gorge, and started to walk up a lovely glen that falls into the main gorge, both being cut out of the limestone, of which the region north and west of Ichang is composed, in contradistinction to the conglomerate mountains, which cover the country to the south and east. This glen has a level bottom, varying in width from 50 to 200 yards, entirely occupied by the bed of the stream, which flows through it, and bounded throughout the first few miles, until it widens out and forms cultivable bottoms, by limestone precipices, perpendicular and overhanging, about a thousand feet high. The side ravines are filled with beautiful ferns and evergreens. Finding that the pace of a coolie-cade (compare cavalcade) is that of its slowest component, I on this occasion had picked out my best coolie, and he alone followed me with my bed and food slung to the two ends of the common carrying pole; the former two thick double blankets, the latter two loaves of brown bread, one tin of cocoa, with a tin of milk. The paths wound up another ravine seemingly endless, and the mountain I was seeking seemed always still twenty li (seven miles) distant. At length, at three o'clock, the ravine widened out, and the path, hitherto confined to the bed of the stream, ascended, by flights of rough steps cut in the limestone, to a terrace upon which stood a first-class Chinese house. I sat down upon the parapet of the terrace, while waiting to make further inquiries as to the distance and direction of our goal.

Two young men came out with a shy manner, but with a politeness common enough in the poor, though unusual in the rich, where a foreigner is concerned, invited me " Ching tso chi cha ! "—" Please sit down and drink tea ! " Chinese good manners would have bid me refuse, but I took them at their word, being tired and wanting their information. They advised me not to attempt to ascend the peak that night, the path being a wild one, with no house on the way, and that I had better stay where I was and go in the morning. I decided to accept this unexpected hospitality, and I spent the rest of the daylight walking about the grounds and admiring the site. Perched, according to my aneroid, 900 feet above the river, and about 250 above the brawling stream that had cut out the valley, down to which a steep wooded slope extended, the tops of the nearest trees were barely above the parapet level. Looking down-stream a couple of miles, to where the vista was closed by the steep mountain, up the foot of which we had just ascended, the small plateau was enthroned between jagged rocks rising 1000 feet on either side—one supposed to represent a lion, the other an elephant, co-guardians of the site. Behind was steeply terraced ground, by which the path up the valley passes to the higher range beyond, whose fantastic tops the last rays of the setting sun were momentarily gilding. I was delighted with my resting-place, and my congratulations to the owner, on the beauty and auspiciousness of the site, were thoroughly sincere.

As night set in, we all sat on the outrageously uncomfortable Chinese benches round a wood-fire, burning in a circular depression surrounded by a stone rim in the floor, the smoke escaping through the tiles—though first arrested midway by a tier of hams—and, as we sat there passing the hubble-bubble or water-pipe, it was to me most interesting to watch the farm-servants coming in, one after the other, and taking their seats round the fire, some crowding on the same bench as their masters. Supper of rice, cabbage, and bean curd was soon served, and washed down with tea. The servants then sat down to the same table, but were served with mountain rice, grown in dry ground, and very inferior to that grown in a wet soil; the cooks being women and "ya-tou," or slave-girls so called, all unfortunately with artificially crippled feet. The two sisters of my hosts looked on, but neither sat down nor ventured a word while I was present. Before eight o'clock we were all in bed. All travellers carry their own bed quilts in China, the guest-room merely containing a bare bedstead, and often not that.

By conversing with my hosts, I learnt that the terraced lands on both sides belonged to them, and that they mostly farmed them on the *métayer* system. Their nett income was 700 to 800 piculs of grain, making them wealthy landowners for these parts; though, translated into sterling, this only amounts to £300 a year. But such a family, having their own vegetable-garden and farmyard, would not spend one-tenth of this sum. The surplus they appeared to invest in buying more mountain land, and in keeping up the stone dykes of the innumerable terraces. The Government land tax averages one-tenth of the gross produce.

Next morning I made an early start, as the sun was creeping down the valley. I, however, first had breakfast with my hosts, who would not even allow me to give any

View of "The Pyramid," on Opposite Bank, taken from the Promenade on Top of Ichang City Wall. This Natural Pyramid of Sandstone, rising 500 Feet above the River, is almost identical in Size and Shape with the Pyramid of Cheops in Egypt (p. 40).

Ferry opposite Ichang City at Mouth of Small River: Sandstone Cliff (p. 50).

[*To face p. 46.*

cash to their servants, kindly observing I should need all I had before I got back.

We went on by an ascending path behind the house, and continued our route up the valley. The paddy-fields, terraced up the course of the mountain streams, the smallest and highest, terrace containing only a few square yards of land, were covered with a thin coating of ice; the air was fresh and bracing; until by nine or half-past, the rising sun had climbed over the mountain-tops. After an hour and a half's walking, we reached a pine wood, through which the ascent was steep and difficult. Here I found some woodcutters, resting and smoking their pipes round a log fire. I joined them, and having had a smoke with them, prevailed on one of them to act as guide to the top of Yun wu Shan, now at last visible, its white temple towering up, like a doll's house, on the cliff above. The climb from this point was exceedingly steep, and it was only with the best will that my coolie, laden with my bed, managed slowly to clamber up after us. At length the long-expected summit was reached, a small Taoist temple, with balustraded terrace in front occupying the whole of the available ground. The daily weather here is extraordinarily regular, dead calm up to noon, when a light breeze sets in up river (S.E.), analogous to a sea breeze, increasing to a fresh breeze towards sunset, when it dies away again altogether. By going up in the morning, I avoided the cold gale, which meets one on these mountain-tops later in the day. It was a beautiful calm sunny morning, but unfortunately misty, and the view only extended over an endless succession of steep mountain peaks with rich valleys between. Most of these limestone mountains are crowned by a "chai," somewhat analogous to the Maori "pah;" bare limestone precipices form the last hundred feet, and the rest of the mountain exterior is formed of the talus. In these distances the "chai" look like magnificent castles, and in ancient times they formed camps of refuge for the inhabitants of the valleys below in the not unfrequent times of political disturbance. Many of the places about here still have "barbarian" names into which enters the forbidden character "I," which is composed of the hieroglyph for a man with a bow or a man squatting, which used also to be applied to us English in Imperial proclamations. The temple was small, and occupied by a very poor, solitary, old Taoist priest, who was much pleased to receive a visitor, but too *abattu* in manner for me to get anything out of. He lit a wood-fire to cook *mien*, or vermicelli, which we had bought on the way, and gratefully received my present of 100 cash—equal to fourpence of our money—though an empty beer-bottle would have pleased him better.

My aneroid had fallen three inches, making the peak about 2700 feet above the "San yeu tung" glen. We descended by the regular footpath on the Ichang side, which though steep was nothing out of the way; alternately scrambling over rocks, and walking in the bed of the nearly dry torrent, under lofty cliffs riddled with caves, and what are commonly called Ichang rocks. These are half-decayed stalactites, waterworn by the summer torrents, full of the seed of the maidenhair fern, of which they often bear a waving forest in miniature. There is a great demand for these rocks amongst the Europeans at Hankow and Shanghai. As the sun was setting, we left the interminable winding of the ravine, and ascended the side of the valley to a "ling" or gap. This pass, called "Chin fêng po" or "Ascent of the Golden Peak," was occupied by half a dozen mudwalled houses, on the ground of one of which I spread my bed, and squatted thereon while awaiting supper. The illumination of Chinese houses after dark, being barely "darkness visible," I always burden my coolie with foreign candles, which are much admired, and without which travelling in China is simply misery. At the wood-fire on the ground I cooked my "Cadbury"—another indispensable when travelling in winter amongst savourless nations—and enjoyed with it a good supper of mountain rice and bean curd. Porters, the humble beasts of burden of the land-roads in South and Mid-China, with "pei-tz" on their backs —some twenty to thirty—dropped in and shared the floor, each unrolling a mattress of plaited straw from the corner, for the use of which he paid ten cash.

My model hotel bill, on leaving the next morning, was:—

Supper for self and coolie, 4 bowls of rice at 10 cash (copper cash), "fixings" of cabbage and bean curd free	40
Use of straw-plaited mattress for ditto, 2 at 10	20
Breakfast, same as supper	40
Supper and breakfast for "Nigger," my dog	20
Pair of straw sandals for coolie (his old ones being worn out)	12
	132

Total 132 copper cash, or, in English money, 4*d.*

We were off at eight, and after a long tramp, during which we crossed on a single plank bridge a beautiful clear river, 200 yards wide and five to ten feet deep, flowing between conglomerate cliffs, we reached Ichang at two p.m., after a most delightful two days' outing.

CHAPTER IV.

ABOVE ICHANG.

Start for the gorges—Grand *coup-d'œil*—Tourist's inscriptions—A factory of boulders—Advantages of a light boat—A Temple School—A " Feng Shui " problem.

St. Patrick's Day.—A lovely summer morning with dew on the grass and fragrance in the air; violets everywhere. Finished writing my mail, and despatched it by the overland post—a courier who performs the overland journey to Hankow in five days. After breakfasting ashore with my kind host, I now at last set sail direct for the gorges and the Far West. A still sunny day, with a breath from the eastward barely sufficient to fill our big lug-sail; but our crew having been reinforced with three additional rowers, we made good progress crossing the now submerged sand-flat, which two days ago seemed to occupy a fourth of the river's width. For the summer rise has begun, and the level has risen five feet during my short stay at Ichang, and the width is increased by several hundreds. Poling and rowing over this bank, we avoid the deep water and strong current of the cliff-lined shore opposite, until after a distance of three miles, we were compelled to cross the river, and the trackers' labours began. Jumping on the rocks, they scrambled with the tow-line around immense boulders, and along narrow ledges, which afforded a bare foothold to the sandal-shod of our active Szechuan crew.

The reach of the river above Ichang is about three-quarters of a mile wide, and has all the appearance of a mountain loch; no sign of an outlet is visible, and as, toiling against the small rapid or "Chi-pa," you approach the upper end, the river seems lost entirely. Suddenly, on the left, a cleft in the mountains comes in sight, and lo! there is the Great River narrowed to 400 yards, flowing slowly and majestically between precipitous limestone cliffs which, in the distance, seemed to close together, and to leave no room between them. The view and the surprise that burst upon one for the first time are indescribable, and no pen can paint the beauty and impressiveness of the panorama that slowly unrolled itself during the next three hours, as we made our way slowly up some ten miles of the gorge to our moorings for the night. The water in the gorges is extremely deep (50 to 100 fathoms). Not a ripple disturbs its surface, and not a sound beyond the occasional echoes of the trackers' voices breaks the awful stillness. Clouds enveloped the higher peaks and enhanced the gloom of the chasm up which we slowly crawled. Dr. Henry, who had accompanied me at the start, left me at the mouth of the gorge, and I was alone—for the Chinaman can never be a sympathetic companion to the European—and I rejoiced that it had been my good fortune to visit the Yang-tse Gorges before the coming stream of European tourists, with the inevitable introduction of Western innovations in their train, should have destroyed their Old-World charm. Such scenery it is impossible properly to appreciate, if it has to be rushed through with steam, leaving no time to study the details or to fix any one picture firmly in the mind before it is obliterated by the next. The photographs and drawings that have hitherto been made of the Ichang Gorge fail lamentably to convey any idea of the size, which is the most striking feature. The dark limestone strata being disposed horizontally, and the cleavage being vertical, account for the striking forms, the towers and buttresses, into which the mountains have been cut up; the narrow side glens, where small streams enter the river, are equally wall-sided, and each turn in the valleys is a right angle. Vegetation, wherever a ledge affords room, is rich and abundant, and the air in springtime is scented and the gloom enlivened by the fruit-trees, now masses of blossom.

The river no longer presented the pellucid appearance which had delighted me between Shasze and Ichang, the spring freshet being of the usual thick muddy colour. Nothing struck me more than the wild unfrequented aspect of the reach as it opened out, there being apparently nothing but a few isolated sampans to be seen in the whole stretch of the water. As we advanced, however, these seeming sampans turned out to be large junks of eighty to one hundred tons, laden with Szechuan produce, and each rowed by twenty up to sixty men, their masts lowered, as always, for the downward trip, and their hulls dwarfed by the colossal dimensions of the surrounding scenery to the size of small boats.

We passed picturesque little villages nestling in the glens amidst miniature patches of wheat and the white blossoms of the plum trees; other glens were clefts, over the ledge of which, some 150 feet above the river level, tumbled a crystal waterfall. I wished to stop and fill up at one of these, but my Chinaman declared spring water to be unwholesome, and, as we have only one water-holder on board, I desisted. Distance travelled, forty li, say ten miles.

Monday, March 19th.—Second day in the gorges. I am careful to give the date of each day's notes, as the river varies so wonderfully at different seasons that any

House-boat in Ichang Gorge; Dangerous Rock, "the Sleeping Pig" (covered in Summer), in Middle Distance.

To face p. 52.

description must be carefully understood only to apply to the day upon which it was written.

In summer, when the river rises sixty to one hundred feet and more above the lowest level, which occurs in February, the volume of water covers up the rocks, and in lieu of smart local rapids interspersed with long stretches of comparatively still water, we find a continuous whirling torrent running about six knots. Now, in March, the river had only risen a few feet, and I saw it, for the first time, under its winter aspect. At this period the navigation is safer for junks, which crawl along the shore, often bumping against the rocks as they go, while steamers, to whom the current in itself would prove no obstacle, would necessarily be run more easily in the high-water period.

We weighed again at daybreak. After a cup of coffee, I went ashore and observed the quarrymen at work; the limestone, which is extensively used in the plains for building and for facing embankments, coming largely from the Ichang Gorge. No explosives are used, the blocks of stone being separated by rows of iron wedges. Passing these quarries, the river takes an abrupt right-angled turn, and on rounding the sharp precipitous corner, a fresh scene of beauty opens out. This turn of the gorge is known locally as the "Teng ying tse" hsia, or gorge of the "Lamp-shine;" the lower reach, called by us foreigners the Ichang Gorge, being known to the Chinese as the "Hoang mao" hsia, or "Yellow cat" gorge, from the supposed resemblance of one of the worn limestone rocks to this animal. In this gorge the right bank rises again in limestone cliffs, their summits crowned with weathered rocks, looking positively like the walls and battlements of impregnable mountain castles. The left bank, less precipitous, affords room for picturesque villages on its receding ledges, embowered in miniature groves of the tung or varnish tree, the tallow tree, and bamboo. The upper end of the gorge narrows like its mouth, a harder limestone having succeeded marvellously in resisting the constant erosion of the sand-laden water. Here to the left is a striking range of perpendicular white pinnacle rocks and cliffs, 3000 feet high, which rise out of a talus extending about halfway up their sides. These cliffs reminded me of the pictures of the dolomite mountains of Styria, and are probably composed of the same material. On the right bank the black-blue limestone continues; at the narrowest spot an isolated pinnacle, smooth rock below, but wooded on its cone-shaped top, rising 1800 feet from the river bed, and called by the Chinese the Pillar of Heaven, is strikingly picturesque.

Following the boat by an easy path some 200 feet above the water's edge, I felt fairly intoxicated with the magnificence of the ever-changing views, combined with the fresh spring morning air. At the end of the gorge an affluent enters through a lovely valley on the left bank at a place called Nan-To. A conspicuous rock at the junction is covered with sentences in large characters, written in whitewash, probably by travellers delayed in boats moored at its foot. Had I been in the vulgar West, I should have taken them for quack advertisements; but in the æsthetic East these notices were short poetical exclamations at the beauty of the scenery—not very profound, such as " Kiang t'ien yi sai," " The river and the sky are one colour:"—" Shan shui ching yin," " The hills are bright and the waters dark," etc. This stream forms the boundary between the limestone and the district of Plutonic rocks we are now entering. Here, the river, instead of cutting out a perpendicular chasm, has succeeded in disintegrating the apparently far more refractory gneiss and granite, with the result of a total change and

"Pillar of Heaven" in Ichang Gorge; Limestone Pinnacle rising 1800 Feet above River.

marvellous contrast in the scenery. A valley, over a mile in width, has been excavated, and the ruins are strewn about in gigantic piles of boulders through which the now narrowed winter stream winds its way in a series of small rapids. The view from one of the surrounding heights is an extraordinarily wild one, and one might, looking down on the stony river-bed, imagine one's self rather on the desolate shores of the Red Sea than in the midst of one of the most fertile provinces of China. The hard gneiss, where still in sight, is traversed by curious dykes of green-stone and porphyry which run at right angles to the river's course, the strata inclined almost to the perpendicular. This granitic axis of the mountain range, through which the Yang-tse forces its way, and which bears the limestones and sandstones on its flanks, barely exceeds 4000 feet in height, although to the south the mountains appear to rise to double this height, but they have never yet been visited and measured by Europeans. This stretch of river is known as the "Yao-tsa-ho," and is much dreaded by the boatmen; in some places piles of loose granitic rocks rise out of the middle of the channel, and everywhere the unfortunate trackers have to scramble up and down hills of broken rock masses which would puzzle a chamois to climb. The main channel is comparatively broad and deep; but the junks prefer the narrower channels near the shore, where they can track almost continuously. This "Yao-tsa-ho" extends for about fifteen miles, until the "Tunk-Ling," as the next gorge is called, is reached. Here we had a gale of wind aft, and it was possible to sail up in midstream between the rocks instead of being tracked up in comparative safety alongshore. The Lao-ta (skipper), nothing loth to save a few cash, reckoned without his host in the shape of his mate, who, when ordered to hoist up the sail, remarked to me, "He orders me to risk my all, my life, for I possess nothing else; it is well enough for him, the owner of the junk, and a rich man, to put only his life in jeopardy!"—a fine Gilbertian fallacy! In this distance we passed up three rapids, the only really difficult one of which was the "Ta-Tung," or Otter's Cave rapid, the current of which in the main channel, where it was unbroken, was running seven or eight knots for a distance of half a mile. We passed up by a small inner channel, with a regular waterfall at the top; but with our own four trackers, and a dozen additional coolies engaged at an additional cost of fourpence in all, we gradually scraped through, although our progress was so slow as to be hardly perceptible. With the elastic oak bottom of our little craft bumping occasionally on the boulders, we ascended with comparative ease; but for the large junks, that have to keep far out in the stream, the surmounting this, one of the minor rapids, is a troublesome business, and a whole day is well spent in its successful negotiation. We passed several big junks thus toiling up, our low mast and tow-line passing under theirs, and I congratulated myself upon having put up with the discomforts of a small boat, rather than spend double the time over the journey in a big one.

Our light canoe-shaped vessel seemed to suffer no harm from its occasional bumping on the rocks, but the big junks do not always get off so easily. We passed a cotton junk bound up-stream, which only the previous day had knocked a hole in her bottom at this very spot. Her crew were encamped on the bank under the mat roof taken from their boat, and had got out the bulk of her cargo of cotton bales, and spread them out on the bank to dry, the bales having been all opened, and the cotton scattered over the rocks. The junk herself they had managed to bring into a quiet little bay, where they had careened her for repair. I was told of the bad fortune of another Lao-ta (Chinese captain) last year, who met with a similar accident, which he successfully repaired, and had just re-stowed his cargo and started again, when he made a total loss only five li higher up.

A big junk of 120 tons carries a crew of over 100 men, viz. seventy or eighty trackers, whose movements are directed by beat of drum, the drummer remaining on board under the direction of the helmsman; a dozen or twenty men left on board to pole, and fend the boat off the boulders and rocky points as she scrapes along, and also to work the gigantic bow sweep formed of a young fir-tree. Another half dozen of the crew are told off to skip over the rocks like cats, and free the tow-line from the rocky corners in which it is perpetually catching: besides a staff of three or four special swimmers called "tai-wan-ti," or water-trackers, who run along, naked as Adam before the fall, and may be seen squatting on their haunches on rocks ahead, like so many big vultures, prepared to jump into the water at a moment's notice and pounce upon the tow-line, and free it when it catches on a rock inaccessible from the shore. These tow-lines are made of strips of bamboo plaited into a cable as thick as the arm, requiring great skill in coiling and un-coiling, which is incessantly being done, as the necessities of the route require a longer or shorter line. Notwithstanding its enormous toughness, owing to constant fraying on the rocks a tow-line only lasts a single voyage, and when one sees deep scores cut by the tow-lines into the granite rocks along the tow-path, the fact is readily accounted for.

The trackers of our humble craft stripped themselves of everything but one jacket, being in and out of the water all day long, and, as it was, we at times caught the tow-line, when the boat would drift back on the rocks before it was freed again; but we managed to start ahead again just in time to avoid incurring serious damage.

I spent most of the day ashore, in light flannels and pith hat, and found clambering over the rocks in the wake of the trackers at times a serious matter. Part of the day I walked along the right bank, on the upper path clear above the river's summer level, and on *terra firma*, distant a quarter of a mile inland from the present shore, and so escaped the boulders and sand-hills, which, although I was at an elevation of two hundred feet, entirely concealed the water of the river from view. The aspect as thus seen was that of a vast desert valley filled with loose piles of rocks enclosed in barren sandbanks. The peasants here carry everything in a bamboo crate on the back, held in position by bamboo straps across the shoulders; and it is a relief to be rid of the eternal carrying-pole on which the Chinese sling all their burdens in the Eastern provinces. One man I met was loaded with a huge sack containing seed of the T'ung, or Dryander (the varnish tree), weighing 220 catties (300 lbs.), with which he was merrily climbing the steep ascent. At sunset we rowed across to the left bank, rounded the last rapid-making point, and moored in a quiet bay at the entrance to the " T'ung ling hsia," the " Pierced Mountain " gorge.

I went ashore, and gazed into the mysterious black-looking cleft we are to pierce to-morrow, not without an eerie feeling at the thought of being shut up in these wild valleys, struggling with the inexorable water, for another fifteen or twenty days.

On a ledge of the steep rise I ascended to get a view of the gorge before us was built a row of five small towers, a series of which, at intervals of about every three miles, are

One of our Crew on Tow-path near Niu-kan Gorge.

erected right along the river from Ichang to Chung-king; the towers are white, with a bright red sun painted on the face of each. They are called "Yen-tun," or smoke-towers, and a fire of shavings is lit up in them to give the alarm by their smoke in the troublous times which so often occur in the Middle Empire. But most of them are in a ruinous condition, like all other Government property in this decaying country. Distance, 130 li, not more than twenty miles. In a difficult part of a route, the li are reduced in length accordingly.

Tuesday, March 20th.—Third day in the gorges. We started at 5.15 a.m., and rowed through the T'ung ling hsia, a long narrow ravine of about four miles, between which and the romantic "Niu-kan ma-fei hsia," literally, Ox-liver, Horse-lungs Gorge, the river opens out, a rocky boulder-covered island blocking the way and dividing the stream into two foaming channels. The exceptionally unromantic name of this gorge is derived from some curious stalactites, high up on the face of the entrance cliff, the form of which portrays the intestines. Nearly all the gorges have been named by the boatmen from like marks on their walls. Aided by a fair wind, we ascended the T'ung-Ling rapid, which intervenes between these two gorges, without difficulty; but the channel at this period is strewn with rocks, and the navigation requires great care. It was here that in September last, the wealthy General Pao-Chao, the T'i-Tu, or commander-in-chief, of Hu-Peh province, which we are now in, was wrecked proceeding up stream, through the junk's tow-line catching on a rock simultaneously with a sudden failure of the wind, which otherwise might have enabled the junk to steer clear of the danger. Two of his sons and several of his suite were drowned by the capsizing of the junk in the whirlpool, and he himself was only rescued by the lifeboat, one of which, as before mentioned, is stationed at the foot of each rapid.

We moored the boat for the men's breakfast at the entrance of the gorge, in a quiet bay, at the foot of a Taoist temple, called the "Ching Kiang Sze," or Pure Stream temple, from which this gorge enjoys a second name of the "Miao Ho Hsia" (Gorge of the River Temple). On the chart it is called the "Lukan" gorge, a misspelling of Niu-Kan; it is the entrance to this gorge which forms the frontispiece of Blakiston's famous work. But this drawing gives but a slight idea of the size and grandeur of the original.

The Taoist temple stands on a steep rise of 150 feet, with a curtain of lofty hills behind, and precipitous mountains opposite, rising to 3000 or 4000 feet. Inside the temple—charmingly situated, like all religious buildings of the Middle Ages, both in the West and in the East—notwithstanding the early hour of seven a.m., school was going on, amidst the usual din, and among the little scholars I noticed one girl, many of whom, in this part of China, I find attending school as well as the boys. One boy was reciting his repetition with his back turned to the master, who at the same time was employed dictating a fresh lesson to another urchin—my presence causing no interruption. A steep glen, with a tiny stream at the bottom, separated the temple from the village of Miao-Ho, composed of a few scattered houses, embosomed in poplars, now in the bright green of the early spring, and peach trees in full blossom. The village rises in successive terraces, built up of boulders and backed by groves of cypress and bamboo, as it creeps up the steep mountain-side. The gorge winds for three miles between sheer cliffs of limestone, 1000 and 2000 feet high, with higher peaks towering behind, taking a sharp rectangular turn in the middle, until the deep ravine opens out slightly, making room for the extensive scattered village of Shin T'an, or, as it is locally pronounced, Ching-t'an, on its flanks.

Shin T'an * means new rapid, and, as its name implies, is of recent formation, having been created by a fall of rocks from the precipitous mountain on the right bank, which occurred in the second year of the reign of the Emperor Chia-Ching of the Ming dynasty—about 250 years ago. This is considered the most formidable of all the rapids on the navigable portion of the Great River. It consists of a race of water broken into three rapids, the whole extending over a distance of two miles, in which I estimate the fall in the river-bed at about twenty feet. The first rapid is due to a small stream called the Lung-ma-chi, which enters the river at right angles on the left bank, issuing from a narrow glen, and which has deposited a huge fan-shaped moraine of boulders, of nearly half a mile radius, damming up the river and causing the first of the three rapids of the Ching-t'an. The other two falls are due simply to barriers of rocks athwart the stream, the latter like a weir with deep still water above it—the channel of the Ping-shu Gorge.

While our boat was delayed here awaiting her turn, below tiers of big junks moored bow on to the shore, I landed for a walk, in company with our "Ta-kan-tse-ti," or bowman, who took me up a beautifully shady road through the village, consisting of a steep flight of steps. Arrived on a terrace, about 300 feet up, on which I had stopped for breath, my companion pointed out two substantial brick houses, one on the right and one on the left, and asked what I thought of their respective Feng-shui, or site. The Chinese, as is well

* Another and more formidable Shin t'an now exists above Yünyang, formed by a huge land-slip in September, 1896.

known, place enormous value upon a well-chosen site for a grave or a house, not so much for the healthfulness of the position (though this probably is the fundamental conception of Chinese geomancy), as for its influence upon the descendants of the corpse in the one, or upon the fortunes of the inhabitants of the other. The lower classes in China seem to have great faith in the superior knowledge of this vital subject possessed by the Chinese-speaking foreigner. At any rate, I have been often consulted on the subject, and having picked up some of the principles of the science, all of which accord with natural conditions, and profiting by the vague latitude allowed to the seer in all ages, I am seldom at a loss when questioned. In the present case, I remarked that one house, from which there extended a magnificent view across the rapids to the gloomy Ping-shu Gorge, seemed to draw in prosperity from the waters rolling towards it, while the other seemed to have its fortune wafted past its door by the up-river wind which here blows steadily all the year round. My companion was delighted, and asked me, to my surprise, to enter with him the latter, pronounced by me the less fortunate, house. I went in, and he then told me this was his home, and that he had led me this way without warning me, in order to get my true unbiased opinion. We seated ourselves in the reception-hall, the family and friends delighted at being able to gratify their curiosity in a Chinese-speaking foreigner. The old mother, who served me with the customary tea, was much exercised over the Feng-shui of her home. They then told me that misfortune had followed misfortune; the father had lost his junk and been drowned in the rapids, and now the eldest son, my companion, was reduced to the hard work and small pay of a Ta-kan-tse-li. Could I suggest anything? I recommended a brick screen should be built on the edge of the terrace,

facing the doorway, and that the energetic youngster who accompanied me should try for employment on one of the big trading junks—and so satisfied everybody. But shipping here, as at home, is temporarily much depressed, junks having been largely overbuilt in the late good times, and in every quiet anchorage along our route we find big junks laid up, generally opposite the homes of their owners, who often possess nice terraced gardens and diminutive farms, carefully laid out, up the steep ravine in which the river flows.

My little boat occupied just six hours making her way inch by inch through the foaming water. Meanwhile we had walked on through the long terraced town to a tea-house picturesquely built on a cliff above the uppermost rapid, whence I looked down on the fleet of junks painfully toiling upwards. At this rapid the junks are stripped of their cargoes, and crowds of men and boys, from the mountain country round, are glad to toil as porters over the boulders for a few cash. Local pilots, too, are always taken on here, a big junk paying as much as one dollar for the five minutes occupied in the descent. These pilots are swells in their way, being well-dressed, and their comfortable homes adorn the surrounding slopes.

This tea-house, from which I looked down on the smooth basin above the natural weir of the uppermost rapid, and in which the junks that had successfully passed up were noisily re-stowing their cargoes, is situated nearly 200 feet above the present level of the water, but yet not high enough to save it from the disastrous floods of 1870 (9th year of Tung chih). Traces of that famous flood, which swept away whole cities, as far down even as the plain of Hankow, are seen in the fact of nearly all the houses forming the long straggling main street of Ching-tan being of recent construction. This street goes up and down long flights of stone steps at intervals, to the great grief of the Pei-lo coolies traversing it, with their piled-up loads on their backs.

We at length got off again with a strong fair wind, through the "Ping-shu Pao-chien" hsia, or "Gorge of the Military Code and the Precious Blade." This name, too, is taken from the supposed resemblance of a big group of stalactites on the cliff to this celebrated emblem in Chinese ancient history—now often seen as a favourite decoration on Chinese porcelain and embroidery. This gorge is not named by Blakiston, nor in the Admiralty Survey. It is about two miles long and a little over a quarter of a mile wide, and its walls of perpendicular cliffs are said to descend as far below the water as they rise above it, 1200 to 1500 feet; behind are the precipitous mountains rising to over 3000. The strata dip to the south and west at an angle of about thirty degrees, and the rocks appear to be formed of a compact greyish sandstone with shales; in these the water has in many places eaten out caverns and worn the walls into columnar shapes. Towing is, of course, impracticable; but we came through with a slashing breeze, which enabled us to stem the two-knot current with ease—a current without a ripple on its surface, and which seemed like still water after the "races" of this morning and yesterday. However strong the gale, the deep swirling water effectually forbids anything like a sea getting up; and hence the small freeboard of the junks, which at first sight, to one accustomed to the big seas that every gale raises on the Lower River, looks uncommonly dangerous. We had a tough job to get round the point which forms the western limit of the gorge, the boatmen clinging on to the crevices in the rock with long bamboos armed with small steel hooks. Beyond the gorge the valley again opens out; still, however, enclosed by mountains, one peak on the left bank rising to 4000 feet. Near to, and just

Home of Retired "Armateur" at Shin t'an, Mouth of Pingshu Gorge.

To face p. 64.

outside the exit of the gorge, I noticed the poplar-trees all inclined to the west, being grown somewhat in the form of a capital S, showing that the prevailing wind, much to the benefit of the ascending junks, is here, as usual, up-stream.

From here we came to the city of Kwei-chow, a distance of six miles; the channel, as is usual where the valley widens, is encumbered with huge rocks and boulder-covered sandbanks, forming a succession of rapids and races through which we struggled, aided by the strong breeze, and crossing from side to side to take advantage of the different eddies, until at last, at five p.m., we made fast to the bank opposite Kwei-chow, prevented from ascending farther by a couple of junks which had taken up their position here for the night, while the roaring stream outside them ran too strong for us to attempt to work round past them. We thus lost the benefit of the strong breeze which was still blowing, and had to put up with a day's work of sixty li, say fourteen miles, but which, on looking back, owing to the extraordinary interest of the journey, seemed more than ten times that distance.

Kwei-chow is a picturesque walled city, situated on a bluff some 200 feet above the river, and at the mouth of a small affluent; at the back rises the mountain range, up part of which its walls, which enclose many gardens and trees, creep in pear-shaped outline. It looks from this distance (the opposite shore) a well-built city; but it has no trade, not a single boat or junk being moored near it. From under its walls, reefs of black rock run out, and the current rushes past like a mill-race. Before we came to our anchorage, I had been walking along the shore, following the trackers. At length the towing-path rounded a smooth, almost precipitous rock, about 100 feet above the river level, until at last the narrow footway came to an end, and the elbow of the slope was rounded by some ten or twenty single footsteps cut in the face of the smooth limestone, just large enough for the small feet of a Chinaman. I was stuck. I could not go forward, and dared not turn round to go back; the trackers were far ahead, and the short twilight was fast merging into night. I was almost in despair, when fortunately one of the trackers came back to look for me. Carefully divesting myself of my boots, avoiding a glance at the foaming water below, and holding the man's hand, I soon got over; but what a path for men harnessed to a tow-line to risk their necks on!

The sun was very hot to-day; though the latitude is the same as Shanghai, and the altitude 500 or 600 feet greater, the spring here is fully a month in advance; the wheat is already over a foot high, and the air is fragrant with the bean-fields in flower. Every bit of sand left dry by the river's winter fall is sown in wheat, as are many of the apparently inaccessible slopes of the mountains; and the wonder is that it is not all blown away, or that any is harvested before the rise now going on, at the rate of two or three feet a day, overwhelms it. With regard to the Shin-tan pilots,—these men, our Lao-ta tells me, earn from one to eight dollars a junk, according to its size; this includes assistant-trackers for junks bound up, and no junk ventures to negotiate the rapids either way without them; they are smart, active men, and are licensed by the officials. Our humble Shen-poh-tse, creeping up under the bank, required no pilot, and the only extra charge for ascending the Shin-tan was twenty-five cents for a dozen supplementary trackers; but down-stream she has to take a pilot at a cost of 300 cash—say one shilling. (I am writing to the accompaniment of the roar of the rapid, up which we start at daybreak.)

Wednesday, March 21st.—Fourth day in the gorges. An exciting day. We ascended two fierce rapids, the Yeh-tan and the Niu-kou-tan, one minor rapid, called the Heng-liang-tse, and innumerable Chi-pa or races. These latter are caused by a projecting point of rock, behind which we paddle up in the eddy, then land the trackers at the point, and ease the shock of the boat's head against the rocks by a stiff pole over the bows, round which is twisted a "stopper" rope, which fends her off very effectually. Four of our crew of seven then drag the boat by main force round the point, two men remaining on board to fend her off the rocks, the water meanwhile boiling and foaming under her bows and threatening to swamp her. The helmsman meanwhile takes care to keep her as much as possible head on to the current, and shouts to the trackers when to haul and when to slacken. Oftentimes at the most critical moment the manœuvres are compromised by the tow-rope catching in an almost inaccessible crevice, when we hang in a most uncomfortable position until one of the trackers runs back, climbs with his bare feet cat-like up the rocks, and, apparently at the risk of his life, releases us. Then, when we have safely reached the comparatively smooth water, if the banks are precipitous, as on the greater part of our route to-day, the whole crew jump on board and claw us along under the overhanging cliffs—two men clinging on to the rocks with the sharp iron claws affixed to the end of their boat-hooks, while two others, with poles, keep her off a safe distance from them. The hookers have to be mighty careful never to lose their hold, as that involves drifting back into the current, and bringing up some distance below, losing in a minute or two the fruits of hours of work. Twelve hours of this sort of progress is very tantalizing, as when once an accident has happened, as occurred to-day, one is always in dread of another, and one's nerves are kept on the stretch all the time. Where practicable, I walk; but as the practicable path is usually some 200 to 300 feet above the river, and often, as it crosses a projecting point, entirely out of sight of the boat, this is not always convenient. In one place this afternoon, after walking two miles in as many hours, stepping from boulder to boulder, I was only too glad to descend and come on board again, as soon as a sandy bay allowed the boat to bring up to the shore with safety. It was at the Shin-tan, owing to the catching of the tow-line in the rocks and its subsequent snapping, that Consul Gardner with his two Hankow friends came to grief last month.

Next day we were off again at dawn (5.15), and crossed to the north bank, where I landed on a rocky point, and scrambled up 200 feet to the high level path, above which the villages in these more open valleys are built. By open valley, I mean a valley where the banks are not precipitous, as in the gorges; but they are still steep enough to rank as gorges on an ordinary river. In fact, the whole journey thus far has been in an almost continuous gorge and rapid. The reach above Kwei-chow has a picturesque charm of its own, from the steep mountain-sides being cultivated in patches to their summits, and studded with small villages embedded in trees and bamboo. . . . At one village I noticed a small stack of patent fuel, coal-dust kneaded with clay into diminutive round cakes, just the size for a Chinese portable oven, and I traced the coal to a small adit in the side of the hill, shored up with timber, not more than three feet high, and less than two feet wide. Out of this miserable hole women laden with baskets of coal-dust on their backs were painfully toiling. A small stream of water was running out of the foot of the burrow. Thousands of these primitive workings are seen along the whole length of the ravine, up to and past Chung-king.

At the head of this reach is the Yeh-tan, after the Shin-tan the worst rapid on the river. Here a huge cone of dejection, entirely covered with loose boulders of every size, shape, and colour, juts out from the north bank across three-fourths of the river's bed, narrowing the channel to about 150 yards. Round the point of the cone the current sweeps with a speed of eight to ten knots, a smooth tongue of water in the centre bounded by a sea of broken waves. We had surmounted the formidable Shin-tan in safety, but this rapid looked much worse. The saying puts it—

> Yo Ching wu Yen :
> Yo Yen wu Ching,

which being interpreted means: "When the Ching (or Shin-tan) is bad, the Yen rapid is nothing;" and, "When the Ching is nothing, then fear the Yen."

Now, we had found the "Ching" fair, and so had reason to dread the "Yen."

A fleet of big junks—fifty or sixty—being moored under the point on the left bank, waiting their turn to tow up, our Lao-ta selected the right or south bank, and thus hoped to avoid a delay of possibly two days. But the south bank forming the outer edge of the sweep, the current is more violent and the rock-bank is precipitous. A gigantic whirlpool immediately below the rapid has hollowed out a bay in the rock-bound bank, and, where the eddy meets the downward rush, a sharp point projects, which is a ticklish place for a boat in the hands of trackers to round in safety. Our Lao-ta having decided to take this course, we crossed the river, paddled up the eddy, which was running up almost as fast as the rapid itself was running down, landed our trackers, and drove the boat's nose into the broken torrent while the eddy was still acting on her stern. The rudder ceased to act; our boat, on entering the down current, suddenly shot out towards the middle of the stream; the trackers were thrown down, and two badly hurt by being dragged over the rocks, while the boat heeled over, threatening to capsize on the instant. Fortunately, our trackers promptly cast off the tow-line in the nick of time, and we incurred no other danger than being swept violently down-stream in the eight-knot current. Fortunately, the up-river breeze still held, and the two men left on board were able to set the sail in time to get steerage way upon the boat before she drifted on the rocks below, and the Lao-ta succeeded in steering her into the eddy on the safer left bank, with nothing lost but the result of the morning's toil. As we suddenly broached-to and lay over for a moment in the boiling surf, a cry of "Tachang!" (Broken adrift!) rose from the crowds on the shore, this being the technical term for this often disastrous accident. Our Lao-ta now decided to wait his turn on the left bank, which we eventually got up successfully, the water being shallow, and with no more harm than a few bumps on the rounded boulders along the shore.

Leaving the Yeh-tan with its animated scenes, we entered a wide reach, bounded by steep crimson-coloured hills, about 2000 feet high, patched with bright-green wheat-fields, the easier slopes affording sites for Alpine villages, surrounded by fruit-trees and evergreens, the former still in blossom. In this valley are more coal burrows, and at its head is the rapid of "Niu-kou," or Oxhead. This is almost a reproduction of the Yeh rapid, except that the current sweeps round an angular bend in the river, and the danger is increased by a circular rock right in the centre of the channel, from which the rapid takes its name. From below, this rock appeared to stand four to five feet out of water; while looking from above, it seemed just awash; its surface,

Seven-storied Pagoda below Patung. Note Fluted Rock, about 50 Feet High, on Right Hand, being Ancient "Pot-holes" in the Limestone worn through by the Current (p. 70).

To face p. 70.

flat, was about ten square yards. Above the rapid, we crossed and recrossed the river, rowing vigorously to catch favouring eddies, and to avoid numerous " Chi-pa," or races, and then tracked up to the head of the reach to another right-angled turn in the channel, off the point of which is the rapid called " Heng-liang-tse," *i.e.* " the Crossbeam." We moored under the point, a pile of loose, precipitous rocks, 150 feet high, detained an hour by a strong westerly gust of wind and rain, against which it would have been impossible to have made headway. At length we made another start, and crawled and clawed along the precipitous banks of the Pa-tung reach, past the unwalled district city of Pa-tung, in which a small coal trade alone exists. Its main street is built on a steep bank about 100 feet above the present level, and it is said by unfortunate magistrates appointed to it to be the poorest district city in the province. Poor as it is, however, its inhabitants have come to the conclusion that its poverty is due, not to its isolated situation among barren mountains, nor yet to the prohibition by the authorities of modern appliances for improving its coal output, but to a defect in its " Feng-shui." Great sacrifices have therefore been made to remedy this defect, and evidences of these are seen in six completed stories of a new pagoda, which is being built on a conspicuous point of hard white rock on the left bank, a mile or more below the town. In Eastern China, where we see the pagodas mostly neglected and in ruin, we little imagine that new pagodas still continue to be built in other parts of the empire. Nearly every town on the river has a pagoda, new or old, situated a mile or two below it, and generally on the left or north bank (the river flows roughly east and west), which is supposed to prevent the wealth of the town being swept past it by the rapid current for the benefit of the cities below.

Distance, ninety li ; say, twenty miles.

Thursday, March 22nd.—Fifth day in the gorges. At six a.m. we left the bank under the lifeless city of Pa-tung in a heavy shower, with cold head-wind, which blew most uncomfortably through the mat tunnel in which we live. It is impossible to close up the ends of this tunnel, except at night, when the boat is moored, as the helmsman requires a clear view through it to be able to steer. However, in these parts, the sublimity of the view reconciles one to any amount of discomfort.

The gorge widens out slightly after leaving Pa-tung, giving room for piles of gigantic *débris* from the neighbouring mountains to obstruct the river and create numerous small rapids, which we surmount in the usual painful manner. The country is wild and desolate-looking in the extreme, and well explains the poverty of the Pa-tung district. The Lao-ta tells me, that since the Feng-shui of the district was " puh "-ed by the pagoda—that we saw building yesterday—an improvement is already noticeable, a graduate (named Shu) having at length arisen in the district, which had been barren of this produce for no less than 200 years previously. I landed, as usual, when the coolies stopped for breakfast, about seven a.m. ; not being so active as they in scrambling over rock *débris*, I am soon caught up, and have difficulty in keeping pace with them, until we reach the next landing, when, the eddy being favourable, we all embark, and take to the oars.

Not a house or sign of cultivation is visible in this reach. Two huge, flat reefs of rocks, their sheer face fifty feet high, but which are covered in summer, now stretch out from the left bank, occupying two-thirds of the river-channel and causing a race called by the boatmen a " Chi-kou," after which the great Wu-shan Gorge, twenty miles long, opens its

Our House-boat, with Cliff, in Wushan Gorge.

To face p. 72.

gloomy chasm before us. This is called the "Wu-shan-ta hsia," *i.e.* Witches' Mountain Great Gorge, so named from the district city of Wu-shan, the first town over the Szechuan frontier, which is situated at its upper end. This gorge varies from 350 to 600 yards in width, and, according to the Chinese, is unfathomable. Throughout the whole twenty miles' length of this grand gorge the river winds round the base of precipitous cliffs, rising vertically in places to 1000 feet, with still higher, all but perpendicular, slopes above, and lofty mountain-pinnacles behind. The entrance, as the river seems to disappear behind the mountains—range upon range of which rise above us, the highest summits just projecting above the fleecy clouds—presents a sublime and solemn aspect. The silence is complete; the rare junks are lost in the immensity of the surrounding nature, and as the current is slack, and a favourable breeze enables the crew to rest awhile from their oars, Schiller's verses, written at Koesen in Thuringia, amidst that beautiful but less grand scenery, recur to my memory—

"Bin ich denn wirklich allein, in deinen Armen, Natur!"

Here, as at the Shin-tan, I observed kites fishing; half-naked men and boys also stand out on the rocks at the foot of each small rapid, catching the minute fish, which alone seem to frequent these troubled waters, with a hand dip-net.

We had put our wounded trackers ashore at Pa-tung in the night, and I was not well pleased to see that, when our trackers were ashore, we had now only one man left in the boat, besides the helmsman, to manage her in the event of our again executing a "Ta-chang," as at the Yeh rapid yesterday. The crew's cook, who formed the spare man on board, was taking the injured man's place, and he proves a most active and powerful worker, although he makes the boat reek with opium fumes every night from seven to nine p.m., while the rest of the men are fast asleep, after their hard day's toil. He tells me he has smoked one mace (about 90 grains) daily for the last ten years; but the native drug is milder than the imported, which may account for the fact of his health being apparently not injured in the slightest degree by the habit. He is thirty-one years of age, and looks much younger. Like nearly all the trackers, his naked body is entirely covered with itch sores, which do not appear to incommode him in the least.

The mountains here rise to between 2000 and 3000 feet, but glimpses of higher peaks behind are occasionally caught through a break in the walls, where a tiny affluent has cut out a narrow side glen. Two such glens, which open into the gorge on either bank, form the boundary-line between the provinces of Hu-peh and Szechuan, which we passed at four o'clock. A wilder spot could hardly be imagined. The gorge is not over 500 yards wide; the cliffs, about 700 feet, with lofty peaks behind. A solemn stillness reigns, only disturbed by the splash of our oars as we advance slowly, first on one side, then on the other, as we take advantage of the eddies crawling past the projecting points where the stream runs strong. One feels at times the lonelinessi of the ocean, and, as at sea, should anything happen to the frail craft, the best swimmer would fail to make a landing. The rocks are still limestone, with super-incumbent sandstone; and where the softer rock has been washed away, the hard limestone forms a colossal terrace to the cliffs above. This lower terrace is fluted along its water-face. Perpendicular pot-holes have been bored right down through it, and the outer walls having been broken through, this curious fluted surface is the result. In more than one place, at several hundred feet above the water-level, I observed natural caves under an overhanging ledge, the entrance to which was partially walled up. These inaccessible nooks had formed the retreat of the sparse inhabitants during the Tai-ping and other rebellions. In another spot, at a break in the cliffs, lay a pile of square blocks of what looked like black-leaded rocks—some as large as a house, fallen apparently from the summit of the mountain behind them, all curiously fretted by the water, and looking as though burnt and blackened in a furnace—and called by the Chinese, not inappropriately, " Ho yen shih," *i.e.* Fire Smoke Rock.

This reach is named the " T'ieh kwan tsai hsia," or Iron Coffin Gorge, from a projecting, coffin-shaped rock in a towering cliff on the left bank. At its entrance is a rock-strewn rapid, called the " Mu-chu tan," or Sow Rapid, up which we struggled in the usual way. Above the Coffin Gorge, iron chains are affixed to the cliffs, fifty feet above the present level, for the use of the upward-bound junks in the time of the summer freshets. A junk stole these chains some time back, when, upon arriving in Hankow, lo! the chain had been metamorphosed into a snake! The alarmed junk people hurried back to the violated spot, and replaced the snake on the rocks, when it at once resumed its original form, and now hangs again in its place on the rocks in evidence!

The last inhabited spot in Hu-peh is the village of " Nan Mu yu'rh," *i.e.* Cedar Garden, romantically situated astride a steep glen, down which flows a small mountain burn, which has its source in a cavern about one-third of the distance from the summit of the 2000-feet-high mountain upon which it is built. The two portions of the village are united midway by a covered bridge. I landed at the foot of a flight of five or six hundred steep stone steps, which form the main street of the village, the houses being terraced up on either side. Behind the houses are groves of orange, lemon, and loquat, all evergreens, besides peach and plum-trees, now in full bloom. Above this charming spot the gorge closes in again, and leaves no room for habitation, until about six miles higher up a colossal limestone ledge, backed by precipitous hills, affords standing-room for the village of " Pei-shih " (Back to the rock), the first place we come to in the Szechuan province. It consists of a long, straggling street, perched up well out of reach of the summer floods, with an imposing Taoist temple in its midst. The houses are of the usual flimsy brick, but stand upon a ledge of hard, smooth, bare blue limestone, the inhabitants depending upon the passing junks for a livelihood. Immediately below it is a narrow glen, now dry, the floods from which in the rainy season have thrust out a huge cone of sand and boulders, narrowing the channel and forming a small rapid, which it took us over an hour to surmount. The upper edge of the terrace, on which the town is built, is scored in places four to six inches deep with ruts formed by the fraying of the bamboo tow-lines. The owner of a small drug-shop—a very poor one, but which possessed a flag planted on the balustrade before the door, announcing its owner to be captain of the volunteers of the place (Twan-lien)—invited me into his house. After serving me with the customary tea and hubble-hubble pipe, he informed me that ever since the great Tai-ping Rebellion, which, it must be remembered, broke out after the empire had enjoyed a long peace for over 200 years, and the leader of which, Hung siu chuen, was one of Mr. P. Roberts' Christian converts made in Canton, the Szechuan people had organized themselves into trained bands, which, said my host, would render another outbreak of the kind impossible. His large family, comprising four generations, stood at a respectful distance, and did not crowd round to feel me and ply me with inane questions, as in the less highly civilized provinces to the east. Upon my asking him whether he was a "Pen-ti" (native of the place), he answered, "No!" that his family had immigrated from Kiang-si in the reign of the Chien-lung, two centuries ago. At this period, Szechuan had been almost depopulated by the rebellion suppressed by Wu-sankwei, which took place during the disturbances which followed upon the Man-chu conquest of the country. This was preceded by the rebellion of Chang chung chien, a monster of indiscriminate slaughter, who is said to have made a pyramid of women's feet, crowning it with those of his own wife, who remonstrated at his cruelty. Szechuan was thereupon repeopled from the eastern provinces, and these immigrants still call themselves natives of their forefathers' original homes.

I walked on, a mile past the town to the end of the ledge, crossing the mouth of another cliff-faced glen, looking up which I again caught a glimpse of mountain-peaks against the clouds. Turning to the gorge, up which lies our to-morrow's course to Wu-shan hsien, I gazed upon the chasm, looking dark and gloomy in the twilight, the silver streak forming its floor scarcely recognizable as the representative of the magnificent Yang-tse. Our boat came round at last, and moored for the night in the little bay formed by the terrace end, down which I climbed, and went on board for dinner.

Distance, 100 li; say, twenty-five miles.

Friday, March 23rd.—Sixth day in the gorges. Off at daylight; a cold wind and rain blowing through the boat. We scrambled up several small rapids, formed by avalanches of gigantic rocks from the mountains on the left bank; rounded one sharp point, where the river seems to disappear altogether, until at last we came in sight of the opening at the end of the gorge, with the welcome sight of Wu-shan city in the distance, where we landed in the afternoon. I am getting positively weary of the endless rapids, especially as, being two men short—a second having succumbed to his accident at the Yeh-tan—we are decidedly undermanned; and this day's whole progress was a hard but gallant struggle, in which one would gladly have taken part, but which was almost painful to witness in inaction. The current in this, the upper end of the Witch's Gorge, runs fully five knots, and the crew had to claw us along under the cliffs with small hooks attached to the end of long bamboos. In one or two places they managed to track us short distances, crawling over almost inaccessible rocks. Crossing one bay cut out by a whirlpool, we took in the tow-rope, leaving the trackers to walk round, while the one man left on board besides the helmsman rowed the boat slowly up the eddy, intending to throw the line out again, to be caught by the trackers just below the rapid. He miscalculated the direction, and the boat's nose, caught by the descending "race," was turned sharply round, and we went flying back, as at the Yeh-tan. But here there was no danger. As we were not attached to the tow-line, the boat took no sheer, and, after half an hour's delay, we got back again into the returning eddy, and then rounded the point successfully. Although many of these whirlpools are a quarter of a mile in diameter, and have a deep depression in the centre, there is, where no rocks obstruct, little danger, the flat bottom and light draft and great beam of the junks giving the water little hold upon them. Still, I cannot say, with Mr. Donald Spence, that with the rapids familiarity breeds contempt, for I find the long, ceaseless struggle with them beginning to tell upon the nerves. Probably Mr. Spence never tried them in a shen-po-tse, *i.e.* a small sailing-boat, such as I am now in.

Travelling House-boat, with Tender, moored in Wushan Gorge: Nude Figure in Foreground, Man who swims out to disengage the Tow-lines: Tender is steered by Long Stern-sweep: House-boat with Long Bow-sweep.   [*To face p.* 78.

The rapid opposite Wu-shan is due to the obstruction caused by the moraine of a small affluent, navigable 180 li, up to the district city of Ta-ling (Ta-ling Hsien), and through this terminal moraine (if it may be so termed) the stream has cut down a narrow channel. The district of Ta-ling produces, from brine wells, the invaluable commodity, salt. The brine is here evaporated by wood-fires, and not by natural gas, as further west. The boats which bring down the salt seem an exact copy of the Venetian gondola, with their cocked-up sterns, stern-oar, and small mat-house amidships. The boatmen are stark naked, and tanned copper colour by the sun, having constantly to jump off into the shallow water and either help the boat along, or else stop her from grinding too rapidly over the shifting boulders.

The cleft in the limestone hills, in which the long gorge ends, opens suddenly out into a charming valley, the slopes of which are cultivated halfway up with tallow-trees and other sub-tropical fruits. The city itself is picturesquely situated on the slope immediately facing the gorge, its walls climbing halfway up the mountain from which it takes its name. Crossing an extensive sand-flat not yet covered, I ascended the steep, rocky bank, sixty or eighty feet high, and entered the south gate, followed by a wondering but respectful crowd. The little urchins ran on in front, shouting, "Yang-jen!" (Ocean-man or Foreigner); but no "Yang-kwei-tse" (Foreign Devil) was heard any more from this time forth. This opprobrious term, by which foreigners are universally designated in the eastern provinces, is happily unknown in Szechuan. I ascended the walls, the summit of which forms the only available promenade in Chinese cities, and looked down on the smiling valley of the "Siao-ho," or Lesser River, as these affluents are similarly called at each place, and walked on until where the wall begins to ascend the hill at the back. Here the wall, its top reduced in width to six feet, is now a succession of steep stone steps, and it encloses a large extent of fields and farms, the streets proper being confined to the more level ground near the river. Like many mountain cities, and as typified in the Great Wall itself, the walls follow the crests of the hills, apparently lest the town should be commanded from the neighbouring heights; but it results in extending the line of defence beyond all reason.

From this height the Yang-tse, though nowhere less than 500 yards wide, looks like a mountain torrent meandering between rocks and sandbanks, the roar of the Hsia-ma rapid, a few miles above the town, being distinctly heard. Wu-shan shares the apparent ruin and decay common to all Chinese towns; but the houses are more spacious, and the streets wider and cleaner, than in the average of the towns in the eastern provinces. The left portal of the Wu-shan Gorge is a steep, conical mountain of about 1500 feet, on the top of which is a temple, in a grove of evergreens, called the Wen-feng shan, or Temple of Literature; behind rises a range of 2500 feet.

For some inscrutable reason—probably to increase the number of its literary graduates—Wu-shan is erecting a brand-new pagoda on this peak, of which our boatmen highly disapprove. They say the site is ill-omened; that it dominates the Wu-shan rapid and whirlpool; and is bound to cause disaster. I here had to send in my passport, with my Chinese card, to the Che-hsien (District Magistrate); and I received a fresh pass, together with an escort of two Ting-chai (Ya-men runners), appointed personally to conduct me to the next city. This is a custom peculiar to the West, and exists since the time when the Chinese local authorities were rightly made responsible for the murder of Margary in

Yunnan. These delegates from the local magistracy (Ya-men) now attend every foreigner travelling in the "Four Streams" province, merchant or missionary alike.

Wu-Shan was our Lao-ta's home, and we discharged, on his account, from the bottom of the boat, four bales of native cotton-cloth, six sacks of rice, and several packages of incense, which he had taken advantage of the presence of the foreigner (dreaded by the officials), in his boat, to bring up from Shasze without paying tax at the numerous Li-kin stations we had passed on our voyage up. The sun was now getting powerful, and I was glad to regain the shelter of the boat, and enjoy our frugal dinner quietly moored in the calm bay off the town.

Distance, 110 li; say, twenty-seven miles.

Saturday, March 24th, 1883.—Seventh day in the gorges. Off at dawn, and proceeded up the small rapid just above the town, the "Siao mao-rh," or "Kitten," running five to six knots; and then, four miles farther up, the "Hsia ma tan," or "Get-down-from-horse rapid," running seven to eight knots. This rapid, like many others, where not due to a reef of hard rocks *in situ*, is caused by the *débris* brought down from the mountains by a small side stream issuing out of a narrow glen. Up this glen is a wonderful cavern, called the "Lao-lung-Tung," or Old Dragon cave, in passing which mounted men are supposed to descend from their steeds and do obeisance. Hence the curious name of the rapid.

Five miles above Wu-Shan the valley closes in again, and we enter the "Feng-hsiang," or "Bellows," gorge, so-called from the imaginary resemblance of a prominence on the entrance cliff to a Chinese blacksmith's bellows, which is an oblong wooden box. This is the last of the great gorges. Its vertical walls, which appear to run up from 1500 to

G

2000 feet, have been clean cut by the river, which here flows directly athwart the mountain range. Where side ravines break through the walls, we have piles of broken rocks forming points on alternate sides of the river, round which the current rushes in alternate rapids and whirlpools. At one rapid, called "T'o tu tze," the eddy ran up and broke over the rocks with the same force as the rapid proper, into which it shot us with a jerk that showed the wisdom of the Lao-ta in having sent five men ashore with two separate tow-ropes, leaving two men upon the deck forward to promptly sweep her head round to the current with the bow sweep. Here lay two big junks—their cargoes of raw cotton neatly housed on shore under a tent made of the sails and mat covers—hove down on the beach, having their bottoms replanked, both having come to grief at this spot while towing up to Chung-king. Another of the red life-boats, each of which has a crew of four men, was patrolling round this rapid. We afterwards passed the "Yo sha Chi" race, the "Likwei Tan" rapid, and the "Hu-shu-tse," or Tiger's Beard, the rapid being so named from a dangerous rock in its midst, round which the current rushed in a circle, as with water twirled round a washing-basin. The last and most troublesome rapid is formed by a boulder spit, due to an affluent on the right bank, in the angle of which, high up the mountain side, stands the picturesque village of "Ta-chi kou," celebrated as the residence of several retired "armateurs" or junk-owners, who, our Lao-ta informs me, wisely retired before the present wretched times afflicted the transport business.

The spit at its mouth dams up the water in the deep reservoir of the Feng-hsiang Gorge, and we hung fire in the current formed by the overflow, our five trackers clinging, on their hands and feet, to the jagged rocks as they pulled

Entrance to Bellows Gorge; Cliffs 3000 and 4000 Feet. In Cliff on the Right are cut the Square Holes of Mêng-liang's Ladder.

To face p. **82.**

the boat up inch by inch. I cannot sufficiently admire the pluck and endurance of these poor coolies, earning but two dollars in cash for a two months' voyage, and getting from the Lao-ta three meals of coarse rice, flavoured with a little fried cabbage, for their sustenance, upon which they are called to put forth all their strength from dawn to dark daily. This place is well named the "Tsei-ka-tse," or "Narrow Barrier," and it seemed to produce a sudden drop of four feet, which, with the bad foothold on shore, it looked an impossibility to surmount.

The Feng-hsiang Gorge is about four miles long, and it took us three hours to get through it, the crew rowing hard against the current, which above the Tsei-ka-tse seemed otherwise hardly perceptible. At its mouth, narrowing the channel to 200 yards under the right, and to barely 100 on the left bank, right in the fairway, stands a square-shaped rock mass, now forty feet out of water, black-polished, as at the Tsei-ka. This dangerous obstruction is known as the "Yen-wei shih," or "Goose-tail" rock. During most of the time of the summer floods it is about awash; but whenever it is covered, the authorities at Kwei-chow-fu detain the junks, and will not allow them to descend until the reappearance of the Goose-tail above the surface. A mark on the embankment of Kwei-chow city, five miles above, coincides with the top of the rock. At the present season, this dreaded rock has all the appearance of a castle built to command the pass.

All this neighbourhood teems with legends of bygone days, notably of the wars of the Three Kingdoms in the second century, when the then kingdom of Hu-peh invaded the kingdom of Shu or Szechuan by way of the Great River. The Hu-peh fleet was arrested by a chain stretched across the narrowest point in the gorge, near its western exit, and the posts to which the chain was affixed are still shown. But more remarkable is the famous "Mêng-liang ti," or Ladder of Mêng-liang, which adjoins this spot. There can be no doubt about the genuineness of this relic, for no sane man would undertake such a work unless he had Mêng-liang's object to gain by it. At the time this ladder, so-called, was constructed, the "Shu" army was encamped upon the mountains above the precipice, and felt secure in their unassailable position, the river being barred, while the cliff appeared to be insurmountable. But the Hu-peh general, Mêng-liang, got his army up the vertical cliff, surprised the enemy's camp, and reaped a victory which ended the domination of Shu. His plan was effected by making a ladder up the cliff, here 700 feet vertical. He had square holes cut in the hard limestone rock, six inches square by about fourteen deep, into which were inserted wooden beams, up which his men climbed. The wooden beams have long since perished, but the holes remain as clean-cut now as on the day when they were made. These run in zig-zags up the face of the vertical cliff, until they reach the point where the slopes above are just practicable for an expert climber. The day has long past since the now effeminate Chinese were capable of such heroic exertion, but "Mêng-liang's ladder" will remain in evidence for many centuries yet as a testimony of the valour and determination which inspired their warlike ancestors.

A grand overhanging peak, with a sheer face of white limestone, with strata nearly vertical, marks the portal of the gorge; issuing from which we enter the more open valley, in which stands the famous prefectual city of Kwei-chow-fu, in a position analogous to that of Wu-shan city at the exit of the Wu-shan Gorge.

On the sandbanks below Kwei-chow, which now occupy

three-fourths of the river's bed, is the colony of salt-boileries. The brine is collected in pits dug in the sand, and then evaporated with the native hard coal. It is the only place in China that I have seen present (in the distance) a faint resemblance to a manufacturing town, due to the quantity of escaping steam. Rounding this bank, which will be deep under water again in a few weeks' time, and a huge boulder flat beyond, we at length bring up under the walls of Kwei-chow, and our seven days' voyage through the gorges proper is at an end. So many exciting incidents have occurred in this week that it seems to be more than a month since I started from Ichang.

Kwei-chow-fu (commonly called Kwei-fu, to distinguish it from Kwei-chow in Hu-peh, which I have described above) is a fine city, picturesquely situated on a bold slope, and is surrounded by high, crenellated walls, with turreted gateways, and four tiers of stone bunding on the river-front below, all in an unusually good state of preservation. Built out of the reach of the summer floods, the foundations of its walls are a good hundred feet above our boat, and the wide sandy slope between is green and yellow with wheat and rape-seed, the latter now in flower, and which will shortly all be reaped before the water rises. At the foot of the bank, and along the water's edge, is the usual winter street of temporary, mud-plastered houses, with opium-booths, tea, and other shops, for the needs of the boat population. In one is a fearful din of gongs and drums going on, making night hideous as I write, which I am informed is a grand "chin-chin joss pigeon," a favourite function for the benefit of one of the inmates reported sick unto death.

Five miles below Kwei-fu, perched up on the cliff that forms the left portal of the Bellows Gorge—Mêng-liang's Cliff forming the right portal, going down-stream—is a fine temple, with gardens and courtyards adorned by handsome stone pavilions, commanding magnificent views in all directions, which marks the site of the old city of Pai-ti Chêng. Pai-ti Chêng, or "Stronghold of the White Emperor," was a famous place in the days of the warring kingdoms, and its ruined walls are still traceable.

CHAPTER V.

IN SZECHUAN.

The customs at Kwei-chow—Transit passes—Their effect on the provincial officials—The drought—Anthracite at Kwei-chow—Visit to a mandarin—A concert—Management of the junks.

KWEI-CHOW-FU, or, for short, Kwei-fu or Kwei-hwan (*i.e.* "The Kwei-chow Barrier"), as it is more commonly called, is the great Li-kin "barrier," which taxes all the trade passing by the Yang-tse route between the "Four-streams" province, with its population of 40,000,000, and its fertile territory of 200,000 square miles, and Eastern China. The local Li-kin office, or custom-house, used formerly to be, next to that of Canton, the most valuable post of the kind in the empire. The transit tax averages about five per cent. on the value of the goods, which are all carefully examined by gaugers attached to the Ya-men, whereby a delay of three or four days is entailed on every junk passing up or down, their number amounting in the year to over 10,000. Hence, although situated in a poor, mountain district, a large population finds subsistence, and the town is studded with the numerous mansions of the wealthy officials and their dependents. These customs form the main source of revenue of the Szechuan province, the land-tax having been reduced to an almost nominal sum in order to attract immigrants after its depopulation at the end of the Ming Dynasty, and having been never since increased. But now a blight has fallen over the place, due to the machinations of the intruding foreigner, who has insisted upon opening a new treaty port at Chung-king, whereby all imports are now admitted into the heart of Szechuan upon payment of one single import duty in Shanghai. The unfortunate Szechuan officials fought as hard as they could against the innovation, which in this decentralized land meant nothing else than their total ruin, but in vain. A few junks carrying local merchandise, and so unprovided with "foreign" customs' passes, still pay Li-kin duties on the spot, as also the salt junks, this trade being a government monopoly by treaty. The result is to replenish the Imperial coffers at the cost of the local authorities, which latter pay a fixed tribute to Peking, retaining the balance of whatever they may collect for their own benefit. Thus, the revenue of Kwei-chow, formerly estimated at 2000 taels a day, is being gradually reduced to *nil:* the central government, whose expenditure in relation to the size and resources of the empire was smaller than that of any other civilized state, is now draining the provinces in a way diametrically opposed to the genius of the Chinese constitution, and one cannot wonder at the consequent hostility of the provincial authorities to foreign intercourse. These provincial officials, deprived of their perquisites, their salaries being purely nominal, have to resort to all kinds of oppressive devices to make up their incomes. What the eventual result of our thus forcibly strengthening the Imperial Government at the expense of the provinces will be, remains to be seen. At present it acts in favour of supporting the Foreign Customs Service, as only by means of foreign officials in the Chinese service, backed as these are by outside foreign influence, can the system be maintained in the face of the persistent and natural opposition of the provincial governments. It is true

Kwei-chow Fu, Five Miles from Upper Entrance to Gorges; Entrance shown in Split Hill on Left.
Height 3000 to 4000 Feet.

that a certain proportion of the revenues thus collected at the foreign customs is handed back to the provincial governors; but the amount is nothing compared to the revenues obtained by them when the taxation lay exclusively in their hands. One thing is certain, viz. that, until some arrangement is made more favourable to the local officials, we shall never see mining and other enterprises willingly thrown open to foreigners, and the illimitable resources of this rich empire properly developed. The same obstacle hinders the introduction of railways and all the other elements of Western progress.

Upon ascending the Kwei-chow bank, the mountains behind the hills, that form the opposite shore, become visible. The high peaks in the rear appeared to be of the same white formation which puzzled me in the Ichang Gorge. Like all the mountains bordering the river, they range from two to three thousand feet, and the stream appears to have forced its way through the hard limestone mountains in a direction at right angles to their main axis. What has determined the actual course of the river cutting its way through such cliffs as that of the Bellows Gorge, which, as seen from Kwei-chow, looks like a slit cut with a knife across the mountain, it is difficult to say. This whole question of the gorges would present a most interesting problem to a competent geologist for study on the spot. Probably, when the Szechuan basin was filled by a vast inland lake, the water found an outlet to the sea by cutting its way down, in the course of æons, through the rocks of least resistance.

Distance (Lao-ta's reckoning, as usual), ninety-five li; say, twenty-four miles, making, in all, from Ichang to Kwei-chow, 146 miles.

This total I believe to be nearer the mark than Blakiston's estimate of 102 miles. I hardly think that Blakiston has allowed enough for the constant turns and angles in the gorges; his chart certainly merely gives the general direction. The difference in longitude is one degree, thirty-five minutes, or nearly 100 statute miles, besides a difference of twenty minutes in latitude.

Sunday, March 25th (Easter Sunday).—Moored all day at Kwei-chow-fu, waiting for a clearance. Having two larger junks coming up behind laden with goods under transit pass, besides purposing to despatch others downward from Chung-king, it was advisable I should call on the authorities and make myself known. At ten o'clock I accordingly set out in a chair with three bearers, and proceeded to make my visits, attended by my Shansi guide carrying my cards (Chinese, on red paper) in a leather portfolio. The south gate, below which we lay moored, was closed on account of the drought, no rain having fallen for the past six months. This shutting the south gate of a city would seem to be a kind of silent protest—made in accordance with the Nature-worship, which appears to be the only real, indigenous, and universal religion of the Chinese—against the south, which is the fire quarter, and the presiding influence over heat and drought. Thus, when Auster blows against the south gate and finds it shut, a hint is supposed to be given to him that his presence is *de trop*. We crossed the sloping sandbank, and ascended by a long flight of steps to the west gate. On this sandbank were scattered manufactories of prepared fuel, such as is seen in the cottages of South Wales, made by kneading up the coal-dust with clay. Junks were loading this, together with anthracite coal in big lumps for Shasze, it being used there by the blacksmiths in preference to the local Hunan coal. When steamers run upon the Upper Yang-tse, this will be the coaling-station, after they have exhausted their bunkers climbing up the arduous 150 miles between this and Ichang. Very fair anthracite can be bought here for ten shillings a ton. The coal comes down a small affluent (again called Siao Ho, *i.e.* the Lesser River), which enters through a glen to the south side of the city, and the stony moraine of which forms the big spit, that creates the slack water and also the harbour or anchorage of Kwei-chow, precisely analogous to that formed by the Siao Ho at Wushan. Entering the winding passage through the city walls, jostled by the usual crowd of water-carriers, who make the long, steep journey from the river into the houses in the city, laden with two buckets of water, for five cash (one farthing), the crowded passage narrowed still more by a double row of pork butchers' and hucksters' stalls, leaving barely room for a single sedan-chair to pass, we turned to the right, and then mounted up another flight of steps to the top of the city wall. This turned out to be just upon a level with that of the rising ground behind. For this reason, and being beautifully paved with large sandstone blocks, it forms a busy thoroughfare, protected on the river-side by the usual crenelated battlements, the whole forming a handsome esplanade, with a view of the winding stream below, until it is lost to sight behind the majestic portals of the Feng-hsiang Gorge.

The streets of Kwei-chow-fu are broad, and the houses more spacious than on the east side of the mountains, but the shops are poor, and the place shows unmistakable signs of rapidly progressing decay. Add to this the destitution caused throughout the prefecture by the total failure of the winter crops, and we can sympathize with the unfortunate mandarins whose sins are responsible for the misery sent by Heaven upon the people, and who are now engaged in humbling themselves and praying for rain. Hence, only the official deputed to manage foreign affairs, Yang wu sze, was open to an interview. This gentleman, known as Wang sze Ta Jen, *i.e.* Wang, the Fourth Excellency, received me very politely; but after the customary ceremonious compliments had passed, and we were duly seated on the daïs at the head of the reception-hall—the cynosure of the ragged crowd who never seem to be refused admission—the poor old gentleman seemed so discomfited at the barbarian irruption, that I truly pitied him. And, indeed, much. as one may abuse the mandarinate in general, it is the system more than the individuals—mostly kindly, well-meaning men—which is to blame. And as all the responsibility of any hitch in dealing with the aggressive, unscrupulous foreigner devolves upon the local official concerned, while his duty is to oppose a *non possumus* to every request, he stands between two fires, and his life is not a happy one. At length, having got through the regulation business, we sipped our tea—the conventional sign that the interview is at an end—and I took my departure, greatly to his Excellency's relief. Being a Hunan man, his *patois* was difficult to understand, even had he been conversationally inclined. The Tao-tai's yamen still bore the traces of ancient grandeur, court above court rising by successive flights of steps, each courtyard adorned with two superb Hoang-ko trees, but the buildings looked like those of a deserted ruin. The Hsien's or Magistrate's ya-men was equally ruinous, but in no way deserted. A large, dirty crowd, including three cadaverous-looking wretches with big, square *cangues* (wooden collars, three feet square) round their necks, which seem to trouble their neighbours more than the occupants, surrounded my chair, until I ordered my coolies to make a dash and get clear of them. But the absence of any rude remark, such as one is inevitably greeted with in the east of China, was surprisingly noticeable.

Upon returning, I found an altercation going on on board

my boat between the Lao-ta and the li-kin officials. The former wanted to escape paying tonnage dues, on the ground that he was conveying a foreign Excellency. Instead of frightening the officers away, as he had expected me to do, I ordered him to pay, the amount on this small boat being 700 cash, or about three shillings. The day was hot and close—80° in the shade—and though thick clouds, to the joy of the crowd, gathered round at sunset, not a drop of rain fell, the clouds melting away completely, as the full moon rose behind the mountains.

Owing to the drought, a strict fast had been proclaimed throughout the district, and the beef I had been expecting to buy here, let alone pork or fowls, was unobtainable. I had calculated upon replenishing my stores with the rich products of Szechuan, but got nothing but a few eggs at four times the usual cost. These, with rice and coarse cabbage, will form our daily food until we leave the drought country. The harbour here is gay with flower-boats and singing-girls. The boats in which these latter live ply up and down in the rear of the long tier of junks tied to the bank, and our evening was enlivened by my Chinese having engaged one of them, which was now moored under our stern. It was a picturesque scene, with the moon rising over the gorge, the black, rugged outlines of the mountains opposite sharp-cut against the illuminated sky. The sing-song boat was a sampan, with a steeply-arched awning amidships, and with the big sweep used in these parts hanging over the high-peaked stern instead of a rudder. In the arch of the mat, lit by a big paper lantern on one side, sat two gaudily-dressed, pretty-looking girls, aged respectively ten and thirteen years, and behind them an old man of eighty, playing the fiddle. The two girls sang in a high falsetto, one accompanying on the guitar, while a second man in the bows beat time with a big pair of bamboo castanettes in his left, and a drum-stick in his right hand. With this latter he hammered away upon a drum on his knees, which consisted simply of a section of a colossal bamboo, made at one of its joints. One hundred cash (fourpence) was the cost of the entertainment, and for this we were allowed to select three pieces from a long *répertoire* tastefully inscribed upon an extended fan. Barring the hideous accompaniment, the singing was not inharmonious.

Monday, March 26th.—While delayed at Kwei-chow-fu, I watched the big junks towing slowly round the flat boulder-point below the city, above which is the quiet bay in which we are moored. The lively cry of the trackers rings in my ears, and will always be associated in my mind with the rapids of the Upper Yang-tse. This cry is "Chor-chor," said to mean "Shang-chia," or, "Put your shoulder to it," "it" being the line which is slung over the shoulder of each tracker, and attached to the quarter-mile-long tow-rope of plaited bamboo by a hitch, which can be instantaneously cast off and rehitched. The trackers mark time with this cry, swinging their arms to and fro at each short step, their bodies bent forward, so that their fingers almost touch the ground. When coming into a station like this, the long, thick tow-line is coiled up on the bank as the trackers advance, each man promptly casting off his own hitch as he gets to the front, and running back to take up his place and hitch on again in the rear. Eighty or a hundred men make a tremendous noise at this work, almost drowning the roar of the rapid, and often half a dozen junks' crews are towing like this, one behind the other. From the solemn stillness of the gorge to the lively commotion of a rapid, the contrast is most striking.

The larger junks are all accompanied by a tender, to land

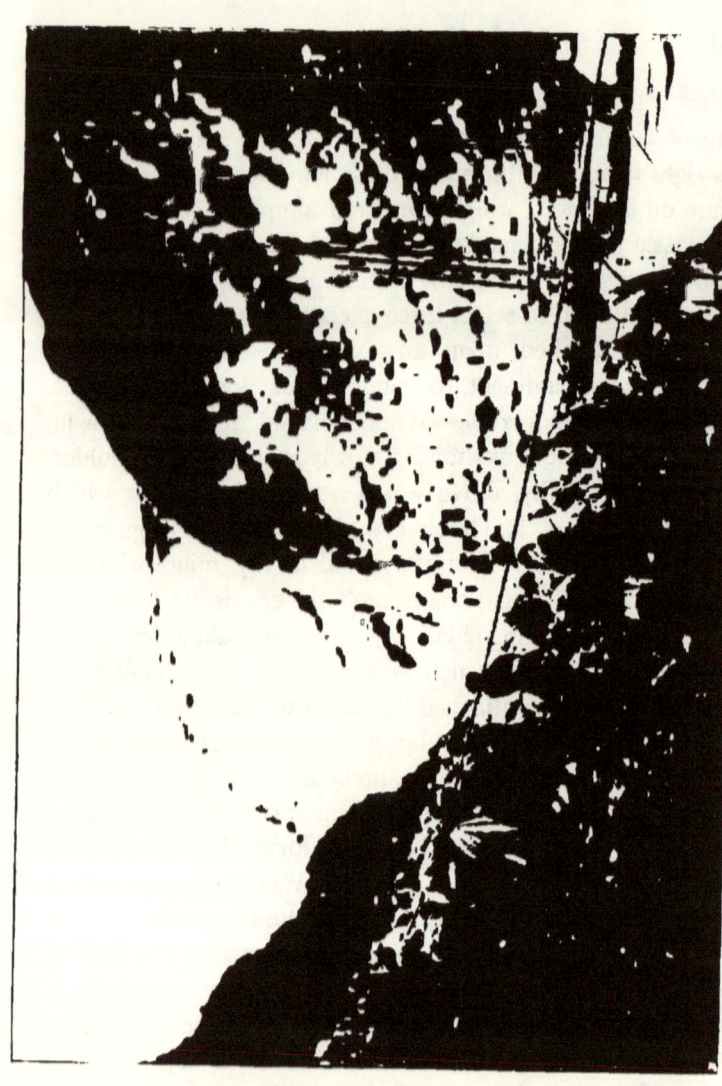

Trackers hauling on Bamboo Tow-lines at Entrance to Ping-shu Gorge.

[To face p. 94.

the trackers and the tow-line, which in inaccessible places is taken on by the tender and made fast to a rock ahead, and hauled on by the crew on board the junk. Many of these tenders are fine vessels, forty feet long, eight feet broad, and four feet deep. A mast forty feet high, and rising in the form of shears from each gunwale, carries a huge square lug-sail with a heavy wooden yard, and a boom of bamboo at the foot, round which the sail is furled, and which then stands perpendicularly up and down the mast. The wind being almost constantly up-stream, this big sail, which can only be set when the wind is directly aft, sends the tight boat along flying. On the Chuan Ho, the Szechuan river, or Upper Yang-tse, only two winds are known by the boatmen—the "Shang fêng," or "up wind;" and the "Hia fêng," or, "down wind."

Meanwhile, the drummer-man on board the big junk drums away as hard as he can, as a signal to the trackers to exert their utmost force, alternating with a rum-ti-tum, rum-ti-tum—the signal to cease hauling. Away from the rapids the river seems deserted; the surroundings are on such a grand scale that the scattered junks are lost, and in such a spot one would be led to believe that there was no traffic on the river at all. The high-water marks, far away above the masts of the largest junks, and which at a distance appear to be only a few feet above the river level, add to the deception. At Kwei-chow these are fully 100 feet high, and in exceptional years the water, dammed up by the narrow gorges below, rises many tens of feet higher. The order, discipline, and promptness displayed by the crews on the Chuan Ho is a striking contrast to the lax way in which, in other parts of China, bodies of workmen seem all to be giving orders together.

Our progress to-day was through a succession of eddies

and small rapids. In the words of Tennyson (slightly altered), "The rapid runs by every rocky point," and it was a constant succession of jumping out to haul us up by main force round these points, and in again to paddle the boat up the eddies. This work culminated in the fierce rapid of Lao-ma ("Old Horse"), at which we were detained some time, waiting our turn to get through, while the Ting-chai, my official conductor, jumped ashore in his official hat, and pressed extra trackers into our service, not one of whom would have received a cash but for my insistence.

I delayed the boat nearly an hour to-day through being unable to keep up with the trackers. The shore was a pile of broken rocks of all sizes, over which they with the tow-line hopped like cats, while I toiled painfully along bathed in perspiration, though clad in nothing but a pair of flannel trousers and a shirt. Somehow I lost the beach, and gradually ascended until I struck a mountain-path five or six hundred feet above. I crawled along this until in view of the precipice below me, and, the path getting almost too narrow for foothold, I came to a stop. The view from this height was very imposing. George Sand discusses somewhere the relative charm of a river gulch viewed from below and from above, and, I think, decides in favour of the former. To me, however, the view from about halfway up is the most striking: the size is then better appreciated. This valley is highly cultivated, and the mountains are as gay with the colours of the different crops as a patched quilt. To conclude: the crew spotted me in my white flannels wandering aloft, and one of them climbed up and put me in the right path, and brought me down in safety.

Distance, seventy-five li; say, eighteen miles, making total from Ichang, 164 miles. One month out from Hankow.

The Miao Chi-tse and Tung Yang Rapids

Tuesday, March 27th.—The crew roused me at five, as usual. With the first glimpse of dawn, the night-mat and awning framework having been stowed away meanwhile, we started, rowing up a long eddy: the valley still narrowed to the river-bed, almost steep enough to be called a gorge. Very little cultivation, the hills being strewn with rocks, which, where fallen into the river, formed points and consequent rapids: the strata are mainly of sandstone and horizontal; the current four to five knots. We passed the minor rapid of Miao chi-tse (Temple Stairs), the water rushing over a succession of rock steps with, however, a clear channel, but an eight-knot current in mid-stream. Here a local passenger-boat discharged its fares to walk over the boulders, while it was being hauled up the rapid empty; and it was characteristic to see the men run down the landing-plank, leaving the women, with their hideous, crippled feet, to get along as best they could. The babies were taken ashore and carried round the rapid, strapped to the backs of boys. Shortly afterwards we pulled up at the foot of a foaming cataract, called Tung yang tse. An eddy rushing up to this, and tumbling over the rocks with little less fury than the main stream, brought us up at a run, and it needed two stoppered bamboos to fend the boat off the rocks, upon which I alighted with the trackers.

This rapid is interesting, as showing what many other rapids need, an attempt at artificial improvement. The rapid is formed, on one side, by a ledge of solid rock jutting out from the mountains on the left bank; and, on the other side, by a huge cone of dejection, consisting of gigantic boulders, the *débris* brought down by a small affluent, at this season little more than a brook, running through a cleft in the hills opposite. Its mouth is diverted by a great barrier of neatly morticed stones, with a paved summit

H

some fifty feet wide. This is built on to and below the rock ledges, and diverts the stream into the whirlpool below the rapid. On its face is a fine stone tablet, which has engraved on it the four characters, " Yung ching ngan lan "—" To tranquillize the waters is a perpetual boon." In smaller characters at the side, we are informed that the tranquillization was effected in the seventh year of Tung-chih, or just thirteen years ago. But, alas! for the perpetuity of modern Chinese work! The lower end is already partially washed away; and the centre, instead of being constructed of modern masonry, is filled up with loose rocks, offering a convenient hold for the current to work upon. Masses of white sand everywhere intermingle with, and in many places entirely smooth over, the rugged rocks. The river continues to vary from three to six hundred yards in width. Above the Tung yang tse, or Temple of the Eastern Ocean, the left bank recedes, yielding room for a few green slopes and picturesque, tree-embosomed villages. Shortly afterwards, 1500 feet up on the right bank, appeared a white pagoda, the portal to the walled city of " Yun-yang hsien," five miles off, higher up.

Yun-yang hsien, or Clouded Sun City, is situated on the left bank of a picturesque gorge formed by pyramidal mountains, horizontally stratified, and 1000 to 1500 feet in height. Its walls run along the river 100 feet or more above the present level, and, as usual, extend some distance up the mountain, on the slope of which it is built. The mountain crest itself is crowned by an additional mud wall, and the summit is surrounded by a ruined castle or fort—all of which proved of little value as a defence against the local rebels or Tu-fei, who, in conjunction with a roving band of Tai-pings, devastated all this country in the early sixties.

Chang-fei's Temple, opposite Yünyang, Winter Level. In Summer, Foreground covered to a Depth of 50 Feet. On the Left the Author in Chinese Dress.

[*To face p.* 98.

In the city and suburb, which has little trade, are several imposing temples—one, the "Wan sho kung," or "Temple of Longevity," has a highly decorated front wall, with inlaid bronze tablets, the most conspicuous bearing the inscription, "Hsien li tsung," *i.e.* "Genii recorder bequeath footsteps"—a phrase, like most of those adorning temples, having little meaning except to those versed in Bhuddist and Taoist lore. But, on the opposite side of the river, on a picturesque cliff backed by wooded hills—such a spot as in the United States would be selected for an advertisement of "Smith's Liver Pad," or "Jones's Liniment,"—our attention is drawn to a colossal inscription in those elegant Chinese characters, which are a decoration in themselves, of the four words, "Ling tsung chien ku," *i.e.* "Ethereal bell one thousand ages." When a fire breaks out in the district, this magic bell rings of its own accord. Immediately above this rock inscription stands a gay-looking range of buildings comprising a temple, dedicated to the hero-saint, Chang-fei, a pork butcher who died fighting for his country in the wars of the "three kingdoms."

The temple is solidly built, in splendid repair, and gorgeously decorated; it comprises three courts and a two-storied pavilion, extending along the river-front. On one side is a handsome stone bridge, looking up which is seen a waterfall, which comes down a steep, narrow glen, the whole forming a scene which would make as pretty a picture of Eastern scenery as I have ever seen. We are moored on the opposite bank, waiting for the new Chai-jen (official messenger), who is to accompany and pass us on to the next district city, Wan Hsien; and I take advantage of the enforced delay to cross over in a ferry-boat and visit the place. We climbed up the almost perpendicular rock until we reached a flight of about a hundred stone steps, which landed us at the door of the temple, looking westward across the bridge. The walls are of brick on stone foundation, as usual, the superstructure supported on morticed wooden columns. One of the courts we found filled with well-dressed women, comprising apparently the rank and fashion of the city of the " Clouded Sun." They were about fifty in number, and had just feasted, and were now playing cards and dominoes, seated in parties round the usual square tables. They are all stump-footed, but healthy-looking, and, though curious to see him, are not at all put out by the irruption of a tall barbarian in a flannel suit, on his head a bath-towel twisted into a huge but graceful turban (the only really effective sun-shade). The priest, an unusually polished Chinaman, showed me round, and told me that this new temple replaces an old temple washed away in the terrible flood of 1870, when the water rose to a level with the present roof—nearly 200 feet above the actual low-water level. This rebuilding cost 10,000 taels, about £1500, being little more than half what such a work would cost at Shanghai.

Wednesday, March 28th.—The sun's heat in the morning is intense. I go ashore to enjoy the morning air, and get violently heated in scrambling over the precipitous towing-paths. Up to noon it is dead calm; then the up-river breeze gradually rises, and a chilling gale is upon you before you are hardly aware of the change. This regular easterly breeze, which sets in daily after the sun has gained power, is invaluable to the crude native crafts which navigate this river. In many long stretches the cliffs are vertical and no towing-path exists, so that without a fair wind they would never get up at all.

Such was my experience to-day, after a long morning's walk over a succession of rocky points and intervening sand-hills, the former looking as though but yesterday a cartload of Brobdignagian paving-stones, varying in size from a house to a dog-kennel, had been shunted off the mountain ridge behind. I was recalled to the boat as we were entering the " Pa ngai hsia," or " Gorge of the Eight Cliffs." This is a bed of hard grey sandstone, through which the river has cut itself an even channel about 300 yards in width, and thirty li—say, six miles—in length. The cliffs are perpendicular, fluted by innumerable " pot-holes," and generally worn into rugged, fantastic outlines. The gorge sweeps round in a curve, the stream entering it with an easterly, and leaving it with a northerly course. My boatman informed me that the gorge had no bottom. At top the cliff extends an almost level surface of one to two hundred yards, to the feet of the broken mountains which rise from and behind it. The summit of the cliffs is only forty feet above the present level, and in the summer rise they are entirely hidden, the water then reaching to the bordering mountains. At such a time the down-going junks are indebted alone to the force of the current for keeping them in the channel.

This curious gorge terminates in a wide ridge of the same formation, of the same height, and with the same level top; but instead of one grand channel, the river finds its way through it in five small ones. All through this gorge a chilling wind blew, and I caught a severe cold. We had four men to tow along the top of the now dry cliff, with one following behind to clear the tow-line—no easy task, as it implies climbing to the edge of the slippery rocks. Rounding one of the projecting points we again met with the mishap known as " Ta chang," *i.e.* " break adrift," but which I should rather translate, " taking charge." I was, as at all difficult places, lying in the central hold under the mats, so as to leave the limited deck space clear for the "Tai-kung" (lit., "Great Work," *i.e.* "Bow-man"). He was busy sounding ahead, and poling the boat's head off the rocks, when suddenly I heard the ominous cry, "Ta-chang!" felt the boat heel over, and looked out to see how soon the trackers would cast off, as she was taking a sheer in the current, which, unless something gave way, must end in our immediate capsize. Fortunately, the bamboo tow-line was cut by the rock and gave way, and we went careering down stream again at the rate of six miles an hour. In this there was no danger from rocks, the channels throughout all the gorges being perfectly clear; but we managed to collide with a small junk towing astern of us, and lost our flagstaff and the house-flag, which I was proudly displaying for the first time on the Upper Yang-tse.

At the entrance to the gorge, on the left bank, are carved three josses, painted and gilt in full canonicals: they are called "Shui fu san wan," or "the Three Guardians of the Water." Our boatmen informed me that they only "Kwan" the river by day, and are off duty at night, and that therefore no good boatmen move in the dark. On the opposite rock wall is carved a "Pai Fang," or triumphal arch. Of course, josses and all undergo a long annual submersion in the summer floods. Below and above this gorge are boulder and shingle-covered spits, upon which gold-washing was being carried on in a most methodical manner; but I could not find out that any of the cradles I visited had found any gold that day, and I imagine the gleaning here must be infinitesimal. After being towed through several small, shallow rapids, and constantly grounded on submerged gold-digger's spoil-heaps, we moored for the night a few miles below the celebrated city of Wan.

Distance, 110 li, equal to twenty-seven miles; total from Ichang, 223 miles.

Thursday, March 29th.—Still the same picturesque mountains and clear river, winding amongst sand-flats and gravel-banks. I landed after early coffee, and soon walked ahead of the trackers. At length I came to a pebble-covered point, to pass which the boat would have to make a long round, while I descried a fine, straight path across its neck, which I followed. On mounting the bank, I saw a white pagoda, a thousand feet above the river, on the apex of one of the many pyramidal hills scattered about, which announced the approach to a city. Further on and lower down, a second pagoda, similarly placed, also white and of nine stories, perfects the Feng-shui. The bank of pebbles I was crossing, and which is called "Hung sha chi," or "Red Sand Point," seemed endless; and, on asking, I was told it was ten li across: I should judge it to be over two miles. The river-bed is here one mile wide, the present stream being about 400 yards. Just below the town the bed narrows, and, passing through a short gorge, enters the Valley of Wan. Wan means myriad. Overlooking the gorge is a handsome temple, called "Chung-ku lo" ("Drum and Bell Lodge"), with a three-storied pavilion surmounting its stage, the platform upon which strolling companies perform in honour of the gods; the whole place well built and remarkably clean. From this terrace, in front, is a fine view of the city and the busy port below.

"Wan hsien," "The Myriad" city, is situated in the midst of a rich and beautiful country, and is the first fair specimen of a Szechuan city we have come to. It faces south and east, and looks down two reaches of the river, which here again, owing to the horizontal stratification and vertical cleavage of the mountains through which it has forced its way, makes a sharp rectangular turn, compelling us to change our course from west to south. We are now in latitude 30° 57′, the highest northing since leaving Ichang (latitude 10° 41′), and from here our general course is south-west, Chung-king being in latitude 29° 33′ (Blakiston). The agricultural land here is formed of the talus of sandstone hills, from the midst of which the picturesque, vertical, flat-topped peaks still peep out. These peaks rise from seven to fifteen hundred feet (and in the distance higher), and are evidently the remnants of a once solid range. They are of all sizes, from a few yards to as many miles in width. On the steep slopes, which in places almost reach to the summits, wherever the angle is not more than 30°, grow wheat, barley, rape, beans, and poppy; the former now in full ear, the latter in flower. The poppy, which I now see cultivated for the first time, is a solid-looking, substantial, dark-green plant, with white, pink and white, and purple flowers, three to four feet in height, springing from well earthed-up ridges, like celery. The harvest is collected in April, by making a sharp incision in the stem, below the capsules overnight, and scraping off the white, escaped sap in the morning; after which it is pulled up, and the plant given to the pigs, and its place is taken by maize or cotton. The valuable Tung, or varnish-tree, from the seed of which is pressed the famous Tung-you (tung varnish), also yields an important article of trade in this flourishing city, the surrounding mountains being covered in places with its dark-green foliage.

The "Feng-shui" of Wan is perfect. A distant range protects it from the evil influences of the "Yin" (Darkness, *i.e.* North). A curtain of lower hills on the opposite bank screens it from the south, yet without hindering, by their height, the benignant influx of the genial south ("Yang," *i.e.* Light). A smooth point of rock juts out into the river just above the city, and constitutes the "Lung" (Dragon), without whose presence no site is complete. This bank, rising landwards, is crowned by a three-storied "Ting-tsze" (pavilion), which overlooks the city and commands a charming prospect. This protruding dragon checks the current and makes a smooth bight behind, in which moor the large fleet of junks that frequent this busy place—a characteristic Szechuan town. Situated on a bend, the descending river pours its wealth into the arms of Wan, before which it halts for a while ere pursuing its onward course. But lest when leaving the city in its downward course it should carry away too rapidly the gifts it has brought down, not only is it checked by the natural gorge below, but on the jutting points, which here keep the river back, the Feng-shui is perfected by a couple of pagodas and the elegant "Chung-ku lo!"

Apart, however, from all these fanciful, yet poetical, advantages—which were kindly pointed out to me by an enthusiastic old gentleman, a big junk-master and owner, who volunteered as my guide in an evening stroll—the extraordinary way in which the peculiar sandstone hills are broken up gives an unique appearance to a landscape, which once seen is never forgotten. I would advise all tourists to the rapids not to stop at Kwei, but to extend their trip two days further to the lovely Vale of Wan.

A river, now almost dry, winding through steep banks, divides the small, walled city from the extensive suburb above it, and is crossed by a semi-circular bridge with no visible abutments, giving it the appearance of a bent bow, the highest and most elegant structure of the kind I have yet seen. Down this stream comes the "Hwang piao tsz'," a yellow paper, manufactured from macerated bamboos, for which there is an unlimited demand throughout the empire for the manufacture of spills, for the universal hubble-bubble, as well as for the piles of paper "cash" burnt at tombs, which are a speciality of this district. Many of the large Szechuan junks which carry on the transit over the rapids are built here, of a tough cypress which grows plentifully on all the hills hereabouts. The planking is only an inch thick, and they are all clamped together in the usual way, the object being to leave them "limber" and to combine strength with lightness. A junk to carry 200 bales of shirting up stream—say, forty tons dead weight—costs here, new, complete, a thousand strings of cash, or £110.

Distance, forty-five li (eleven miles); total from Ichang, 234 miles.

CHAPTER VI.

ON TO CHUNG-KING.

Iron workers—Census taking—Site of old Chung-chow—A rain-bringing opera—Deforesting of the country—Feng-tu—The temple of the Chinese Pluto—Fu-chow—Chang-chow—First sight of Chung-king.

AFTER departing from the city of Wan, we journeyed on through a beautiful country, the sandstone mountains eroded into marvellously romantic outlines. On the left bank a range of the same picturesque hills, about 800 feet high, and in many reaches too steep for cultivation. On the right bank rise gentle ranges of from four to five hundred feet, cultivated to the summit, and backed by mountains rising to 2000 feet. The air is balmy in the bright morning sunshine with the odour of the rape and bean, now in full flower; the water is pellucid, and flows with a smooth current of from two to three knots, except where it is intercepted by and rushes round the numerous rocky points, which at intervals contract the channel when it flows at double this speed. I mounted up to one of the villages, which are mostly situated at 200 feet above the present level, safe from the summer floods. This, like many others, is built astride a steep glen filled with tall cypress, and is called "Tung tsz'yu'rh," or "Dryanda Garden." A steep flight of steps, the lower portion neatly cut in the solid rock, leads up about a thousand feet through this prettily terraced hamlet. Leaving

Dryanda village embowered in its rich spring foliage and flowers, we passed up the "Fuh t'an," a rapid formed by immense masses of projecting rocks, but dangerous only in the summer floods. The sun was most oppressive, and at ten o'clock I returned to the boat, and sat there in pyjamas till sunset, when I got another hour's walk across one of the interminable boulder banks which are the common feature of this section of the river. All these spits are covered with the deserted piles of stones left by the gold-washers who have been driven off by the rising water. Brought up at seven p.m. at Wu-ling chi, a steep point, on which is a busy town of blacksmiths, working Yun-Yang iron with excellent local, bituminous coal. Forest fires were visible on a distant range.

Distance run, ninety li (twenty-two miles); total, 256 miles.

Saturday, March 31st.—Our voyage continued through beautiful and characteristic Szechuan scenery. Steep, cultivated hills, well wooded round the villages, flat-topped sandstone cliffs forming their summits; the wheat, barley, rape, and poppy fields covering the talus. At their foot lie big rocks, the *débris* of these ancient mountains, which obstruct the river channel and form a succession of small rapids, the average speed of the current being barely four knots. Behind the hills on the right bank runs a range of mountains of about 5000 feet, of even height, and, from their appearance, probably of limestone, in a direct line N.N.E. and S.S.W., like all the main ranges through which the river forces its way between this and Ichang. The windings of the river among the sandstone hills now approach, now recede, from this range, through which it cuts its way in the gorge below Wan Hsien. I landed early, and walked across one of the interminable, boulder-covered flats which here alternate with the sandbanks, sprinkled with great, angular, unrolled rocks, all, however, under water in summer. At noon, passed a remarkable and picturesque rock, called "Shih Pao chai," or "Stone Precious Castle." This rock rises a hundred feet from its talus in perpendicular cliffs, its summit being flat and of about two hundred feet by fifty—just sufficient space for a temple of three courts which covers it. The talus rises steep from the river for 200 feet, making the height of the whole about 300 feet. Against the south-east face is built a nine-storied pavilion, about sixty feet wide at the base, springing from a handsome temple built of wood, with a projecting, curved, pagoda-like roof extending from each story. This forms the ascent to the rock above. On this, again, is built a two-storied pavilion, the whole, when seen end on, appearing like a huge eleven-storied pagoda. At its foot is a village, at which it was market-day, and the crowd, in the white turbans common in Szechuan, and in their long blue gowns, looked uncommonly smart and un-Chinese. I saw here, for the first time during my many years' travel in China, men with red staves in their hands, and with large shields slung across their backs, called "Men Pai" (Door Shields), meaning "Census," and reminding one of our sandwich-men. They are engaged in numbering the people (or rather the houses), a custom apparently more honoured in this orderly province than elsewhere. We passed on until we came to a reach, where the native rocks have got the better of the river, which forces its way through them in intricate channels with a deafening roar, the bed being here nearly a mile wide. We made here one of our many daily crossings, in which we usually lose a mile of our hardly-earned vantage. This is a dangerous crossing, and a life-boat is stationed here. Only an accurate knowledge of the eddies enabled our men to cross the rushing waters in safety. We regained a good lot of our lost ground by the men suddenly ceasing their vigorous rowing, jumping out with the tow-line, and tracking us up to the head of one of the rocks, when we began again our involuntary descent, until we reached an eddy on the opposite bank, up which we rowed in peace. All these rocks are perfectly level, having been originally all one piece, through which the river has carved out an infinity of channels, are of the same height, and are covered in summer. Above this stretches another extensive, flat, rocky point, until we come to a basin some four miles by six, in the centre of which is a steep, beautifully-wooded island of the same height as the banks (about five hundred feet), with the two thousand feet mountains immediately behind. This is called "Hoa Hoa Chen" ("Flowery Walls"), and is the ancient site of Chung-chow, the city at which we are due to-morrow, and which is now situated ten miles higher up. The site of the old city was changed to that of the modern one owing to a parricide which occurred there—a noteworthy custom of ancient times, the unfilial spot being razed level with the earth.

A curious legend is attached to the "Shih pao chai." Formerly this remarkable rock possessed a hole, from which flowed a stream of rice sufficient for the wants of the three priests living there. The head priest, wishing to have rice to sell, enlarged the hole, when at once the flow of rice ceased. Unfortunately, my boatmen would not stop to allow me to land and verify the existence of this supernatural opening.

Walking along the shore, a constant source of amusement is to watch the army of trackers attached to each big junk as they toil along, harnessed to the inexorable tow-line, over ground, which practice alone is enabling me to get over, armed with a big stick and comfortable boots, and choosing the easiest path at my leisure. Rounding a point where the junk hung fire, and the trackers were giving way step by step, notwithstanding the vociferations and blows (harmless) of the half-dozen overseers, I saw the gang-master quietly divest himself of his clothing, which was carefully gathered up by a colleague, rush into the river, and then roll himself in the sand, taking special care well to plaster his face. Then, like a maniac, he danced, howled, tumbled, crawled on all-fours through the ranks of the trackers, jumped at and struck them. After having thus warmed them to their work, and the tight place being successfully passed, he washed himself, methodically resumed his clothing, and became restored to his senses. At a distance, a group of these trackers on all fours, howling and bellowing like cattle, and surrounded by six or eight overseers walking erect and belabouring their men with split bamboos—which make more noise than hurt—has all the appearance of a drove of donkeys being forced along a difficult path, the junk itself, the *corps de délit*, being generally out of sight in the rear. Each of these unfortunates gets a couple of dollars, besides his rice, for his two months' arduous work, and coming down-stream, he works for his rice alone. These big junks are also a curious sight, descending the river. The mast is unshipped and slung alongside, the deck is covered with seventy or eighty men with white turbans, brown, naked bodies, and blue trousers, some working the big bow sweep; others rowing erect, with their faces forwards; others, again, working the gigantic oars, called the "Che" (carriage or wheel), formed of the trunk of a cypress, the stem in-board, each of which takes eight or ten men to work it. The larger junks have six or eight of these, in addition to oars and yu-loes (hugh sculls, working screw-fashion over the stern or alongside, parallel to the ship's rail); and yet, such is the deceptive size of the gorges, I at first took these lumbering machines in the distance to be only sampans. Each big junk, both in ascending and descending, has a sampan in attendance, which acts as its tender throughout the voyage. With all this apparatus the junks barely make steerage way; and when a dangerous place is approached, the shouting to make the men work is terrific.

Day's run, eighty li (twenty miles); 276 from Ichang.

Sunday, April 1st.—Weather still fine and warm, with light, south-westerly breeze. Our ragged escort was exchanged at Wan Hsien for a new "despatch bearer." From one district city to another, the news of my progress is thus communicated by one magistracy to the next. This is a polite attention, happily as unnecessary in this favoured province as it is to the traveller vexatious. These messengers have to be fed and housed, and in this small boat we have no room to spare; and also custom demands a present of two hundred cash for the man's return expenses at each stage, which at our rate of travel extends over two days. A writer from the "Ya-men" also comes on board, and carefully engrosses a literal copy of my voluminous passport. Red tape is not confined to England. At Kwei-fu the officials had the additional trouble of sending each a Sze-yeh (clerk), with a card, to return my calls. The messenger from the rich city of Wan is a great contrast to the poor devil we received at Yun-yang. He is a dandy in his way. Though his feet are bare, he wears most elaborate straw sandals, in form like those of the ancients, with a blue, rose-shaped tassel over each great toe. His underclothing of grey shirting is scrupulously clean, and he is one of the few natives hereabouts I have yet seen not covered with itch sores. He made himself useful, assisting in the kitchen, our cook proper being still laid up with a scald. I was quite sorry to lose him at Chung-chow, where we exchanged him for an ordinary specimen of the Yamen-runner—a pale, sickly, opium-smoking youth covered with sores and dirt. Not bringing their beds, these men have to find a lodging ashore for the night. On inquiry, I find our itch-covered gentleman obtained his, including use of quilt, for eight cash, or two-fifths of a penny, while our exquisite paid just double for his. While on the subject of official messengers, I may add that each of the big whitey-brown envelopes enclosing the despatches with which I am being convoyed, has stated upon it the names in full of the two messengers deputed to deliver it; but, Chinese-fashion, one man only is really sent: and this man often takes the pay, and then engages some poor tramp to take his place at one-third the pay, he pocketing the difference. This sub-letting of contracts is reduced to a fine art throughout China.

Early this morning, a few miles above Wu-ling Chi (Five-mountain Point), the river takes a sharp bend to the westward, and we turn our backs upon the high range we have been coasting since leaving Wan Hsien, and enter the reach in which stands, again on the left or north bank, the district city of Chung-chow, the "loyal" city. We track round the concave shore of this bend, where the current is at its strongest; but the reefs of rock on the convex side, which boats towing up usually affect, are too extensive and scattered for even a woman of Shên to thread, at the present low stage of the water level.

I notice here, for the first time, a properly constructed towing-path, consisting of a stone embankment, built up twenty feet high against the rocky cliff, so that the trackers need not jump like goats from stone to stone, as in most similar places. The embankment is, like all the useful public works still extant in China, ancient and out of repair; and, of course, it enters into nobody's head to repair anything nowadays. If you ask why "the stitch in time" is not taken, you get the same answer in each of the eighteen provinces, viz. this : that the emperor, meaning the government, has no money, and the old 'public spirit of the many wealthy grandees seems totally to have died out. All over the country you see scattered large houses, the homes of the gentry, and so-called Literati. Of the buildings, you see nothing but the four blank walls and a heavy, closed door; and their inmates seldom emerge, but spend their time in selfish idleness, managing, however, their incomes with frugality. This is the class opposed to all progress, which stirs up the otherwise indifferent masses against the foreigner. I confess that I loathe the bespectacled Chinaman, whenever I meet one, with his rude stare. The civility we meet with in travel is almost entirely confined to the lower and middle classes.

Not long after rounding this point, we recrossed the river, here three-quarters of a mile wide, and, tracking under some wooded sandstone cliffs, arrived at the city of Chungchow, which is built immediately above them, and thus raised on a ledge 100 to 150 feet above the river. This city is remarkable for the number of temples and pavilions, surrounded by fine trees, which give it a picturesque aspect, apart from its beautiful setting in a steeply-sloping amphitheatre of groves of tall bamboo and wooded hills. The walls, as usual, run back, and enclose a lot of waste land. Rounding a bend above the city, the river widens out, and the hills on either side enclose a lake-like expanse. The scene is very beautiful. During the quarter of an hour our crew devote to their mid-day meal, at which time the boat is moored alongside the bank, I ascended one of the many well-nigh endless flights of stone steps which on these steep hills lead up to the villages situated on the greater heights behind. The path led upwards for about 400 feet, through a wood of cypress, Tung, or wood-oil trees, poplars, and bamboos, until on reaching the first summit, as it passed directly inland, I had to carefully descend by the way I had passed up. I followed our boat along the shore, walking, as usual, alternately in the loose sand, on boulders, or over jagged rocks, sometimes at the water's edge; at others, 200 feet above it. Suddenly I heard a great outcry, and could just distinguish the hair of a man in the water ahead of our boat. I ran quickly down to go in after him; but before I reached the shore our boat came up with him, and dragged him on board half-drowned. It was one of our trackers, who, in fording a shallow between two reefs of rocks, had got out of his depth, and been just saved in time. I still do not understand how he floated so long and quietly, with only just his hair above the surface.

It is pleasing, in contrast with the carelessness of Shanghai boatmen, to note the careful way in which the *voyageurs* of this river coil up their enormous plaited bamboo tow-lines, with which the after part of the big junks is entirely covered, two big additional coils being suspended over each quarter, and another on a special raised platform over the steering-house, of which one man has sole charge. As the tow-line is being constantly lengthened and shortened and frequently changed, this entails much work on the dozen men or so left on the junk, and the will and system with which these men handle the bulky coils are refreshing to a yachtsman to witness. They coil alternately in and out. We now recrossed the river below a small rapid, on the rocky banks of which a junk had been recently wrecked, and her cargo was being dried, while the junk herself was careened for repairs. This is the fifth or sixth big junk laden with raw Shanghai cotton that we have passed in a similar condition since leaving Ichang. One or two days back, at a similar wreck, a temporary stage had been erected, in which the "pockets" were slung while the crew were treading down the cotton into them. After having been fourteen hours, as usual, under way, we ultimately brought up for the night at Yang tu chi, a large village on the right bank, noted for its earthenware factories, where very artistically shaped vessels can be purchased at nominal prices.

After supper, it was proposed we should adjourn to the opera, a celebrated company having come up from the city of Wan to aid the villagers in propitiating the rain-god. The performance was then proceeding in a temple on the bank. Lighting a length of worn-out bamboo tow-line, which our Tai-kung, or pilot, furnished us with, and which made a most efficient torch, we threaded our way up the steep sandbank and among the dirty temporary huts, largely composed of opium dens, which in winter cover the low ground adjoining the junks' halting-places. We at length entered a handsome and solidly-constructed temple; and there, upon the fine stage in the first courtyard, was the usual gay scene of a Chinese historical play. The stage was lit by two staring oil-lamps suspended from the proscenium, reminding me of those of the London costermonger, and by about a dozen red-wax dips. The auditorium was in darkness. My intrusion was quickly detected by the crowd of turbaned coolies, but I was not in the least disturbed, and I stood looking on at some very good acting until ten o'clock. These performances, usually of historical plays, like Shakespeare's, and processions in honour of the gods, if they do not always produce rain, at least serve to educate and amuse the people, and to divert their thoughts from their troubles.

Day's run, 110 li (twenty-seven miles); from Ichang, 303 miles.

Monday, April 2nd.—Heavy rain at last, in the night; a fine warm day, with light south-westerly breeze. We started this morning against a freshet, which had come down in the night, and raised the river some two feet, while the current was increased to four or five knots. We passed the rapid, dangerous in summer, of "T'ieh men ka'rh," or "Iron Threshold." A few women, not professional or mutilated beggars, had taken up their station on the ledge, along which all upward junks pass tracking, and begged importunately. Our messenger said it was owing to poverty caused by the four years' drought. Is it possible that the deserts of Central Asia, once the "manufactory of nations," after invading Kan-su and Shan-si, the latter once the granary of the empire, are stretching their octopus clutch towards this, the fairest jewel in the Celestial crown? Will the recklessness of the people, and the carelessness of its governors, allow the country to decay and become obliterated, like Nineveh and Babylon and the once flourishing cities of Asia Minor? Or will Western influence interfere, and by force or persuasion turn this magnificent country and its industrious inhabitants to some real account? The deforestation of the hills and mountains is so marked and persistent that the demand for fuel and building alone will hardly explain it. Père David believes it to be due to the dread of wild beasts, and the consequent attempts to root up and destroy their cover.

Turning a bend and quitting this scene, we entered a fine straight reach, about one mile wide, and ten long, running nearly due north and south. Both banks are formed of gentle hills of from four to five hundred feet high, with higher ranges behind. The bed of the river was entirely covered, but the left bank, up which we tracked, was very shallow, and, notwithstanding our light draft, we had to keep out some distance from the shore. It was in this reach, on the right bank of which is situated the market-town of "Kao-chia chen"—the 'mart of the "Kao" family—that Blakiston found his least depth of two fathoms. A market was in progress, chiefly interesting from the number of cattle —"wet" and "dry," *i.e.* buffaloes and zebus—and the number of long, blue-coated, white-turbaned Chinamen covering the sand-slopes. The whole long valley was beautifully cultivated exclusively with poppy, the brilliant dark-green of the plant, sprinkled with the white flowers, giving the hills the appearance, in the distance, of being covered with rich pasture, from which the sun had not yet dissipated the morning dews. The picturesque two-storied farmhouses— white, with dark wooden framework showing through, and with large overhanging eaves, situated amidst the trees, now in full leaf in every glen and on every projecting knoll, and looking not unlike Swiss chalets—added to the charm of this lotus-eater's home. From noon till four, in the hot spring sunshine, our men tracked steadily up this reach, until at its upper end, where a steep cliff on the left bank seems to shut it in, we got entangled in a nest of rocks, and made little progress until our mooring-time of seven p.m. A seven-storied pagoda on the right bank, modern and a sham, having neither windows nor buddhas, but doubtless none the less efficacious in "Pu"-ing the Feng-shui; and the sacred hill of "Tien tsz'" ("Son of Heaven") right before us, told of our arrival at the (Chinese) world-renowned city of "Feng-tu."

In this part the local passage and ferry-boats are roomy, and possess a high, open, steeply-arched mat awning, with a front platform for the rowers, and, in place of rudder, have

all a single gigantic stern-sweep. Walking towards Chung-chow yesterday morning, it being market-day, numbers of country people were making their way into the town, and ferry-boats, some containing cattle, were stationed five and six miles below the city. I was induced to enter one of these, on the assurance that there were none higher up (which proved to be false), for the stipulated fare of sixteen cash (three farthings), when my own boat, which I thought must have crossed over below, turned up. A pleasant feature in these parts is the carrying of everything in and on baskets, called Pei tsz, attached to the back, with plaited bamboo straps round the shoulder. The eternal bamboo carrying-pole, with the weights dangling at each end, and its accompanying "Hee-haw, Ah-oo!" no longer mars the scene. Frogs croaked steadily through the night for the first time this year.

Day's run, eighty li (twenty miles); total from Ichang, 323 miles.

Tuesday, April 3rd.—Fine warm day; light south-westerly wind still ahead. We were off at 5.30 a.m. I landed at seven at the foot of the "T'ien tze Shan," "Mountain of the Son of Heaven," which is situated on the left bank below and immediately adjoining the walled city of "Fêng tu," *i.e.* "The Abundant Capital," commonly called "Fêng-tu-Chêng. This is one of the many steep, isolated hills abounding in this level sandstone district. Being a sacred mount, it is wooded to the summit, upon which is a collection of ancient, solidly-built, but now ruinous, temples, said to date from before the Tang dynasty, at which period (eighth and ninth centuries), however, the existing buildings—with wood pillars supporting tiled roofs—were erected. This temple is dedicated to the Emperor of the "Yin," or Dead, as the Imperial palace at Peking is to the Emperor of the "Yang," or Living; and as that is the visible home of T'ien tze, or Son of Heaven, so this is the type of the shadowy Emperor of Hades. The only curious thing in the uncomfortably dirty range of building, and courtyards, filled with grimy josses of all sizes and shapes, is the figure of a woman in an elegant modern dress, and with the usual gold or gilt face, who sits enthroned on the left hand of the image, representing the "Yin chien T'ien tze," which latter is a gilt figure, in no way, that I could distinguish, different from the ordinary Buddhist idol. On its right is a gilt female figure covered with dust, the god's chief wife; but the figure on the left contains a real skeleton, to whom the women in the neighbourhood annually present a new embroidered silk dress. This second wife of the "Infernal" Emperor was only acquired by him about fifty years ago, in the twelfth year of the reign of "Chai-king," in the following manner: A maiden of Ho-chow, a town situated above Chung-king, was being carried in her bridal chair to the home of her betrothed, when, half-way en route, the chair door was opened, but the bride had disappeared. The husband's family entered an action for breach of promise against the bride's family, which, after proceeding over two years, was stopped by the lady herself appearing in a dream to her parents, and informing them that on her marriage day the "T'ien tze" had claimed her for his second wife, and carried her off from her chair; and that her body, of which only the skeleton now remains, would be found alongside her new husband's effigy on the T'ien tze Shan. Of the fact that the earthly bridegroom lost his bride, I have no doubt, nor of the ensuing action at law; of the rest of the legend, which is universally believed as I have narrated it, each barbarian sceptic must form his own explanation. Fêng-tu-Chêng is celebrated over the whole eighteen provinces, as at every death the

"Full Moon" Pavilion in Garden of Temple dedicated to Changfei, Hero of the Wars of the Three Kingdoms (A.D. 200), opposite City of Yünyang: Wall and Pillars Stone, Roofs Thatch (p. 100).

Five-storied Pagoda in Grounds of Buddhist Temple near Chung-king (p. 120).

officiating Taoist priest indites a despatch to the T'ien tze, duly addressed to Fêng-tu-Chêng, notifying him of the new-comer. This despatch is, however, not sent through the terrestrial post, but by the celestial road, being burnt to ashes. No Chinaman will enter the precincts of the T'ien tze Shan alone, nor venture near it at all after sunset, as it is haunted by innumerable ghosts, as befits the residence of the ruler of Hades. Their presence is known, not only by their cries at night, but the priests put out every night a bundle of birch rods. Sometimes these disappear altogether; at other times they are found all in splinters, having been used to flog refractory, drunken, and other vicious spirits at the ghostly tribunals.

My Chinese companions, who are usually too lazy to leave the boat, and who do not care how long the voyage lasts as long as they can eat and sleep their fill, became genuinely excited upon arriving at Fêng-tu. They climbed up the steep hillside—about 300 feet—bought incense and candles, and performed a general Kow-tow all round. Another show-place—for cash, be it well understood—is a dry well, said to communicate with the river. We bought paper cash of the priest, which was set alight and dropped through a stone grating immediately in front of the altar, thus contributing our mite to the aid of the struggling souls in purgatory below. The burning paper soon lodged on the bottom, and hence it would appear that the ash of the billions of cash deposited in it have filled up this wonderful well to within a few feet of its mouth. We descended by a fine, broad, easy, stone path through the wood, which, interspersed with opium patches, covers this sacred mount. At each turn are small temples adorned with Buddhas; and by the roadside are inlaid stone tablets with hortatory texts engraved upon them; such as, "The affairs of life are all vanity," etc.; the whole arrangement of the zig-zag path reminding me of the path adorned with the stations of the Cross such as is often to be seen in Roman Catholic countries.

We passed through the city, which is a poor place with low walls and gates, and the usual crowded Chinese streets, filthy in fine, and impassable in wet weather; then to our boat across the usual long, steep sandbank, covered with a temporary bamboo town, which is moved up higher and higher as the river rises. I was followed by the customary crowd, for whose benefit I sat on the bows of the boat while delayed waiting for the relief Ting-chai (messenger).

We got away at nine a.m., literally threading our way through a huge reef of rocks, which extends across the river just above this city. On emerging from this labyrinth, I was not a little surprised to see on a bluff, separated from the town by a lofty, almost perpendicular, sandstone hill, the walls of another city, with the usual gates, crowned by handsome two-storied pavilions or guard-houses, its walls enclosing a large area of highly-cultivated ground and a few, possibly fifty, scattered houses, the intended yamêns or residences of the officials. This city without inhabitants might, I at first thought, have been built for the mysterious Son of Heaven and his shadowy subjects, from whose presence Fêng-tu has acquired so great distinction. I was informed, however, that Fêng-tu-Chêng proper having been entirely washed away in the terrific flood of 1870, the then magistrate "Ma" had built this new city at a safe height above the river, and had ordered the surviving inhabitants to remove to it. This they refused to do, preferring the risk of inundation to the inconvenience of having to carry their daily supply of water up a height of two hundred feet. They appealed to Peking; and it having been discovered that out of a total cost of £250,000 Ma had embezzled £50,000 (his real object in undertaking it, the natives say), he was incontinently degraded; but having disgorged a portion to the officials of the capital, he was permitted to retire, and the inhabitants were ordered to rebuild their houses on the old site. Meanwhile, Ma has a monument which will ensure the handing down of his name to all posterity. The walls of this uninhabited city are splendidly built of the local sandstone, and the inscriptions in the stone plaques, let in over the open and deserted gateways, I could read with my field-glass, although a mile distant.

The view of the river from the T'ien tze Shan is not unlike that of the entrance of the Niukan, or Ox-liver Gorge. The stream seemed to lose itself behind a succession of lofty points, backed by mountains of fifteen hundred to two thousand feet, each range separated from the other by the morning mist, in which the distant valleys were concealed, the rich vegetation in the foreground, and the curved temple-roofs peeping out behind the trees, adding to the beauty of the scene. On passing up we found, in fact, the banks very steep, cliff-like in many places, and strewn with huge rocks, which render the navigation dangerous in summer-time.

Making another of the usual rectangular turns, this time to the west, the river widens and flows between steep banks, every available spot being carefully cultivated with the poppy. We proceeded slowly past several small rapids, and brought up under a steep sandbank, on which poppies were growing almost to the water's edge; opposite the busy market-town of Sheng-chi Chang, the river, including a boulder-covered sandbank near the left shore, being fully three-quarters of a mile wide.

Distance run, seventy li (seventeen miles); from Ichang, 340 miles.

Wednesday, April 4th.—18th day from Ichang; 36th from Hankow; 56th from Shanghai. Very hot sun. On waking this morning I found the sun shining straight in on my bed, showing our course to be about due east, though our goal is due west. At seven I landed on a rocky ledge, called "Pai-Chien," at an elbow, where we turned up to the north, and looked out on a vast spread of rocky islands and promontories, all flat-topped, and about twenty feet higher than the present level, the remains evidently of a continuous sandstone stratum, which the river had gradually broken down. I walked inland by a direct path through the poppy-fields, now a mass of white flower, enjoying the balmy air of this bright summer morning. At length I heard a noise ahead which made me ask myself if it were possible a pile-driver had invaded this wild and remote district. I listened attentively; the thud was clear and unmistakable above the roar of the river, and the intervals corresponded exactly with those of my old Shanghai acquaintance. Walking on, I found the sound proceeded from one of the roomy farmsteads which are scattered throughout these valleys. I climbed up the usual long flight of stone steps, and found an extensive, tile-roofed shed, in which the full process of T'ung oil manufacture was being carried on. Opium and T'ung (Elaocacoa, or varnish-tree) oil are the two main staples of Eastern Szechuan. The T'ung nut, which yields the oil, was being ground up in a circular stone trough by iron wheels dragged round by a blindfold ox. The resultant coarse powder is then made into circular cakes with straw, and a horizontal pile is then placed in a very rough but solid wooden press, and long wedges are successively driven in, and the oil expressed. These wedges are iron-capped, and are struck by a huge ram slung from the roof and worked by two men, the taking correct aim being apparently an affair of much nicety. The oil-cake remaining is a valuable manure for the poppy.

The reach we were now in, at the head of which is situated the city of Fu-chow, runs north-west, and is straight for about four miles, when the river turns to the south-west, and the reach opens up. It is lined throughout with loose rocks, which produce a succession of points and small rapids. The hills are steep, and are, together with the back range, entirely covered with the poppy. Along the left bank, about sixty feet above the present level, runs a fine broad path—" Ta-lu " (*i.e.* high road), the Chinese call it, and well may it be dignified with such a name, in comparison with the goat-paths which usually pass for roads. It is of dressed stone, solidly built up upon the rocks. As the sun was getting uncomfortably hot, and there was no prospect of being able to descend to the boat as far ahead as I could see, I was congratulating myself on the easy progress, when all at once I found the road broken up by an avalanche of rocks, which were not overcome without much sweat of brow. In this reach I noticed my boat boarded by a small vessel bearing the Fu-chow " Chih-chow's " (Prefect) flag, with two well-dressed Ting-chai sent to meet me. They returned ahead of us, having made the necessary inquiries and prepared an escort of a Sze-yeh (clerk) and four messengers, who accompanied us, in a separate boat, from Fu-chow on to the next prefectural district—Chang-sho.

Fu-chow stands at the head of a broad reach enclosed by steep hills about a thousand feet high, on one of which is a white, modern, nine-storied pagoda about sixty feet high, on the lower slope of a steep hill which appears to close the reach at its western end. Raised tier above tier, the site of Fu-chow reminded my Chinamen of that of Hong-kong. Though on a smaller scale, the situation of Fu-chow is certainly very impressive, and unequalled by any of the many picturesque cities we have passed these last 300 miles. Like Coblentz, it is situated at the confluence of a clear-water river and a thick stream, the two descending together a long distance without 'mixing. The clear river is "Kung t'an Hŏ," the only affluent of importance which the Yang-tse receives between this and the Tung-ting Lake, a distance of 600 miles. This river has its source in the neighbourhood of one of the feeders of that vast artery, and is navigable some 800 li, or about 200 miles, and is utilized at times as a way of transit to Hankow and to Canton, when the Yang-tse itself is in too violent flood for the junks to navigate in safety. The boats used on this river, which is about 200 yards wide at its mouth, are the most extraordinary I have ever seen. The curious, fiddle-shaped boats of the Poyang Lake, built for cheating the local customs' measurement, are nothing to them. It is just as though a giant had taken an ordinary junk in his two hands and wrung it a quarter round, so that the stern deck is actually perpendicular, being at right angles to the forward deck, into which the slope gradually merges. I was told that only a boat of this shape could twist through the rocks and whirlpools of the Kung rapid (t'an), from which the river takes its name of "Kung t'an Hŏ" (River of the Rapid of Kung.) These boats are called "Wai pi-ku'rh," meaning "twisting stern." The only object of their peculiar shape which I could discover, after a narrow inspection on board, was to bring the fulcrum of the gigantic stern-sweep into a line with the keel, and at the same time on to the edge of the usual raised quarter. This sweep is worked from a bridge crossing the junk amidships. On the perpendicular quarter-deck are rungs, to enable a man to climb up if needful. They have no rudder, but a second smaller sweep on the *depressed* corner of the quarter, worked under the big sweep from a spot where the deck approaches to the horizontal.

The Kung t'an Hŏ enters the Yang-tse immediately south of Fu-chow and in line with the main river, which here takes a sharp bend to the north. The angle of the bend opposite the town forms a lake-like expanse, in which many reefs and sandbanks are now visible. On the latter are some of the Wai pi-ku'rh hauled up for repair, so that I had an opportunity of carefully investigating the extraordinary shape I have described above. A violent whirlpool, the feeble remains of which swept us rapidly past, forms off this town in summer; and if a descending junk happens to get caught in it, she is inevitably swallowed up; so said my informant. This was a native of Shantung, the captain of a hundred men (part of the garrison of three hundred), who called on board while we were relieving Ting-chai, and who, having had much intercourse with foreigners while in the Chinese navy, was one of the few men who have it in their power to give an approach to accurate information. Fu-chow is full of spacious temples; one holding a commanding position on the point, and overlooking the suburb under which we moored, was under repair. On inquiry, I found that, although the knoll on which it stands is sixty or seventy feet above the present river-level, the temple was completely washed away in 1877. It is surprising that they should have rebuilt it on the same spot.

Above Fu-chow another long reef of rocks runs out parallel with the right bank, outside of which we tracked; a few miles further is the picturesque town of Li-tu, built on a sloping ledge sixty to a hundred feet above the river, and running with the strata, which here dip to the south-southwest. Above and below are the sandstone cliffs, which crop up in every direction throughout this region.

Distance run, ninety li (twenty-two miles): total from Ichang, 362 miles.

Thursday, April 5th.—" Ching-ming," or first day of the fortnightly period of the Chinese calendar—" Clear bright."

A very fine day, without wind, but with very hot sunshine. We started early as usual, and passed through several lake-like reaches, mostly running at right angles to each other, obstructed at the ends by extensive rock ledges now dry, and forming smaller rapids, and in their middle by extensive boulder-covered sandbanks. The hills are from 500 to 1200 feet high, beautifully cultivated to their summits with the dark-green poppy, interspersed with cypress and large bamboo groves. The water latterly is a rich chocolate colour, the same colour as the ferruginous soil which covers all the hills from Wan Hsien upwards. We passed the village of Lin-sze, noticeable from its large three-arched bridge, decorated with three handsome, new, carved stone " Pai-Fang," or triumphal arches, which spans a gully now dry. This bridge, they say, gets washed away once every twenty years. On the opposite or left bank of the river, here three-quarters of a mile wide, stands out another of the many cliff-sided, flat-topped, isolated hills which distinguish this sandstone country. This one, about 300 feet high, was remarkable from a distance for the fine, thick wood of big trees which covered its talus, and the tops of which half concealed a range of buildings which I thought must be a temple. It turned out to be the residence of a wealthy family (" Tsai-chu," *i.e.* Wealth-Lord, or Plutocrat), such as are scattered about in picturesque and isolated situations, testifying to the peace and quiet that now reign throughout this rich province. On the edge of the cliff was a large, ornamental gateway, and two two-storied pavilions, or drum-towers, appeared to adorn the outer courtyard. Above this place we threaded our way through extensive flat reefs, and passed under a steep cliff on the left bank, into which were built two stone archways, as though opening into the rock. Landing in a broiling sun, I climbed up the steep talus, and found these to be archways of trimmed sandstone, built into a cave in the rock, in the rear of which sat two colossal, gilded Buddhas—the images of a bean-curd seller and his wife, who resided near this spot when in life, and after death were canonized for their good deeds.

Shortly above this quaint evidence of the religious spirit which still pervades the Chinese, we enter the "Chien-tao," or "Scissors" Gorge, where projecting points narrow the river to about 300 yards. The strata of the steep banks, above 1000 feet high here, dip at an angle of about 45° to S.W., and several burrows of soft coal have been opened. It is noticeable that hereabouts, not only the houses, but all the local boats, large and small, use coal for fuel, for burning which they have specially-constructed stoves, with low, tile chimneys. On emerging from this gorge we entered a wide reach, bordered by less precipitous hills, and the city of Chang-sho * rises up before us on the left bank. This place is peculiar, in that the walled city proper occupies the flat summit of a hill some 500 feet high, nothing but the outside of its walls, with their crenelated battlements standing out against the evening sky, being visible from the river, with which it is connected by a straggling suburb creeping down the hill a mile and a half long. A small affluent, now dry, runs on the south-east side, crossed by a lofty (fifty feet) four-arched bridge. A handsome Confucian temple adorns this suburb, in which the business of the place, which consists principally in the export of bamboo matting for packing goods, appears to be transacted. Much of the matting used

* = longevity.

in Hankow comes from this place. I went ashore, and walked through some of the streets, which were wide, well paved, and the houses roomy, as everywhere in Szechuan, but the people and surroundings little less filthy than throughout China generally. We brought up here for the night at six o'clock, instead of at seven, as usual, in a position where my Lao-ta and crew could sleep at ease, there being no fear of thieves (of which notices, warning boatmen not to moor for the night in remote spots, were painted on the rocks in several places coming along), and too conveniently near the usual along shore latrines.

Distance, nine li (twenty-two miles); total from Ichang, 384 miles.

Friday, April 6th.—Thunderstorm with heavy rain in night; cleared at eight a.m., with strong north-easterly wind and lower temperature.

The five Chai-jen (messenger-men) who escorted us from Fu-chow in their own boat left us here, and neither asked for nor received a present. They were relieved by two sickly wretches, the hands of one being covered with leprous sores; happily, they too had their own boat. These Chai-jen, or, as they are commonly called, "Ya-men runners," are attached to every Hsien or magistracy (Sub-prefecture) in large cities, to the number of 1000 or more, and pick up a living as best they can, being paid by the job. Their great source of income is the law-suits, which are always going on, when both parties have to spend freely to get a hearing. Taking their cue from their superiors, who are here most agreeably polite to the foreigner, I found this usually truculent and detested class obsequiously civil.

We started at nine a.m. The river had fallen two feet in the night, and our boat grounded in consequence. The water was very thick after the heavy rain. The country

Free School in Szechuan: Characters "I Shuo" (Free Teaching) over Door.

To face p. 130.

is more open; the hills are from three to six hundred feet high, cultivated to the summit with the poppy, and backed by higher ranges, steep, with the precipitous peaks well-wooded. We nooned at Lo-chi, a large village built on a wide and steep boulder-heap, and remarkable for its mat industry, the shore being lined with booths in which the manufacture of the large, neat, double-plaited bamboo matting, used for junk housing and also for the walls and roofs of dwellings, was being carried on. The men's midday meal over, we continued under sail with a true fair wind, against a moderate current of not more than two knots, through the "Shan-pei To" ("Fan Loch"), a lake-like expanse five miles long and a mile wide. We thence threaded our way through an archipelago of rock islands, the left bank being precipitous and only cultivated in patches, the right bank hilly, and having at its foot an extensive embankment between it and the river. Like those scattered throughout the river-bed all the way from Kwei-fu upwards, these rock islands are of the same height, now twenty to thirty feet out of water, precipitous, and level-topped, and generally bare, being all under water in summer; but those in the Shan-pei To had a more pleasing aspect, their tops being green with moss and scattered grass patches.

Turning sharp round to the right, we passed through a short, narrow gorge, called the "Coal Gorge," with precipitous peaks a thousand to twelve hundred feet high on the right bank, and entered the expanse of the Lu-tsz' T'o. This was filled with piles of boulders of all colours, and about the size of ostrich eggs, rising some twenty feet above the river, and with sides so steep that in tracking along them our boat almost rubbed against the pile while still travelling in deep water. We continued for two hours after dark, until eight p.m., cautiously feeling our way, and occasionally bumping on a rock midst the roar of rushing water under the opposite left bank, until we brought up at the village of Lu-tze To.

Distance run, 120 li (thirty miles); total, 414 miles.

Saturday, April 7th.—Between Ichang and Chung-king the Yang-tse is universally known as the "Chuan Ho," or River of Szechuan. Above Chung-king it is commonly called the "Sêng Ho," or River of the Provincial Capital, *i.e.* Cheng-tu-sêng. The junks only attempt sailing when going up-river with a fair wind, when they hoist large square lug-sails without any bamboos, not unlike those of the picturesque Japanese junks, except that the foot is stretched on a yard, which is lashed to the mast amidships and stayed by two guys (they can hardly be called sheets) leading aft. They are useless with the wind abeam, and are simply lowered and furled when the wind ceases to be fair. However hard the wind blows, it never seems to raise any sea; the Chinamen say because the river runs too fast, but the cause is the perpetual "chow-chow" or vertical motion of the currents, due to the sunken reefs, which effectually check each nascent ripple. Aided then by an up-wind, we tracked up the fierce "Yeh-lo tze" ("Wild Mule Rapid"), the river and banks being strewn with rocks, and rowed through the "Tung-lo hsia" ("Brass Gong Gorge"), a short but very picturesque gorge, with nearly vertical walls, between hills about eight hundred feet high, and entered the expanse of "Tang chia t'o" (the Loch of the Tang Family) in the steep hills, surrounding which are many lime-kilns.*

Thence we passed into a tamer reach, with low, steep, conical hills on the left bank; and low, rounded hills, highly

* Since the formal opening of Chung-king in 1891, the Imperial Maritime Customs have opened a station at this place, in charge of an European. All "chartered" junks, *i.e.* junks under "foreign" flags, have now to report at this station for examination of cargo and "papers."

cultivated with poppy, tobacco, barley, and beans, on the right. We nooned for the men's dinner at the foot of a romantic-looking temple, called "Ta Fo Sze," or "Great Buddha's Hall," situated in a large, walled enclosure of bamboo groves, orange, camellia, and other trees. Outside was a colossal stone Buddha, gilt, sitting in a stone pavilion open to the river, and approached by a long flight of stone steps, before which our boatmen, as is the invariable custom with the crews of upward bound junks from Ichang, thankful to have concluded their perilous voyage, reverently kotowed.

I landed and inspected the temple, in one court of which are five more colossal stone Buddhas, the grounds in front being prettily laid out in stone terraces, gardens, and fish-ponds, all in a fair state of repair. I then walked on along the right bank, until, on rounding a point on the left, a high-peaked range was visible to the south, and between this and the point I stood on extended an amphitheatre of rocky cliffs and hills, entirely covered with shining-white houses as far as the eye could reach; while the river at its foot, divided by rocks into several arms, was crowded with thousands of junks of all shapes and sizes securely moored in every bight and backwater. This was the walled city of "Li-min fu," usually known as "Chiang-peh Ting," or "North-bank Suburb" of the great metropolis higher up. This town is situated on the left bank of the Yang-tse, and immediately below the mouth of an affluent, the "Kia-ling Ho," which here flows in from the north-west. On the opposite or right bank of this affluent, and built on a lofty sandstone peninsula, formed by its junction with the main river, stands the sister-city of Chung-king (both, in the Mandarin language and locally, known as Chung-ching)—the commerical metropolis of Szechuan. The shore on which I was standing—the right or south-east bank of the Great River—is also covered with a long and busy suburb, the three towns together forming a most imposing spectacle of animated movement on land and water, backed by a magnificent amphitheatre of richly cultivated and finely wooded hills, rising steeply fifteen hundred feet above the water. There is no doubt that we have now safely arrived at the great commerical metropolis of the West. The position reminded me forcibly of that of Quebec, with the difference that here the river is narrower and the hills are far more lofty. Estimated population, 400,000.

I stood a long time on one of the many rocky platforms by which the stream is broken up, watching the busy gangs of coolies loading and discharging the vast fleet of junks laden with the mingled produce of the east, north, and west. Conspicuous as they climbed up the long flights of steps were files of porters toiling under huge bales of white, unpressed cotton, looking in the distance like regiments of busy ants carrying their eggs. I gazed at leisure on the busy scene, enjoying the novelty of being allowed to look on unmolested by the crowd, as well as the contrast with the stillness of the wild, natural scenery, amidst which so many long days had been spent. Yet I was sorry that this must necessarily be the goal of my present journeyings, business requiring me to be back in Hankow in the following month. The farther one travels, the farther one wants to travel.

Szechuan, the westernmost and at once the richest and the largest of the eighteen provinces, has an area of 167,000 square miles, being little less than that of France, and is credited with a population of thirty-five millions.* The

---

* Such was the area of the province as drawn in the maps of twenty years back. Latterly, the Chinese have added large stretches of the Tibetan border behind and beyond the great mountain wall to the administrative region of Szechuan, so that to-day (1898) the province is said to comprise 220,000 square miles, and 40,000,000 inhabitants.

province may roughly be described as a high basin situated at the foot of the great snow-mountains that wall in the Thibetan table-land, and cut off from free communication with the other provinces by wide mountain-ranges less lofty than these, but hardly less precipitous. Hence it has been even more independent of the Central Government than is elsewhere the case in the loosely attached organism known as the Chinese Empire; and since the great cataclysm which overspread it during the wars consequent upon the Manchu invasion in the seventeenth century, it has enjoyed an almost uninterrupted peace. Under these circumstances, its prosperity is assured by an exceptionally fertile soil, a general sub-tropical climate, and a purely nominal land-tax. The people are amiable, and their civility to the stranger is a delightful surpise, after the rude treatment he has been subjected to in the coast and central provinces. Of course the few foreign travellers here all speak the language, and hence we are not regarded, as we are on the coast, as "speechless" barbarians who have never learnt manners.

I was received here most hospitably by the proprietor of a large piece-goods hong, in which I proposed to stay while making a hurried investigation of the capabilities of the place, in view of the clause in the Chefoo Convention, stipulating for the opening of Chung-king to the foreign trade, being carried out.

We terminated our long voyage in the *Old Lady of Shen* by running her nose up against the steepy rocky slope at the foot of the east gate of the city, standing about two hundred feet above us. While my Chinamen were gone ashore to announce our arrival, I waited in the boat, and amused myself watching the naked gamins chasing the rats which were being washed out of their holes by the rapidly rising river. This rise was seriously disconcerting the inhabitants of the many well-built bamboo houses, who crowd to the extreme margin as the water falls, and have now to beat a hasty retreat. At length a sedan chair was sent down to the boat to receive me, and we quickly ascended the long stone staircase, and having entered the city gate, I was carried through the narrow, crowded streets to my host's residence in the "Pai-hsiang kai," or "Street of the White Elephant." This is the main business street of the bankers and wholesale merchants of Chung-king, and contains many fine hongs. A hong of this description consists of a series of two-storied buildings situated one behind the other, and separated by intervening courtyards, the whole comprising the warehouses, offices, and residences of the clerks and servants employed in the establishment. The ground floor is very lofty, and elaborately decorated with gilding and carving in wood and stone; the upper story, mostly bedrooms for the numerous staff, being low, unwholesome attics. In many instances, as in the present one, the proprietor ("Tung-chia," *i.e.* "who sits on the East") resides with his family at a distance. My host lived in the "Upper Town," which stands on a sandstone plateau about one hundred feet above and immediately in the rear of the business quarter. I had here a little room assigned to me, and messed with the "Ho-chi"—literally, "partners," but who would be better described as assistants, and was glad of the opportunity thus afforded me of free converse with the natives of the place during my stay.

I had made the journey from Ichang in twenty-one days. Had I hired a large passenger-junk usually employed, called "Kua-tsz," I should have occupied double the time, the chief delay being in waiting one's turn to tow up the rapids, while a small boat scrambles through on the unoccupied bank, and thus often escapes a detention of two or three days.

Distance of Chung-king from the Sea

Twenty-first day from Ichang; fortieth from Hankow; and fifty-ninth from Shanghai.

Distance, according to Blakiston, 358 geographical miles; equal to 412 statute miles; and from Hankow, 721 geographical, equal to 829 statute, miles. From Shanghai, 1309 geographical, equal to 1506 statute miles.

NOTE.—I cannot but think that Blakiston has hardly allowed for all the windings of the river when he makes the distance from Ichang to Chung-king 358 geographical miles. The Chinese Gazetteer of the Upper Yang-tse, which gives the distance from town to town the whole way, sets down 1800 li as the total. This, at the usual reckoning of $3\frac{2}{3}$ li to the geographical mile, would give a distance of 491 geographical or 566 statute miles. An Admiralty survey is much wanted to decide the point with final accuracy.

CHAPTER VII.

CHUNG-KING.

The weather—Morning calls—Visit to a Chinese country house—A fine road—A tedious meal—Personal uncleanliness—The Tung family—"Feng Shui" again—A tough yarn—An inscription.

SZECHUAN is noted among the Chinese for its overcast skies and showery climate. During the month of April that I spent there, we had heavy showers regularly every night. The province seems to lie beneath a cloud-belt, a peculiarity depicted from ancient times in the name of the adjoining province of Yün-nan, which means, "To the south of the clouds."

Since the murder of Margary at Teng-yüeh, in Yünnan, in 1875, British consular agents have been successively deputed from Peking to reside and travel in Western China, with their head-quarters in Chung-king. These officials have been appointed, under the Chefoo Convention of 1876, to see that the promised proclamation, stating the rights of British subjects to travel unmolested throughout the Empire, was duly posted in all the large towns, and generally to report on the capacity of these remote regions for trade. Much most interesting and valuable information has been thus collected, and issued to the public in the form of consular reports, where they lie buried. Baber the

Cargo-boat rowing down Stream (p. 135).

Entrance Gate of Temple outside Walls of Chung-king City ; the Chinese Characters are, "Cave of Genii and Spirits." (p. 139).

To face p. 138.

inimitable, Spence, and Hosie, have all earned the thanks of their countrymen for their arduous labours in collecting original facts in this field. At the time of my arrival, Mr. Hosie was away in Kwei-chow (the province lying to the south-east), and the consular office was in charge of H.M. "Writer," Mr. Mai, or, to call him by his title, Mai-sze-yeh. The consular Ya-mên is situated in the upper town, and consists of a substantial modern Chinese courtyard building. Mr. Mai, who received me when I called, is a native of Yünnan, and a Mahometan ("Hui-hui"). He has visited Singapore, and is consequently familiar with the barbarian "Chi," or restlessness, which so astonishes and worries the untravelled Chinese. He therefore responded to my multifarious inquiries, and introduced me to Mr. Tung, or Tung-Loa-yeh, an owner of coal-mines, who wishes me to import foreign pumping machinery for him. These all breakfasted with me at the hospitable table of my host, Mr. Hsing-hsi-tang. The upper and business classes in China take but two meals a day—breakfast at ten, and dinner at five; late people, however, as the merchants mostly are (much business being transacted at night over the opium-pipe), have a supper in addition. I accepted an invitation from Tung to visit him at his country house to-morrow, and stay over a day or two. I witnessed from the steps of our hong, an elaborate Buddhist procession, which occupied over half an hour passing the door. The numerous *tableaux vivants* represented various fairy legends, each composed of a group of four boys gorgeously dressed, and borne on a platform supported on bamboo poles, and carried on the shoulders of two men. Children dressed up as sages, with flowing white beards, followed in the procession on horseback—all pretty conceits, and novel to me.

In the afternoon I called on Dr. Wheeler, D.D., to whom

I had a letter of introduction, and who lives in the "Shang Cheng," or Upper City. I went there in a chair, up steps all the way. The streets are broad, busy, and filthy, and might have been those of a hundred similar towns I have visited in China. Dr. Wheeler belongs to the American Methodist Episcopal Mission, and came up here from Kiukiang last winter with his wife and three daughters, none of whom care to walk out of the compound, European women being still a novelty and objects of insuperable curiosity to the Western Chinese. The site is charming, with a magnificent prospect across the Siao Ho (affluent) to "Chiang-peh ting" ("City on the North Bank").

Monday, April 9th.—I carried out my promise to Tung Lao-yeh to accompany him to his country seat, to which I set out in a sedan with three bearers. Tung Lao-yeh's dwelling is situated near a gap in the hills, through which passes the main road to Chêng-tu Sêng, the capital of the province. This road is the sole "Han-lu" (dry road) out of Chung-king, the city being built on a narrow peninsula formed by the Yang-tse, locally the Tsz' shui Ho, or "Letters' Water River," and the great affluent locally known as the Siao Hŏ. The Yang-tse here is so-called from the curls, like Chinese characters, which the innumerable eddies form on its smooth, glistening surface. This affluent, the Siao Hŏ, is about half the size of the main stream, and drains a large area of country to the north and north-west of the great river's main valley. This river has its sources in the boundary ranges of the provinces of Kan-su and Shen-si, and furnishes water communication—obstructed by rapids which are the concomitant of all Szechuan rivers—with the cities of Ho-chow, Pa-chow, Suilin, and Pao-ning-fu. This dry road is one of the best in China, being fully five feet wide, and paved with heavy stone slabs laid crossways.

Quite half the road was composed of long ascending and descending staircases, the hills here, as throughout China, being remarkable for their steepness. After going for over a mile through the city streets, we went out at the west gate, and descended for about a hundred steps on to a road which passed along the edge of the sandstone cliffs some hundred and fifty feet above the river-bed, now two-thirds dry, and having a fine stone parapet guarding the path on the outside. Thence the road ascends by steps over a hill about five hundred feet high—one mass of small, mostly nameless, graves, with not a single tree or shrub to break their monotony, but with a grand prospect of the rushing river and the lofty hills rising from the opposite bank, all green with the spring crops of opium, barley, and beans, and picturesque, tree-embosomed villages and residences scattered throughout. A marked feature of Eastern Szechuan is the total absence both of plain and of barren hills, every inch of land being either under cultivation or wooded—except round the cities, where the monotonous cemeteries occupy more ground than do the living inhabitants. After travelling thus up and down three miles of grave-covered hills, we ascended through a narrow wooded gap, and passed under several elaborately carved stone triumphal arches, or "Pai-fang," more numerous and handsome in Szechuan than in any other province; then through a small village on to a high hill commanding a glorious prospect of river and valley, upon which is built the "Tang," or family residence of the Tungs, until at length we rested in the formally set-out K'o-tang, or guest-hall, looking on to a handsome enclosed courtyard filled with orange, camellia, and azalea trees growing in large pots placed on stone pedestals. I was at once surrounded by the children of the family, which consists of three brothers, having eighteen children amongst them—ten boys and eight girls. The women were only allowed to peep in at the barbarian through curtained doors.

As soon as we sat down, cloths wrung out of hot water were handed to us to wipe our faces—a most refreshing custom in a warm climate, and the usual hot tea, which the two assiduous servants would never allow to cool, marching round with a kettle of hot water to replace each sip taken by the guests. Then, in my honour, followed the usual Chinese dinner-party, which to the western is an intolerably tedious affair. Seven of us sat down to a small square table, I, as the guest of the day, having a seat at the top all to myself, the others sitting two each on short benches. The table was adorned at starting with sixteen large set dishes of highly-flavoured mincemeats, fruits, and vegetables, and about a dozen saucers containing melon-seeds, pea-nuts, candied orange-peel, etc., the centre being occupied by the "removes," which are replaced successively a dozen times or more throughout the feast, and consist largely of fat pork cooked in various ways. The business of the day commenced with swallowing endless thimblefuls of hot "samshu," a fiery spirit made from millet, interspersed with the cracking of melon-seeds and pea-nuts, and the tasting of the different dishes with chop-sticks, the Lilliputian saucer in front of the honoured guests being heaped up with tit-bits fished out with the chop-sticks of the too polite hosts. Gradually, after all have drunk well, the removes are seriously attacked, when the company, after about two hours' time, being absolutely unable to swallow any more food, wine-drinking recommences, stimulated by the noisy and, to the Chinaman, highly exciting game of Morra, in which I am fairly proficient. All this time not a morsel of bread or grain of rice to assist the deglutition of the greasy dishes, only occasional hot cloths to wipe the mouth and the perspiring brow, and a few whiffs of the common hubble-bubble, which a lad is told off to constantly hand round to each guest. This he does, the burning match in one hand, the pipe in the other, presenting the long brass stem to the mouth. Little red paper napkins, five inches by two, are folded before each guest, but are totally insufficient to wipe away the grease-spots with which the varnished table at an early period gets covered, bones, gristle, etc., being spat out on the floor to mingle with the tobacco from the perpetually relighted pipes. All the while one is seated on a high, hard wooden stool, which is torture to a weary western traveller, but on which the Chinese loll about from morning to night. At last, to my intense relief, appeared a dirty servant with the wooden rice-tub, which he placed on a sideboard, along with a pile of little rice-bowls. Then with a wooden scoop he filled a bowl for each guest with the steaming grain, and the dinner was practically over. But the bowl, if accepted, must be emptied to the last grain, or you are set down as totally wanting in manners. To assist in this, some of the greasy and now cold soup out of one of the dishes on the table is emptied by each guest into his bowl, thus enabling him to pick up the last grain. After the rice, tea is served, and no more wine can be touched. I never could find any other reason given for this inexorable rule than that wine is made from the seed, and tea from the leaves of plants, and to take wine on the top of tea would be placing the son above the father. Such fanciful reasons for possibly practical customs abound in China. Chinese dinners have been described over and over again, but I have narrated this one, as I think few have given an idea of their tediousness and the absence of all that we deem comfort. Still, to mix with the people, one must swallow one's antipathies, and conform to their habits.

We retired at nine, the hours from dusk to bedtime being most uncomfortably passed sitting about on hard, high, square chairs in a state of darkness made visible by a dim oil-lamp, consisting of a tilted greasy saucer, on a high stand, filled with oil, from the edge of which a smoking pith wick protrudes. There being no privacy in China, I held a levée in my earth-floored bedroom, furnished with a gorgeously carved and heavily gilt bedstead, and rows of red, lacquered, brass-locked wardrobes, and the usual stiff chairs at little tea-poys. Here I was carefully put to bed on a mattress of plaited straw, with a not very clean cotton quilt, and exceedingly dirty flowered-silk bed-curtains. The Chinese, like our own ancestors, dress in magnificent silks and satins, their underclothing being often filthy in the extreme. Though they acknowledge the value of cleanliness theoretically, their whole life, public and private, is an almost total negation of it. Rich and poor are all alike, nor do I find the Szechuan people one whit better than their neighbours in this respect. Coming up, every man of our crew was covered with itch-sores, and some ointment I offered them they would not take the trouble to apply. There can be no doubt that the Chinese possess a much less highly developed organization than do the Caucasian races, and hence their indifference to discomfort and suffering. They seem, too, nowadays to be quite wanting in the imaginative faculty, and have long since ceased to invent anything new; and while doubtless they are thus spared many of the pains that a superior development of this faculty afflicts us with, they lose nearly all the highest pleasures which our more sensitive organization affords us. Like the animals to a great extent, their procedures follow instinct or hereditary tendencies rather than reason, and their ambition seems limited to the gratification of the senses.

Courage, in the highest sense of controlling their instincts, they rarely possess; hence, while apathetic in the presence of sickness and death, they are cowards in the presence of dangers which call for energetic resistance.

Their religion consists in propitiating evil spirits, and abjectly kotowing to such saints as they believe may aid them in worldly enterprises. Such a people, seemingly incapable of chivalrous feeling or loyalty, can hardly appreciate the Christian ideal which we are making such costly efforts to place before them. Their own system of ethics, based upon filial piety and "custom," works well; and endeavours to upset it produce at first much harm, whatever the ultimate good. With all their faults—say radical defects—they possess many virtues. They are easy-going, kindly disposed towards one another, clannish in supporting their relations, hospitable, attached to their employers, and public-spirited, where their feelings are aroused, to a degree unknown in Europe. But the whole social system is undermined, from the highest to the lowest, by peculation and deceit; and, from armies which only exist in the commander-in-chief's wardrobe, and public granaries containing nothing but chaff, down to presents not intended for acceptance, and proclamations never meant to be observed, the whole empire is one vast sham. Yet such is their persistent industry, that, with more highly gifted leaders to guide and lead them, they may yet be a great people. As an instance of what resolute leaders may do with this people, witness the celebrated "P'ing-fen," or "grave-levelling law," promulgated at the accession of various invading dynasties. This law was enforced, notably at the accession of the Mongols in the tenth century, when, finding so large a proportion of the cultivable area of the empire given over to cemeteries, Kublai Khan ordered them to be ploughed up remorselessly. It is to be regretted that their Manchu conquerors two hundred years ago were persuaded to rescind a similar edict.

To return to the Tung family, who are rich and influential. The father, now deceased, bought official rank of the fifth grade for himself and his sons, who are now addressed as "Lao-yeh" ("Old Sire," *i.e.* Honourable). The family have lost a good deal of their money, chiefly by shipwrecks in the rapids, though they still own a coal-mine thirty miles distant, a soap factory, silk-spinning, and weaving, and dyeing establishments ten miles distant, besides shops in the city itself, where they retail their produce. One brother is a prefect (Che-fu) in the adjoining province of Kwei-chow, the other three attending to the various businesses. These all live together. One tutor teaches the boys; and the little girls, pretty-looking and gaudily dressed, but piteously hobbling on their mutilated feet, learn needlework, housekeeping, and water-colours. At table I was surprised to see at the upper seat—that is, next to mine—and among my handsomely clad hosts, a poorly dressed, pale young man, who, I was told, was the "Lao-sze" (literally, "Old Scholar)," or family tutor. It is gratifying to see the extreme respect everywhere paid in China to teachers, whose extreme poverty would render them despised in Europe.

Tuesday, April 10*th*.—Another beautiful, warm summer day. I went for a short stroll, accompanied as usual by my hosts, and again admired the view of the river valley hidden in mist, above which the bright-green hills, interspersed with variegated sandstone cliffs, shone resplendent in the sunshine. The hill-summit belongs to Mr. Tung, and upon it some ten years since they opened a stone-quarry. The people, fearing for their "Feng-shui," remonstrated, and entered suit against the Tung family in the local magistrate's Ya-men. After long delays, profitable only to the magistrate, a compromise was effected, the Tung family receiving a round sum, in return for which they guaranteed, on behalf of themselves, their heirs, and assigns, henceforth to leave the "Yin" or Dark, *i.e.* the underground, undisturbed, and to make use only of the "Yang," or Bright, *i.e.* the surface portion of their property. I may add, that in making the stone-quarry, they destroyed three of the artificial cave-dwellings which abound throughout the sandstone cliffs of Szechuan, leaving one intact as a specimen and a cool summer retreat. These caves were inhabited by the Aboriginals or Miaotse, or, as the Chinese here say, by the Man-tze, who occupied the whole of this and the neighbouring provinces of Kweichow and Yünnan before they were gradually driven out by Chinese immigrants from the north and east, about two thousand years back. The public generally are now warned not to touch the "yin" of this hill, in a lengthy proclamation deeply engraved in red and gold characters on three massive black stone slabs enclosed in a kind of stone archway, which is built by the side of the road just outside my host's door. I brought away with me a rubbing of this proclamation for careful examination at my leisure, and which I think of sufficient interest, as showing the nature of the belief of Fêng-shui, to warrant my giving a translation of the document. I must premise that my hosts are members of an old Catholic family, which fact might be thought to prejudice the people against them; but they themselves do not admit that this was the cause of their molestation. However it be, there is no doubt that Fêng-shui, as indeed is superstition in all countries, is a powerful weapon in the hands of the malevolent, and an obstacle to all works of progress in this benighted land. (See note at the end of this chapter.)

Beyond is a large enclosure reaching to the top of the hill, in which is the grave of my host's father. In front is a handsome terrace bounded by two obelisks about thirty feet high, surmounted by lions, and on the terrace three stone tables surrounded by stone stools, all carved in facsimile of their ordinary wooden prototypes. This is curiously the case with all stonework in China: triumphal arches, parapets, balustrades—all imitate the woodwork, to which architecture was exclusively limited originally, as this, in its turn, still takes its outlines from the earlier tent of the Nomad. These stone seats and tables are used when the relatives of the deceased visit the tomb to burn incense and offer rice to the Manes, and make a sort of picnic for the occasion. The enclosure was planted with cypress, the pointed cones of which represent the brush used in Chinese writing—and hence literature. My host was careful to point out to me the admirable "Fêng-shui" of the tomb. Facing a reach of the great river confined between steep hills some five hundred feet below, up which the tomb looks lengthways, the angle of the river, where it turns short off to the left, being hidden in the slope of the hill in the immediate foreground, all the water seen is "approaching" ("Lai-shui"), bringing, as it were, blessings to the inhabitants, and so to his posterity. Yet my same host, who had been thus careful of the site of his own father's grave, had not hesitated to outrage the "Fêng-shui" of his neighbours—the good people of Chung-king—by burrowing into their "Serpent's neck." For the city of Chung-king represents a tortoise, and on it, or round it, is coiled a snake. According to the Chinese, these two species live together—an absurd belief, which, however, I have never been able to shake, and the prevalence of which the subjoined extract from a local English newspaper published at Shanghai testifies. Thus, a correspondent at T'ai-yuen (General Mesney) writes: "March, 1883.—The Chinese generally assert that snakes and tortoises cohabit; and I have seen paintings of turtles and tortoises, and metal castings also, with a snake wound about, the emblem of strength and longevity; and, on inquiry, I have always been told the same story—that it was the only way of multiplying both species. Be that as it may, and let naturalists say what they like, one thing I am certain of, and that is—that one summer afternoon, whilst walking along the banks of the Chung-ngan River, below Kwei-chow, on the look-out for a carp for my dinner, I chanced to see a turtle going across the clear stream, with its head out of the water, some thirty yards off. I directed my rifle towards the turtle; and when I had fired, a snake floated on the surface, cut in two, and a turtle dived to the bottom and swam away out of sight amongst the rocks. I guess his snakeship was just taking a sort of saloon, or rather a deck passage, across the Chung-ngan kiang by the turtle ferry."

The day being hot, we sat about generally, saw the boys with their tutor engaged in their monotonous, noisy repetitions, and discussed the wonders of foreign countries. In the evening we ascended a neighbouring height, on which was the handsome grave of a sister of my host, from which we looked down a precipice some five hundred feet sheer on to the romantic valley of the Siao Ho, which here runs parallel to the main river, the land-neck between the two rivers at this spot narrowing to two hundred yards in width; the city of Chung-king is situated where the peninsula on which it is built widens out immediately above the confluence of the two rivers, which run in deep, narrow valleys between steep sandstone cliffs. At this season of the year, with the trees in full foliage and the crops nearly ready for harvesting, the view is exceptionally beautiful.

The following is a translation of the inscription referred to on page 147 :—

I, P'ENG, by imperial decree, bearing the insignia of the second rank, acting salt transport commissioner, Intendant of Circuit for the districts of Yung-chuen, Nanchuen, and Tung-hiang in Szechuen; Governor of the Prefectures of Chung-king, Kwei-chow, Sui-ting, Chung-chow, Chui-chow, and Shihsien : advanced in office five steps ; the possessor in person of three orders of merit ; the recorded holder of ten honorific degrees :— do hereby issue a prohibitory proclamation upon a case deposed before me.

Whereas Siao Ju-lan, an official of the second grade holding brevet rank, Li Mao-lin, an official of the third degree; Lo Yuen-yi, decorated with the peacock's feather ; the bachelor Wang Ting-chang ; the bachelor Chin teh-chun ; the literary graduate Lin Tao-wo ; the Tung-che and deputy magistrate in Hu-peh, Chen Chi-chang ; the Tung-che Li Chiu, decorated with the peacock feather ; Li Shen-hai and Yeh Wen-siang, officials of the fourth rank ; the sub-prefects Hoang Pang-jung, Lui Wen-yi, Liu Yung-sheng, and Yang Tao-chuen ; the decorated officers, Yao Tsun, Wang Yin-ting, Tang Sheng-tze, Wang Ching-san, Cho Shih-yung, Wang Ta-tze, Chu Ming-hoai, Cho Tso-yi, Kuo Wei-hang, and Chang Shuo-shu respectively, have petitioned, saying—

We, the graduates detailed above, strongly urge the issue of a prohibitory proclamation with a view to cherish and aid the affairs of the locality, the circumstance being as follows :—

Outside the South of Ue (Chung-king), outside the Kee (history) gate, and below the citadel of Fu-tu koan (four miles distant), is a place called Ngo hsiang-ching (goose's neck), joining the hamlet of Shih ma tsao (stone horse manger). Now having investigated the records, we find that this place is in truth the spot whence exudes the pulse (*i.e.* in which are the water-sources) of Fu-tu Koan, and verily forms the throat of the district of Ue (Chung-king), by virtue of which scholars abound, the people flourish, and merchants and traders are attracted to the place, whereby all are mutually benefited together. Now we have further investigated the ancient records of the province and find it therein stated that—" A certain Li yan once purposed to open this ground and so penetrate the two waters (watershed) of Pei and Min, whereupon the Military Expectant, Chu-ko, declared that if this ground be opened, the enclosure of Ue (Chung-king) would lose its life-breath; and it was consequently forbidden to touch it. It is evident that Ngo hsiang-chin is a place of the weightiest import, and must in nowise be injured: hence this prohibition has continued in force from of old without change."

But now one Tung has acquired this ground by purchase, and, giving ear to the deceitful words of stonemasons, has quarried this stone for the sake of inordinate gain. This has been going on for some ten years, until the pulses of the place are being sundered almost past remedy. And now, graduate and military, merchants and traders, are steadily going down. So is the business of the Tai-ping and Chaotien gates, which open on to the two busiest quarters, growing duller and colder. Searching into the cause, we find it clearly due to the wounding of the ground pulse; and, if a plan be not at once devised for repairing it, what answer shall graduates, military merchants, and traders receive? These several gentry see this plainly, and will not stand by idle. They have therefore called together the scholars, officials, traders, and merchants to consider the matter, and they have unanimously agreed to contribute the needful funds and to buy up Ngo hsiang-ching, and make of it a public ground, to be called the Pei shan tang, or "Cultivate virtue hall," and so nourish the Feng-shui. The aforesaid Tung having given his willing consent, the deeds have been drawn up, the price agreed on has been paid, and the transfer is accomplished.

Lest now in the lapse of time the matter should fall into oblivion and the determination now arrived at be set aside and not survive to distant times, which is a matter of weighty import to this city, such as we dare not ourselves decide, we have presented a petition to the Prefect and to the magistrate, and now present the matter to the higher authorities for decision, requesting them to issue a prohibitory edict to the following effect, and to have it engraved on stone, that—"On the ground between Futu koan and Chiao men tung, improvements, whether public or private, are henceforward prohibited by proclamation, that it will not be permitted to disturb the ground; and the range of the ground extending up from Fu-tu Koan down to Chiao men tung is closely bound up with the inflowing pulses of the walls of Ue (book-name of Chung-king). Henceforth, let no one touch this place either for the purpose of public or private repairs. It is forbidden to quarry stone, to burn kilns, or to open a ditch, that the ground pulse may be cherished and handed down (intact) to all ages. Now, after the issue of this proclamation, should any dare to disobey, then it shall be the duty of the Elders and of the Petitioners respectively, to point out their names and bring an accusation against the offenders, notifying the magistrate to arrest them for trial, when they shall in no case escape. Let all yield implicit obedience and not disobey." The proclamation on the right (*i.e.* is for general information).

Dated the eleventh year of the reign Tung-chih (1872).

This proclamation is thrice repeated in the same words on three separate tablets of limestone, each being enclosed in a heavy sandstone frame. The three parallel proclamations are issued by the Taotai (Intendant of Circut), Chefu (Prefect), and Pahsien (Magistrate of the District of Pa, *i.e.* Chung-king) respectively.

CHAPTER VIII.

CHUNG-KING.

Return to town—Catholic and other missions—Visitors—The China Inland Mission—Native post—A Taoist temple—The priests hard-up—Chinese banks—An ephemeral town—Across the river—The Catholic cathedral—Charming surroundings of the city—Filth within—Dull evenings—Chess—Malt liquor—A public garden—The walls—Slow progress of the missionaries.

On our way back to the city on the following day, we turned aside to visit an extensive garden occupying a narrow glen overlooking the Sia Hŏ, in which are the courtyards, temples, reception-rooms, fish-ponds, winding stone paths, and rockwork mountains of the Kiangsi Guildhall, in Chinese, Ning Kiang Hui-kwan. The merchants and traders from the distant provinces, assembled in the larger commercial cities all over the empire, have each a guild-house of their own in every important city. The glen above is filled with groves of magnificent bamboos, and the whole place is redolent of vegetation, and, notwithstanding the sunshine, the air was close and damp, like that of a hothouse. In picturesque spots, scattered about the gardens, are handsome pavilions, where parties come to "drink wine," *i.e.* to dine, and to "shwa," *i.e.* flâner. The usual oranges, camellias, and azaleas filled every vacant niche, besides numberless flowers, the names of which are unknown to me.

Notwithstanding the hospitality of the Tung family, I was glad to leave Mien-hoa pu (the village where they resided), as life in a Chinese country house, and, indeed, in a town house also, is insufferably dull. When the scrolls on the wall are exhausted, the enclosed courtyard becomes monotonous, and to enjoy the view one has to go outside into the street; and when I get up to go out, I am accompanied by such a retinue—my own two servants, as well as those of my hosts, and the members of the family (male only, *bien entendu*), that I could well sympathize with the boredom of royalty. To be followed and stared at, even by a respectful mob, destroys half the pleasure derived from beautiful scenery. The weather, too, was very hot and close, and moving resulted in much perspiration, while baths are as much unknown to the modern Chinese as they were to our own forefathers.

In the afternoon I called at the French Catholic establishment, situated in the Upper City (Shang pan cheng), known as the Chen-yuen Tang, and was received by Père Vinçot, the same bishop who entertained Blakiston's party in 1860, and whose characteristic letters are printed in " Five Months on the Upper Yang-tse." The missionaries occupy spacious premises, which are now being rebuilt. Szechuan is the most promising field these missions possess, there being in Chung-king close on four thousand converts, and in the whole province nearly fifty thousand, mostly, however, the descendants of families who were converted by the original Jesuit missionaries in the seventeenth century. This does not appear to be a great result of two centuries of work, and of the efforts of some of the ablest men of the Catholic priesthood, who are specially selected for China, there being over fifty in Szechuan alone; and I cannot but agree with Père Amand David, who doubts if China will ever be Christianized, especially now that innumerable different sects of Protestantism from Europe and America have entered the field, and rendered confusion worse confounded to the naturally sceptical Chinese mind. The Catholic and Protestant sects are looked upon by the Chinese as different religions, and the contempt entertained for missions is aggravated by the unfortunate disagreement as to the translation of the word "God." The Chinese of all descriptions employ exclusively the word "T'ien" whenever allusion is made to the Supreme Being. This word T'ien, which is also the common word for the material sky, is the equivalent of our word "Heaven;" all saints and all beings to whom prayer is offered, or of whom images are constructed in the different temples, are under "Heaven." To my mind, after many years' conversational intimacy with all classes of the Chinese, the common phrase of "Pai T'ien" is an exact equivalent of our "Worship God." And if the early missionaries had been content to stop there, introducing the teachings of Jesus as that of a Prophet under Heaven, they might have made as much progress with Christianity as has been made with Buddhism—a religion that has had a wonderful effect in softening the character of the ancient Chinese. But wishing to personify *their* God, the Jesuit fathers invented a new name—" T'ien Chu," or " Lord of Heaven." Then came the English, who in order not to be identified with the Roman Catholics, took another name for their God, namely, "Shang-ti," meaning "Supreme Ruler" or Emperor. Later missionaries (American Baptist) have adopted another title—" Chen Shen," *i.e.* " The True Spirit," thus by implication stamping all other spirits as false. The natural result is that the Chinese say, " Foreign nations have each their deities, why not we ours? In any case, T'ien is above all; and whether the relation of inferior deities to High Heaven be that of Sonship or Motherhood" (latterly the Catholics have started separate Shêng-Mu, *i.e.* Mother of God Temples), " or anything else, can never be exactly ascertained, and is consequently a matter of indifference to every thoughtful and educated person." No one can doubt that the Chinese would be all the better for accepting the teachings of the Great Founder of our Western religion: what I do doubt is whether the spending of so much competitive energy and money does not rather repel educated Chinese instead of leading them to respect Christ's teaching.

It is one thing to convert African savages or Polynesian fetish worshippers, and another thing to spend millions of money in attempting to convert Chinese who possess an ancient and admirable system of ethics of their own, adulterated, it is true, by many foolish superstitions. But who is competent to decide where religion ends and superstition begins? The riots and consequent massacres resulting from mission-work throughout Indo-China may be justified by the end; but it is certain our relations with the Chinese would be far more cordial than they are, were our diplomatists not engaged in a ceaseless struggle with the Chinese Government in order to compel the people, *nolens volens*, to respect and accept missionaries of all denominations and with endless idiosyncracies. This leads the Chinese to regard missionaries as political agents, and will always prevent their being cordially welcomed by the ruling classes. Further, how can the Chinese reconcile the treatment they have received at the hands of Christian nations as an example of the superior ethics of Christianity?

My evenings in the hong where I am staying were spent

in holding a levée of Chinese visitors, while seated in state on the daïs at the head of the reception-hall. At times we played Chinese chess, which is a favourite amusement with the youth of this establishment—a game differing from Indian chess chiefly in the addition of two pieces called "cannon," which only check when a third piece intervenes between them and their object. This serves to pass away the time during the dim gloom of a Chinese house from sunset till bedtime. At nine, Shao-yeh (literally, small night) or supper is eaten. This is another characteristically Chinese pastime. By the light of the oil-lamp we peck with our chop-sticks at a few miniature dishes of cold onions, minced leeks, cold peas and beans flavoured with vinegar and soy, apricot and melon-seeds, all which serve as a zest to numerous sups of mild, hot rice-wine—a kind of beer fermented from the glutinous rice. Sam-shu, or distilled spirit, on the other hand, is generally made from millet-seed.

As I was about to establish a mercantile business of my own in Chung-king, which was not formally opened as a treaty port until eight years later, I called on the local officials—the Tao-tai, or Intendant of Circuit, and the Pa-hsien, the local magistrate—to notify them of my intended stay. I found them very communicative and pleasant, and discussed with them the possible opening of the port. The latter afterwards sent me a proclamation, to be posted on the wall of my hong, consisting of a preamble citing the Tientsin Treaty, by virtue of which British subjects have a right to visit the interior for purposes of trade and residence, and exhorting the people to deal fairly with and not to crowd or molest me. The proclamation was hardly needed, for the Szechuan officials and people seem to form an exception to the rest of China in being favourably disposed towards foreign intercourse.

I afterwards called, by invitation, on the China Inland Mission, one of whose chief stations is in this city. This mission is English, and, apart from my commiseration for people forced to live like poor Chinamen, it is always pleasant to meet one's fellow-countrymen in distant parts, and I was delighted to go and see them. The members of this mission, male and female, all adopt the Chinese dress. They rent extensive and rather dilapidated Chinese buildings in the upper and more open portion of the city, and have boys' and girls' schools, besides religious services. Their converts are as yet but few; but these earnest missionaries are, as they say, satisfied to sow the seed, and leave the harvest to a Higher Power. It must be disheartening work thus trying to convert the very poor, whose motives in changing their religion can never be trusted; while, as a rule, the upper classes in China disdain all intercourse with them.

I was accompanied in my rounds to-day by an obliging volunteer guide. He astonished me, however, in reply to the usual questions, by telling one magistrate he was a native of Chili; another, that his province was Shantung; while he was, I believe, really a native of Shansi. I asked him afterwards what was his object in thus concealing his birthplace. He replied it was well not to let the officials know too much. No one who has not been in China (in Shanghai and Hong-kong the whole tone is too European to learn anything really about the natives) can form any idea of the labour to be gone through to gain an exact knowledge of the simplest fact.

The forwarding of letters by post between the treaty ports is now (1898) a monopoly of the foreign Customs, but the bulk of the inland postage is still carried on by private native organizations. During my visit to Chung-king, in

Green and Yellow Tiled Roof of Pavilion in Chung-king City (p. 106).

Graves on Range of Hills opposite Chung-king: the two "Characters" cut in the Landscape indicate that this Mountain is a Reproduction of the Sacred "Mount T'u" in Shantung Province (p. 158).   *To face p.* 158.

1883, the time occupied by overland courier was, from Ichang five days, and from Hankow fourteen days. The new Customs couriers are half as long again on the journey, owing, so say the foreign Customs' officials, to the increase in the mail matter.

The couriers make the whole journey on foot over the goat-paths of the intervening mountains. They are necessarily men of wonderful endurance; they will do forty miles a day over rough ground for days together, going at a sort of jog-trot all the way. Between Ichang and Shanghai the mails are, of course, carried by the foreign steamers.

Several ferries cross the river at Chung-king, occupying half an hour or one hour for the half-mile transit, according to the strength of the current. The principal ferry lands are at the foot of the paved path which leads over the mountains to the adjoining province of Kwei-chow and to Kwei-yang Fu, its capital, distant twelve days' journey, each of ninety li, say twenty-five miles. The road crosses the steep range of hills, 1200 feet high, which faces Chung-king; and thence runs through a continuously mountainous country. Being a main artery of the empire, the road is some five feet wide, and evenly paved with stone flags. A steady ascent, partly by long staircases, leads to a spot where the road forks, a side path taking one up one of the peaks, between which the main highway passes. This, the left peak, is finely wooded, and on it are scattered the temples and pavilions known as " Lao-chün Tung," or The Cave of the Sage Lao-tse. On the other and loftier peak stands a pagoda—p'u-ing, or supplementing, the Feng-shui of Chung-king—from which is a splendid view over the steep mountainous country which embraces the city on this side.

Lao Chün, or, as he is commonly designated, Laotse (the old philosopher), was the reputed author of the

"Tao teh King"—classic of the path and virtue; he lived in the sixth century B.C., and was thus a contemporary of Confucius, who is said to have visited him and to have been overwhelmed by his mystical insight. Lao-tse disappeared in the west after writing his Tao teh King, but it is highly improbable that he ever visited Szechuan, at that period a wilderness in possession of wild aboriginal tribes. The present Taoist religion, with its magic rites and interminable ceremonial worship, is a sad travesty of Lao-tse's pure doctrine—not, unfortunately, an isolated instance of the corruption that has perverted the original teaching of a Great Founder. Lao-tse is reported to have dwelt in the cave near the summit, from which exudes a fine spring of water. The temples are spacious and handsome, the usual terraces and flights of steps with fine stone balustrades uniting the various sanctuaries. From the main terrace one looks over the silver streak of the river and the city, which, though built on a perpendicular walled sandstone bluff rising to 250 feet above the river, from here appears flat, to the distant range, some 3000 feet above the river, which protects Chung-king on the north. Lao-chün Tung is a great summer resort of the festive Chung-kingites; but times here, as elsewhere, are bad, and economy has to be studied in "shwa"-ing as in other things, so that the priests, seventeen in number, complained bitterly that they could not cover their expenses. There are a number of Catholic converts about here whose mites are diverted from the local deities, going to swell the fund from which the distractingly ugly white-washed churches, affected by missionaries, are built. Meanwhile the beautiful old temples, with their cool halls and shady gardens, and every aspect which art and nature can combine to soothe the brain, weary of the outer world, are falling into decay. Even their rich, deep, quiet-sounding bells are being slowly removed by the barbarian curio-collector, to be replaced by the discordant jingle of the chapel adjacent. How often in some quiet, wooded valley have I heard the deep bell sounded with a single stroke at long intervals, of some Buddhist shrine calling to vespers, and rested from my walk and watched the worshippers and smoking incense! "Vicist Galilea!" I feel inclined to say, with the old Roman stoic. As a nineteenth-century European, I say, "Why cannot the exalted teachings of Jesus be grafted upon the results of previous struggles towards a better life, instead of being antagonistic to and destroying them?"

In any case, the priests of Lao-chün Tung are hard put to it for a living. A coal-mine had undermined their chief temple, and the resultant lawsuit, decided against them, has impoverished them. This is the first place, too, of the kind where I have been openly asked for money. Not having anticipated such a long excursion, I had not brought my coolie, and consequently had no purse-bearer with me (a shilling's worth of copper cash weighs a pound and a half). They had regaled me with the usual tea and hubble-bubble, and were somewhat put out at my having nothing to give them.

On another occasion I returned the call of the manager of the Chang-sing-tung Bank, "Chao" by name, and stayed to breakfast, at which small wheaten loaves and vermicelli soup, besides "fahtsai"—hair-herb, a very fine-cut seaweed from Japan—being served, I enjoyed the repast more than usual. This is the chief Shansi bank and hong here; it has existed for 270 years, the chief managing the business from his native place, T'ai-yuen-Fu, in Shansi. These are the most respectable and strictly managed businesses in the empire; their branches extend to every important city in the eighteen provinces, and their staff numbers several hundreds. I asked him how he accounted for one firm remaining in existence for nearly three centuries. He replied, " Our rule is strict. Our inside staff are all from Shansi ; they are apprenticed, live in the hong, and are never allowed out after nine at night." He said the southern mercantile establishments are more lax. These Shansi banks grant drafts for large sums upon their branches scattered all over the empire, and it is wonderful how, with the slow intercommunication, they manage their finances as they do.

Another day I started for a stroll along the foreshore below the walls. I left the city by the nearest gate, the " T'ai-ping Men," or " Gate of Peace," and descended 240 filthy steps crowded with water-carriers going up, and malodorous manure-carriers going down, each with two heavy buckets slung across the shoulders by a heavy bamboo carrier—the " pien tan," or " convenience carrier," in use from Penang to San Francisco and wherever Chinese congregate. All the water used in the city is carried up from the river, through the different gates, by poorly-paid coolies, who get from four to five " cash "—a farthing—for a load of two large buckets. I reached the beach, now dry and crowded with shanties, shops, opium-dens, wood and coal stores, all of which will have to be removed a month hence, when the river makes another big rise. I noticed two gigantic isolated rocks standing on the sandbank ; these had dropped out of the cliff immediately beneath the city wall, a slice of which fell down later one stormy night, carrying with it several adjoining houses and their unfortunate inhabitants. According to local information—not always reliable—these rocks fell down three winters back. The larger is a rough cube of about fifty feet, a considerable portion having been already quarried away, its position on the water's edge being very convenient, and the rock a compact, homogeneous, grey sandstone. Here, on the south-west side of Chung-king, the river-bed widens out, forming a huge sand and boulder bank in the middle, with a wide channel on each side, called the "Shan-hu Pa," or "Coral Strand," the summit of which is cultivated for a space of about one square mile, and sustains several farms and cottages, which have to be removed every year in order to escape the summer floods, when the whole island, now thirty feet out of water, is submerged. The summit of this bank is the only level spot of ground I have yet met with in Eastern Szechuan. I walked for nearly a mile along its edge, until the loose boulders, about the size of cricket-balls, became too much for me. I may mention that I had chosen this uncomfortable path as a means of escape from the large crowd of gamins who had taken to following me. The "Wa-wa'rh," as the children are called in the friendly language of Szechuan, who had collected to the number of some hundreds, were amusing themselves shouting at the top of their voices, "Yang jen p'ao ma'i," *i.e.* "See the foreigner galloping on his horse!" I afterwards found out that this cry (any rallying-cry for a mob) originated in a peep-show of the Shanghai races, which had been recently exhibited by an itinerant showman, and which had excited the sportive minds of the Chung-king youth, to whose bare feet I had hoped the stones would prove a barrier. But it was not so, and I only eluded them by jumping into a sampan, and ordering myself to be set across the river. A tremendous shout arose from the assembled Wa-wa'rh as this feat was happily accomplished.

In crossing to the other side, we were carried down nearly a mile by the five-knot current, but almost regained the lost ground by running up in the eddy on the opposite shore, which leads to the small but dangerous rapid formed by a ledge of rocks, that here juts out from the right bank and obstructs the channel. A large junk, oil laden, had been wrecked here a few days before, and her hull had been towed into shoal-water, where she was floating with the decks gone. The cargo of oil-tubs, made of plaited bamboo lined with bamboo-paper, was stowed on the bank, with the crew comfortably housed alongside to guard it under an awning made from the sail. Landing, I climbed up the steep hillside, and finding a newly-made grave, with comfortable stone seats, just erected on a prominent knee of the hill, I sat down in the hot sunshine to rest and to enjoy the view. From whichever point you regard the city of Chung-king, the view is one full of interest, each aspect forming a new picture of rock, river, wood, and temple, crenellated battlements, and uplifted roofs, crowded with bewildering detail which the photograph cannot do justice to. The view forms one of the most perfect pictures of river and mountain scenery, enlivened by human activity, that the world affords.

In Europe, excepting in purely wild scenery, and more especially in America, the delight in gazing on many of the most beautiful scenes is often alloyed by the crude newness of men's work. This is now, unfortunately, the case even in beautiful Japan—the home of æstheticism—since the rage for copying Western architecture and dress fell as a blight on the islands of the rising sun. But here in the far west of China, nothing has intervened to mar the accord between Man and Nature. Fêng-shui, in its best sense, reigns supreme, and Man harmonizes with the soil as a bird with the air and a fish with the water. The buildings are all in keeping with the environment. Mediæval Italy, before the Renaissance, was much like China in this respect. Man was in perfect harmony with Nature, and Nature seemed to return Man's love for her. This feeling, the foundation

Roof Corner, Guildhall, Chung-king (p. 164).

Dinner-party in Chung-king: Guests facing Theatrical Performance; Intervening Courtyard, or "Pit" filled with freely admitted Audience from the Street (p. 200).

To face p. 164.

of true æstheticism, leads the Chinese to resent our modern innovations; but the force of circumstances is slowly subduing its expression, and the factory chimney and the scream of the locomotive will ere long rejoice the Philistine and be the despair of the Artist. Meanwhile, let us enjoy our short return to the era of the Middle Ages, and profit by the possibility of realizing the life of our ancestors in the "good old times." The hoary battlements which wall in the crowded city seem a natural excrescence on the rugged cliffs, and as the city walls follow the sinuosities of hill and dale, there is no sign of that strife with Nature which our bold Western methods encourage. No braggart upstart building towers rudely above its neighbours, stealing their air and light. The temples and Ya-mêns are the only buildings more conspicuous than the mass, the former distinguished by their green and gold porcelain tiles, the latter by their two quaint flagstaffs—phallic emblems, according to Baber,—very different from the bare poles and square-cut flags of the West. Were such an outrage as are the Queen Anne Mansions to London, to be attempted here; the Dragon and Tortoise (in the shape of an infuriated mob) would rise from their sleep of ages, and overthrow the ill-omened erection until not one brick was left on another. The first display of ill-feeling towards foreigners ever manifested in this city was due to the action of the Roman Catholic missionaries. Profiting by the avarice of the few old surviving priests left in possession, and to whom the trust of this ancient benefaction had devolved, they succeeded in acquiring, as a site for their cathedral, a prominent sandstone bluff, about two acres in extent, which occupies a commanding position in the centre of the city, and upon which stands a very ancient Taoist temple. The people rose *en masse*, and undoubtedly the lives of the

Christians and of their priests would have been sacrificed, had the latter not consented at the last moment to grant the request of the officials, and accept another equally valuable, but less conspicuous and Fêng-shui-disturbing site on lower ground.

In 1885 there was another rising in Chung-king, due this time to the action of the American Methodist mission. Not content with the native building in which I found them, this mission also had secured for itself a magnificent and strikingly conspicuous site on the neck of the Chung-king peninsula, and commanding the valleys of both rivers, upon which to erect a more imposing edifice. The mob rose, and the disturbance was only quelled after several lives had been sacrificed.

The movement on the river, too, is in harmony with its surroundings. Favoured by a fine fresh up-river breeze, the quaintly shaped junks, each with a single square-cut bellying mainsail, make almost imperceptible progress against the rapid stream. Though under sail, they are still attached by an invisible thread to the shore, and a gang of trackers, ascending and descending the rocky path along the slope of the ravine, may just be traced about a quarter of a mile ahead of each toiling craft.

The amphitheatre of hills, which encircle the peninsula on which Chung-king stands, and at the foot of which flows the wide deep stream of the Yang-tse, are thickly sprinkled with farmhouses and villages, distilleries and small manufactories. Unlike the hill-ranges which rise from the plains of the lower river, stark and bare, shunned as a habitation and unused for pasture, treeless and close-shorn by the rapacious wood-cutters, treated as enemies, and looking barren and forlorn in consequence;—the Szechuen hills are as freely and as fondly utilized as those surrounding a

European city, and the country here has a peaceful, happy aspect, totally wanting in the scenery further east. In the Hu-peh plains the walled cities, at the foot of the naked hills, rising abruptly out of the level plain, look like camps pitched in a purposely devastated country, and the prospect, though wild and romantic in the extreme, is deterrent and uninviting. The street in which I lived in Chung-king was distant not five minutes' walk from the south wall of the city, and ran level with its summit; often I used to adjourn with my cigar, from the close hong to a seat on the battlements, and gaze down on the ravine below and the suburbs on the opposite shore. This, owing to the steep rocks, is only accessible in three or four spots, and to these the ferry-boats ply; to watch one of these specks, taking half an hour to creep across, was a curious sight. What an opportunity for steam-launches! Were free scope once given for the infusion of Western energy and methods into an active trade-loving people like the Chinese, China would rival the United States in wealth and resources. The pressure of Western population will ere long force the real opening of the country, willy-nilly, on the mandarins, and in the renewed activity of the people, no time will be left for the *ennui* that drives the Chinese to the opium-pipe.

Graceful and unique in appearance as is an inland mountain city, when viewed from a distance, I regret to say that, as with many a picturesque town in Southern Europe, the charm of a Chinese city vanishes entirely on closer acquaintance. Filth seems inseparable from Chinese humanity, and a total apathy in regard to matter in the wrong place, pervades all classes, from the highest to the lowest. Gorgeous silks conceal an unwashed skin, and from under the rich sable cuffs of the official, protrude finger-nails innocent of soap or penknife. In spring-time the hard-worked coolie doffs his wadded winter garments, and parades his naked skin, happily unconscious of any disgrace attending the exhibition of the itch-sores which disfigure it. In the narrow crowded streets rain-storms are the only scavengers, and if we look into the interiors, we find the mud on the floors and the dust on the furniture steadily accumulating, until the New Year brings round the solitary annual house-cleaning. What, however, can be expected of a race who cripple their women, and incapacitate the natural guardians of the home from all active exertion?

During my stay I received many invitations to dinner-parties. These are generally given in one of the dozen spacious guildhalls in the city, or in one of the many really beautiful club-gardens in the surrounding country. One party, given in the Canton guild-garden, had the most exquisite setting for a banquet possible. The Canton guild-gardens cover some two or three acres, all laid out with paths winding between masses of rockwork and great bouquets of flowers and flowering shrubs. A precipitous slope, rising a few hundred feet and covered by a mass of fine bamboos, forms the background, while the "little river" flows in front in its narrow valley an equal distance below. Spacious houses with courtyards, solidly built and beautifully adorned with wood and stone carving, marble floors, and wide verandahs, form the chief reception-rooms, while elegant smaller pavilions are scattered about the grounds, so arranged as to secure perfect privacy to each party of visitors. For the hot weather, caves have been excavated in the soft sandstone rock, which are much affected by the Chinese as being cool and draughtless. These "halls" are mostly owned in shares by a group of friendly families, and form in fact institutions analogous to our clubs; they differ, however, in that families are admitted, and that the host brings his own cook and provisions.

Another morning early, I received a call from a gentleman named Ting, who offered his services as cicerone in the event of my desiring to "Shwah" in the neighbourhood. This word Shwah, which means to play, is constantly in the mouths of the festive Chung-kingites. "Hao shwa"—good to play—is a recommendation that led me to visit many a local celebrity. On the present occasion, our ten-o'clock breakfast over, I set out with friend Ting to walk round the city walls, a distance of about six miles. Starting from the Tai-ping gate, along the wide-paved roadway to the summit of the wall, we have on our left the crenellated battlements, through which the swift-flowing river is seen two hundred feet below; while on the right is an interminable line of drug-dealers' stores, their fronts open to the road, and the whole air redolent with the heavy fragrance of Chinese medicines, a *mélange* apparently of rhubarb, liquorice-root, orris-root, lovage (*Radix Levistici*), and musk. Turning to the right, and leaving the river to the left, we ascend the broad, paved surface of the wall by long flights of steps following its sinuosities as it ascends the crest of the ravine, which on this side also drops perpendicularly from its flanks. We here visited the Ti-shin Tang, a convivial and benevolent institution, comprising a temple, a three-storied pavilion, with green and yellow tiles covering its steep, tent-shaped roof, a dead-house for the coffins of the poor while awaiting burial, and the usual miniature gardens, fish-ponds, and bridges, not omitting the rock caves, which form a speciality in the pleasure-gardens of this city. The view from the top of the pavilion, like that from every eminence in the neighbourhood, afforded a fresh picture of rock, river, and mountain, combined with wild-looking battlements and curled temple-roofs. Passing the parade-ground in the north-west angle of the wall, and upon which some local volunteers were exercising with bows and arrows, I stopped to look on, and was offered a trial-shot by one of the citizen soldiers. I shot as far, but as wide of the mark as any of the rest. My civil volunteer now begged me to adjourn to his house and drink tea. We descended, and entering the gateway in a high wall close by, I found myself in an extensive nursery-garden, my host proving to be a florist. Dwarf mandarin oranges, about the size of walnuts, composed his principal crop. There was a fine show of other flowers and sub-tropical shrubs in addition, all in their full April bloom. The good wife hobbled in with the teapot, and after a refreshing drink we again set forth on our rounds. The angle of the wall is composed of a large square, three-storied stone fort, loop-holed in three stories; but the wooden platforms, originally built to support the marksmen in position, were, like all other Government institutions in China, in a state of utter decay. Continuing on along the inland wall, and parallel to the river, the rising ground outside on our left a confused mass of ancient grave-mounds, such as universally cover the hill-sides surrounding a Chinese city, we wound on, up and down, until we passed the door of the "Ngai-teh Tang," or "Hall of the Lovers of Virtue," in the courts of which I had enjoyed a sumptuous feed on the previous day. After passing, I found myself called back, and on turning round I was surprised to find my late host advancing to meet me. Some of the idlers or retainers, who throng the doorways of all the large Chinese houses, had informed him of my presence. Mr. Wang was, my companion told me, entertaining female guests, or *Anglice*, had a ladies' party on; but I declined his invitation to come in and join them. I may here mention that Mr. Wang is a member of one of the leading Catholic families of the place, and that, kind as were all the Chung-king people with whom I came in contact, there is no doubt that *bonâ-fide* Christians, such as those, do entertain a fellow-feeling towards us. From this point the wall, turning eastwards, follows the crest of the ravine of the Siao Ho (small river), or, as it is called in the maps, the Kia ling river. This stream, which has its sources in Kansu and Honan, has a deep and rapid current of about half the bulk of the main river; but, unlike the latter, at the time of my visit its waters were pellucid green. It separates the city of Chung-king proper from its northern suburb of " Kiang peh Ting " (" City North of the River "). This much-walled city is under the separate jurisdiction of a "Ting," intermediate in rank between a " Fu " and a " Hsien." The walled enclosure contains many picturesque temples and official residences, the business suburb lying below on the Yang-tse side, where there is a good natural harbour, formed by a fine ledge of rocks, which divides it from the main current. It is either here, or else at Lung-mên Hao, across the main river and opposite the Tai-ping Gate, that we find the best site for the Foreign Concession, the opening of which Chung-king is now (in 1898) still anxiously awaiting.

Continuing our walk along the wall, with the deep valley of the Siao River on our left, and the narrow, thronged streets of the busy city immediately on our right, at a point where the sandstone cliff falls perpendicularly some two hundred feet, between the street and the battlements, stands the spacious native residence which has just been purchased for the American Methodist Mission. The large sum, for these parts, of three thousand taels was the price paid, and the buildings were in course of being Europeanized into a suitable dwelling for the learned missionary, his wife, and three daughters, who have spread their tent in this charming though remote site. This missionary work is the greatest of the many problems propounded to the Chinese by the presence of the barbarian in the Central Flowery Land. From their point of view, it goes without saying that all foreigners are enormously rich, and that there are no poor in our favoured lands, or we should not have money to spend in maintaining corps of missionaries nearly as numerous as our merchants, and in subsidizing outcast Chinese to forsake the family altars to "fêng chiao," or be "sealed" to a doctrine strange and incredible.

Chung-king possesses several Christian missions: the American Methodist, the China Inland, the London Mission, that of the Society of Friends, the Scotch and American Bible Societies, and the Roman Catholic. The latter is the oldest and most important, and its converts in Chung-king alone number over three thousand. The Catholic system, with its unconscious imitation of Buddhistic forms, and its wise toleration of ancestral worship, so called, appeals more forcibly than the others to the ignorant and consequently superstitious Chinese; yet even Catholicism is stationary, and exists mainly through the prestige of its age and its extensive possessions. The entrance of Protestantism into China, with its inquiring and disputatious spirit, is proving fatal to the ingathering of the harvest anticipated by devout Catholics as the result of two centuries of toil in this ungrateful land. As in the West, the door once opened to doubt, *dogmatic* Christianity seems doomed. And it must not be supposed that, to quote one of the many false impressions derived from missionary reports, the Chinese are so steeped in materialism as to be callous in regard to moral teaching, and hence to be dependent on Western charity for their spiritual food. Hortatory works urging men to reform their lives are perpetually being circulated by benevolent individuals, in addition to which the people are stimulated by open-air exhortations by paid preachers. A common sight in Chungking in the evening, after the day's work is over and the shops are closed, is an elevated stand at the street corner, consisting of a raised table draped in red cloth; upon it two flaring red candles, and behind it a man in full ceremonial dress, with the stiff official hat and silk ma-kwa, addressing the crowd. At first sight one would, but for his careful costume, take the man for a story-teller, surrounded as he is by a group of silent listeners, until, on a nearer approach, you find he is expounding the doctrine of the native classics, and exhorting men to repentance. No nation has so many wise saws and moral maxims always at its fingers' ends as the Chinese; scarcely a sentence but is interlarded with a proverb or a text from the ancient sages. That a people so generally well read as are the Chinese, and possessing in the teachings of Confucius a doctrine which, unlike Christianity, has survived unquestioned throughout all the wars and commotions of twenty-five centuries; to expect that a people so unemotional and so eminently practical in the application of their ethics to the wants of daily existence, should ever pin their faith to a work like the historical books of the Old Testament, seems to a layman a hopeless conclusion. That the Chinese fail to live up to their standard is only to say that they are human. Their civilization, not long since, so far before all others, has failed to keep pace with ours; but so have their physical and mental faculties. If they are ever to be raised to our level, it will be by secular contact with the West during many more generations. One of the most accomplished men that has ever visited the country, a traveller and a man of science as well as a missionary—the well-known Abbé David—in a chapter on the missions of Kiangse, the most thoroughly worked province in the occupation of the Lazarists, sums up his judgment in the following pertinent remarks, which I venture to quote in full :—

"Je mets fin à ma digression sur les missions du Kiangsi, en ajoutant : (1) qu'il faut à la Compagnie de Jésus la justice de reconnaître que c'est à des missionnaires de leur active société, que la plupart des anciennes chrétientés des parties de la Chine, que j'ai visitées ont eu leur origine ; (2) que, *les chrétiens de tout l'empire ont été autrefois plus nombreux qu'ils ne le sont maintenant*.

"Pour ne parler que de cette province, j'entends dire qu'il n'y a pas une ville qui n'ait eu jadis *sa* ou *ses* chapelles chrétiennes, mais actuellement on ne compte guère en Chine, qu'un fidèle par *mille* paiens. Et bien que, dans toutes les dix-huit provinces, il y ait à présent des conversions de plus en plus nombreuses, mon opinion est, que la christianisation générale de ce peuple, si jamais elle doit s'effectuer, ne peut s'attendre que dans un avenir très éloigné encore, surtout depuis que la facilité progressive de circuler et de s'établir dans l'intérieur de l'empire y attire de plus en plus les prédicateurs de toutes les sociétés dissidentes.

"Cette déplorable divergence dans l'enseignement et dans la pratique du Christianisme est pour les Chinois un *seminarium d'indifférence*, parce qu'ils s'habituent à croire que chacune des nations occidentales a sa réligion particulière ; et ils pensent qu'ils sont raisonnables eux-mêmes en conservant la leur. C'est là une conséquence qui vient naturellement à l'esprit des hommes qui ne veulent et qui ne peuvent pas étudier pertinemment la question réligieuse."

We left the ramparts and turned off into the town, and, after walking fast through the maze of narrow dirty streets, Mr. Ting landed me somewhat unexpectedly in a spacious mansion of many courts, which turned out to be his family residence. Here I was introduced to his three sons, who were, together with half a dozen young cousins, all engaged with the schoolmaster, and as usual shouting, each his own lesson, at the very top of their voices. In this way the texts of the four sacred books are learnt by rote, and remain indelibly impressed on the memory for ever afterwards: their meaning is expounded later. Absurd as this system may seem, I am convinced that there is no other method equally efficacious for fixing the innumerable characters of this cumbrous language on the mind. One of the youngsters brought us eggs, boiled and floating in a bowl of hot water, which, but that it was unaccompanied by bread, was no bad refreshment after our long walk. Another mile through the crowded streets brought us to the Peh-hsiang Kai, or White Elephant Street, in which was situated the business establishment of my companion—a sugar refinery—where I was introduced to the father, a hale old man approaching seventy, who appeared to be actively engaged superintending the work, which was being carried on upon a large scale, but with the usual primitive methods.

CHAPTER IX.

CHUNG-KING.

Ponies—Silk-weaving—Prehistoric caves—A fine country-house—A Catholic chapel—A Buddhist oracle—The coal workings—Cost of getting and transporting coal—An eviction scrimmage—Ventilation—A huge coal-field—A farm-house—Opium-smoking—Agile ponies—Return by boat—Fine scenery—Legends—The river rising—Trade Guilds—Another country-house—Civility of the Chung-kingese—The women's feet—The Manchus—A pseudo-European dinner.

At eight o'clock on the morning of the eighteenth April, friend Tung and his nephew arrived with three small shaggy ponies, one of which, a well-conditioned little animal standing about twelve hands, and a native of the neighbouring province of Kwei-chow, was destined for myself. My hosts had put a Miao-tse saddle on him. This, like all saddles in China, was made of wood, but it was covered with heavy carved lacquer, precisely like the celebrated Soochow ware. A wadded quilt, topped with a foreign blanket, succeeded, however, in shielding this showy but uncomfortable piece of furniture from the public gaze, as well as from the rider's person. A crowd assembled to see us off; we were soon mounted, and trotted off gaily down the slippery street. My little animal being the best goer, I was requested to take the lead. My natural inclination to walk through

Heangko Sinu, and *Ficus infectoria* with Shrine as usual round Roots, and my Stallion from Province Kwei-chow with whom I travelled 1500 Miles.   *To face p. 170.*

the narrow crowded streets was overcome by my companions urging me to hurry on, as we were due at Shih-ma Tsao, my host's home, where breakfast was awaiting us, at nine o'clock. The collar of bells, with which all Chinese riders surround their ponies' necks, warns the foot-passengers to stand aside, while their merry jingle gives a sense of speed and adds to the festive air of the cavalcade. We passed out of the north gate, descending by a winding staircase, narrowed by the encroachments of the shops and booths bordering on it, to a width of barely six feet. It was covered with black grime as usual, all the water used in the city being carried out by these gates. My wonderful little nag scrambled down without accident, though not without considerably alarming its rider. This descent of about 150 steps led us on to a terrace, a sort of cornice-road, shaded by many fine old banyan trees; the rushing water being below on our left, and steep, treeless, grave-covered hills on our right. The old stone parapet had fallen down in places, and I was not sorry when we turned off inland into the hills, along the road that I had previously traversed in a chair. The traffic on this road is very great, but it is well regulated by the all-pervading *custom*, and difficulties seldom or never occur. Thus, everything gives way to chairs, pedestrians to horsemen, and the toiling carrying-coolies to all: where the path is narrow these unfortunates have to step down into the neighbouring paddy-field, and strings of them had often to stand aside in this way while our cavalcade went by. Each of our ponies had its own mafu, or groom, in attendance, besides which we had two porters with our luggage: my pony was the property of our host, but the others were hired animals, the price being 180 cash (9*d*.) per diem, including the mafu, who supplied his charge with fodder cut from the wayside at our halts. This will give an idea of the astonishing cheapness of life in this favoured province. An hour's hot ride brought us to "Shih-ma Tsao" ("Stone-Horse Crib") and the residence of the Tungs. The ride in the morning sun had been a hot one, and we were glad to rest in the cool courtyard of the house. Breakfast was soon announced, at which my hosts drank freely the hot wine, while I confined myself to tea : my want of "wine-power" (chiu-liang) being a sad defect in the Chinese eyes. It was nearly eleven before we made a second start. We passed over a short "col," being the neck of the serpent whose beneficent folds envelope the city landwards, while the opposing tortoise, in the shape of a projecting crag on the opposite shore, completes the Fengshui and causes the prosperity of Chung-king; and soon found ourselves approaching Fu-tu Kwan, or the barrier of Fu-tu, which is a small walled city or fortress, commanding the one land-road by which Chung-king is in communication with the outer world. Its walls embrace the outlines of a lofty scarped sandstone knoll, one of the many remnants of the old sandstone plateau which must, at one time, have covered the face of Eastern Szechuan. We ascend to the gate by a steep slanting staircase up which my little pony scrambles bravely, and ride through the fort. Its interior is occupied by the usual narrow streets and mean houses of a country town, but no trace of guns or garrison is to be seen. Emerging on the west, we descend by another staircase, and proceed along the great western road which leads to Chêng-tu, the provincial capital.

This road leads up and down over a steeply undulating country, the hills being all richly cultivated to their summits. The chief crops at this season were opium and tobacco, the poppy predominating. In the narrow gullies minute paddy-fields descend in terraces, and occupy the limited amount of level ground to be found in the valley bottoms. The upper sides of these gullies often consist of vertical rocks, and where the road runs along their summit, or has been cut into them, it has in olden times been protected by a handsome balustrade of stone, now in a sad state of disrepair, and in the worse places often wanting altogether. My diminutive steed entertained a most uncomfortable preference for the extreme edge of the narrow pathway, the flagstones of which, where not wanting altogether, invariably seemed to slope outwards. The ascents and descents were by narrow, steep, dilapidated staircases. Originally constructed with an utter absence of engineering skill, these paved footpaths have been rendered still worse by the insidious encroachments of the avaricious peasantry. After leaving the main artery, the road got so bad that, but that there was positively not room for me to dismount, I should on several occasions have resigned the saddle and taken to my legs. Apart from the risk of a fall, it seemed cruelty to animals to ride a pony over such country; but on being assured that he was accustomed to carry double my weight in goods over the Kwei-chow mountains, I hardened my heart, and we scrambled on. At length, in the afternoon, we reached our destination for the day—the mansion of Sha-ping Pa (the "Spreading Sandbank"). Heading our cavalcade over the rugged paths, I had noticed on the slope of a hill to our right a spacious walled enclosure with a broad terrace in front, approached by a handsome flight of stone steps—a noble residence, superior to anything yet encountered in my travels in this dilapidated land. I was not a little surprised to learn that this was our destination, and I trotted gaily up the steps, glad to escape from the blazing sunshine into the umbrageous courtyards and gardens before me. I found that this was the ancient home of the Tung family, now exchanged for the more modest but convenient mansion of Shih-ma Tsao; and that the Tungs had just sold this their old home to their spiritual fathers, the Catholic mission at Chung-king, by whom it was used as a rural retreat and new mission centre. The place was unoccupied at the time of my visit, save that in one of the numerous "dependencies" a "Chi-fang," or silk-weaving establishment, was in operation. The place was still being worked by the Tungs, who have a shop for the distribution of their productions in the city of Chung-king. The Chi-fang was a lofty brick and tiled "godown," containing some twenty looms, as well as spinning gear. About a hundred men were at work; they were paid by the piece, and earn about a hundred cash a day, in addition to their rice. The goods produced are of a very fair quality, but their consumption is mainly confined to the province. At the time of the Tai-ping Rebellion, however, when the Hoochow silk country west of Shanghai was being devastated by fire and sword, large quantities of this silk were shipped eastwards, and an active business was done, and large profits were made; but Szechuan silk cannot compete with that of Hoochow, and the trade is now in a languishing condition. We took dinner with the foreman of the works— a frugal meal of rice, beans, and pork—and then went for a stroll with our guns. My friend Tung was an ardent sportsman, and carried a Kwei-chow gun with a barrel nearly five feet long, a bore about the size of a pea, and firing iron shot. We beat up some of the groves surrounding the scattered farms, and scrambled down the almost perpendicular bank of the Siao river, here about six hundred feet high. The country was lovely, and the waters of the rapid river, at this season clear, and in the pools between the rock barriers almost stagnant, afforded a delightful swim and a grand entertainment to the rustics. Climbing the heights again by the aid of a wooded gully, now dry, we sat down on a stone seat overlooking the ravine, and situated scarcely a hundred yards from the walls of Sha-ping Pa, and enjoyed the magnificent prospect before us. The Chinese, in their love of privacy and retirement, never enjoy a view from the windows of their own dwelling, except it be that of the miniature enclosed gardens surrounding them, hence partly the oppressive dulness with which they afflict a foreigner. The view embraces the steep sandstone cliffs of the opposite bank of the Kia-ling Ho, commonly called the Siao or Small River, and in which were apparent some of the square openings of the cave dwellings which abound throughout the rivers of this province, and the exploration of which has been so interestingly described by Mr. Baber. Behind us, from a green, tree-covered mound, projects the corner of a huge stone sarcophagus. This, my companion informed me, had been opened in the night by the indefatigable "Be-te-la" (Baber), on the occasion of a visit he had made to Shaping Pa. Mr. Baber was rewarded for his exertions by finding nothing better inside than a layer of wet mould; but a short time previously the landlord of the place (my host) had picked out from under the head of the lid a polished stone axe-head of serpentine. This was handed over to Mr. Baber, but in a damaged state, owing to the greed of the finder, who had tried to break it open in expectation of finding gold inside, the only possible object that, in the eyes of the Chinese, can justify archæological research.

The country house in which we were resting was the finest example of a Chinese residence I had yet visited, and merits a short description. It was built in the last century by a retired Fantai, or Provincial Treasurer, at a cost, I was told, of ten thousand pounds. The enclosure occupies little over four acres, and is surrounded by a stone wall ten feet high and five feet thick. Within is the usual succession of courtyards and lofty halls, with no upper story, the tiled roofs supported by massive wooden pillars on stone bases, all looking as fresh and brilliant as they did the day they were put up. The walls are of brick, and the floors of stone. Each court rises behind the other by a few steps, and at the back of all is the scarped face of the rock, covered with ferns, and surmounted by a bamboo grove, and from the face of the rock spurts forth a refreshing stream, supplying the house with spring water. Outhouses for servants, kitchen, and stabling are on an extensive scale, and in front of the lowest court, and between it and the outer hall, is a deep fish-pond surrounded by a stone quay, and crossed by two zigzag bridges of carved stone. In the grounds, which are filled with the luxuriant sub-tropical vegetation of the latitude, long untended, and rendering the winding paths almost impassable, stood an elegant stone stage for open-air theatricals, backed by a grove of the "lettered" bamboo—an elegant variety distinguished by black lines imprinted on the pale-green stem. The main buildings, most substantially erected originally, were in remarkably good repair; but the only sign of occupation was in one of the smaller courts, where a sort of temporary chapel had been fitted up, decorated with coloured prints of the saints, with Notre Dame au Sacré Cœur in the centre tearing open her flaming heart with most unpleasant effect. In the suffering attitudes of our Christian worthies, as represented to their worshippers, the asceticism of the Western creed shows forth in strong contrast to the apparent cheerfulness of Buddhism—as exhibited in the fat, jovial-looking images in the temples. Probably both religions have deviated equally from the doctrines of their founders, the latter being outwardly the more attractive, the ennobling doctrine of self-denial being nowadays more strongly emphasized in the former. The noble examples of the Catholic priesthood are as far beyond the attainment of the Bonze as is the mental capacity of the West above that of the East; but if the symbols of each religion be a true picture of the reward of its observance, I had rather be a "Lo-han" than a saint!

Early dawn of the following day saw us once more in the saddle, prepared again to confront the ups and downs of this most "broken" country. Our course lay parallel to the Small river, across a country more broken and by paths steeper still than yesterday's. The repeated ascents and descents were due to the necessity of crossing the numerous gullies worn in the soft rock by the streams that fall into the main river. These were usually crossed by smooth, unprotected bridges in a good state of preservation; but the stone paths running along a raised dyke between two paddy-fields, or climbing the side of a rocky cliff, were often barely twelve inches wide, and the small flagstones of which they were composed were several degrees out of the horizontal. In places the flags were missing entirely, leaving small chasms, over which our little ponies leapt with cat-like alacrity, making me tremble at times for the landing on the other side. The sun was pouring down with all the force of early summer in these latitudes, and scarcely a breath of air was stirring. During the whole of my stay in Szechuan, from the middle of March to the beginning of May, not a drop of rain fell in the daytime, but regular night showers freshened the air and gladdened the vegetation. We nooned at a small wayside temple, which possessed a spring of deliciously cool water, with which we washed down the small, wheaten, dumpling-like cakes of the country. The temple, approached by a steep flight of steps, was built against the face of the rock, and commanded a most picturesque view. The peculiar formation of Eastern Szechuan renders the country charmingly picturesque, each half-mile yielding a fresh prospect. There are few woods, properly speaking, but small groves surround the scattered farms and temples, and the shade of the magnificent banian is, along the high-roads, seldom wanting for any distance. Under one of these we had already indulged in some excellent cherries, little piles of which were spread out on a table by the wayside, and purchasable for three cash each.

We found the priest gone to market, and his place supplied by a ragged, little, bare-footed "larn-pigeon," or acolyte. A poor woman, accompanied by her little son, both dressed in their newest clothes, came in while we were resting. Taking no notice whatever of the strangers, they proceeded leisurely to disentangle some bundles of red-wax dips which they had brought with them, and to set them up and light them before the different josses with which the hall was surrounded. Then the old lady drew forth one of the circular mat-cushions, knelt down and kotowed to the central Buddha. At each blow of her forehead on the stone floor, the ragged little boy, who had taken up a lounging position near the deep-toned bell to be found in every temple, struck a smart blow thereon, presumably to call the attention of the saint to whom the temple was dedicated to the worshipper's devotions. The kotowing over, the old lady let her son shake a "lot" out of the bamboo vase which stands on the altar in front of the golden image, picked up the slip of bamboo that had fallen out on the floor, and handed it to the acolyte. A big quarto volume in manuscript was then produced, and the page corresponding to the number of the lot referred to. The ragged little priest being himself unequal to the task of deciphering the oracle, my companion read it out to him in all solemnity. It appeared that the old lady's husband was sick unto death, and that she had come to pray for his recovery, and was now receiving an answer to her prayers. The reply was somewhat ambiguous, but generally favourable, and the old lady hobbled down the steep flight of steps, holding her staff in one hand, and leaning on her boy with the other, doubtless highly comforted. Long as I have lived in China, I can never become reconciled to this hideous and painful mutilation of the feet, and I can but wish that some despot like the conquerors of old would ascend the throne and issue an ukase against a practice which entails gratuitous torture on one-half of the population. It would be obeyed, for thinking Chinamen regret the cruelty to which the despot fashion alone compels them to conform. On the accession of the Mongols, the private graves and public cemeteries, which then, as now, absorbed an enormous proportion of the arable land, were all ploughed over by imperial edict, and, as is well known, upon the accession of the present dynasty in 1644, the dress of the Manchus, together with the obnoxious pigtail, was accepted by the whole nation almost without a murmur. This shows what determination among an apathetic people like the Chinese will effect.

Setting out again on our journey, the range of hills, in which were situated the coal-mines which formed our destination, came into view. The range itself is about a thousand feet above the level of the surrounding country, about two thousand above the level of the river, and three thousand by my aneroid above the sea: it runs for some distance in a N.N.E. and S.S.W. direction, and is cut through at right angles by the Siao river, which has thus manufactured a picturesque gorge on a small scale, similar to the magnificent cuttings on the main river below. We traversed one or two flourishing villages, small ports situated at the mouth of gullies opening on the river. The country was entirely under cultivation, with rice in the bottoms and opium and tobacco on the slopes. Ascending the range, however, at the foot of which we arrived at sunset, we left cultivation behind and rode up through scrubby pine-forests along a steep mountain path, winding round the crest of a ravine, at the bottom of which ran a roaring stream which issued from the coal-mine above us. At length a huge talus, or spoil-heap formed by the mine's working, barred our way; but the ponies scrambled up and landed us on a small plateau just as the stars were appearing over the almost vertical hill in our front. There was just enough light to enable us to distinguish some fifty naked coal-begrimed coolies lounging about, and some two-storied wooden shanties built up against the declivity of the hillside and over the horizontal entrance of the mine. Ascending to the upper story, and passing a crowd of curious but absolutely undemonstrative coolies, who had just come off their shift and were lounging after their bath, we entered a small room in the rear, occupied by the foreman of the works, in which—with the aid of the good man's bed there was barely room to seat our party—we sat down to a frugal supper of red rice and broad beans, washed down with a tea so nauseous that I was positively unable to swallow it. My hosts informed me that the leaf was grown on the neighbouring hill, and that its cost dried was only about three-halfpence a pound; the fragrant herb in this instance consisted mainly of stalks and twigs intermingled with a few big leaves, the whole more or less musty. Any infusion of the kind is called "Cha" by the Chinese, and does not necessarily contain any real tea. It is with such refuse that the unfortunate Tibetans are supplied in the shape of brick tea. Could India force the opening-up of Tibet to trade, Assam sweepings would replace this rubbish to the advantage of all concerned. All eat and drink alike at the mine, and as the miners are fed by the proprietors, economy in food is studied more than quality. Still, as I had been looking forward to the usual refreshing cup of tea after our long day in the sun, I was much disappointed. Being pretty well tired out, I deferred my visit to the mine until the morning: meanwhile I noted down the chief statistics as detailed to me by the obliging superintendent of works :—

Coal raised per day	30 tons.
Coal raised per day before workings stopped by water ...	60 tons.
Total number of men employed	120
viz.—Hewers, at work in four galleries	36
Carriers, between the galleries and the mouth ...	36
Pumpers, working the bamboo pumps	36
Fanners, working the revolving fans	12

besides superintendent, foreman, two accountants and landlord's agent appointed to tally the output and collect his royalty of 175 copper cash for each "to-tze," or basket of 260 catties, being the equivalent of 5$d.$ per ton of 2240 .pounds; my friends, the Tungs, being the present owners of the mine.

The men work in two shifts of twelve hours per day of twenty-four; their rice, which is provided by the lessee of the mine, being carried to them three times a day. Their pay is 140 cash per day, equal to sixpence-halfpenny, in addition to their food, worth about half this amount. The wages are paid every ten days, pay-day being a holiday: they thus receive ten days' pay for nine days' labour. On the other hand, each pair of workers, viz. a hewer and a carrier, are bound to deliver daily eleven "to-tze" at the pit's mouth. Thus the delivery of each ton of coals costs in actual labour about one shilling.

The ventilating fans are circular and enclosed in boxes, and are precisely similar to those used for winnowing tea.

The fresh air is driven in through bamboo tubing. Three fans were at work: one at the entrance of the mine, just outside the swinging doors; one at the extremity of the tunnel, 1000 feet outside; and one closely adjoining the workings. These fans are not needed in winter and are worked in summer only, commencing on the third day of the third moon to the ninth day of the ninth moon—say from April to September inclusive.

Another incidental expense is of course that for illumination; this is effected by Tung-oil lamps, one of which each carrier wears on his head and burns ten ounces per shift, the hewers burning six ounces only. According to my informant, this Tung-you is oil derived from the nut of the *Elæococca sinensis*, from the smoke of which the soot used to manufacture the so-called Indian ink is obtained; they told me, that were rape or other oil used the men would cough.

The royalty received by the Tung family for their mine in 1882 amounted to 781 taels, about £200.

The history of the mine is a curious one. It was opened about twenty years ago by a capitalist whose means were exhausted by the time the main tunnel, which runs through 1000 feet of sandstone rock and occupied six years in boring, was completed; he thereupon mortgaged the mine, but, being still in want of funds, sold the mine to the Tungs for 4000 taels, about half its cost, and little more than enough to redeem the mortgage. The mortgagee, who had been expecting to get the mine into his own hands, refused to give it up, and forcibly prevented Mr. Tung from taking possession by stationing armed men round the works. This Mr. Tung naturally resented, and he immediately set about collecting a force wherewith to enter upon his property. Some days later the force was gathered at a farmhouse in the neighbourhood, and a night-attack determined upon. This attack was led in person by my companion on the present occasion—Tung chiu-ye, or the honourable ninth Tung, he being the ninth brother (all first cousins being included) of his generation. At early dawn the party of some twenty men, armed with spears and a few matchlocks, set forth, hoping to catch the enemy unprepared, and so gain peaceable possession of the place; though it was still dark, however, they were discovered, and met with a volley which fortunately injured no one. The Tung men now made a rush, whereupon the enemy fled into the surrounding jungle, not, however, unfortunately for Tung, before one of their number had bitten the dust, transfixed by a spear. Possession was thus gained and the law's delay avoided; the late mortgagee, however, was not a man to neglect the advantage he had gained in losing one of his men, while the Tung force had escaped scot free. A charge of murder was preferred before the prefect, and it cost Mr. Tung another 4000 taels, a very large sum in these parts, before he got clear of the authorities. He now holds the mine undisturbed, and receives from it the moderate income detailed above.

There appears to be no taxation of mining property, the officials contenting themselves with whatever transit dues they can collect while the produce is being transported. This mine is eight li, or little more than two miles, distant from the banks of the river, where there is a depôt for its sale, and whence the buyers transport it by water to Chung-king. Porterage over the mountain to Shih chia-liang (the depôt) costs twenty-seven cash per picul, while the thirty miles of water-carriage to Chung-king cost fourteen cash only. The coal is sold (delivered at Shih chia-liang) for 130 cash for lump, and 110 cash for dust, per picul of 133 pounds, or about six shillings per ton. It is a soft bituminous coal of apparently good quality.

On Friday, April 20th, I was up at 4 a.m., and, donning a native suit of calico and a pair of straw sandals much too small for me, I entered the mine. A tunnel eight feet high by five feet broad, almost horizontal, but with a gentle incline outwards, pierces the rock for a distance of 194 pai, Chinese fathom or length of five Chinese feet of fourteen inches English—thus making the length of the adit about one thousand English feet. In the centre a wooden tramway is laid, upon which run the to-tze or coal-baskets, which rest on four small iron wheels. A double doorway guards the entrance, which is only opened for the passage of the to-tze as they come out laden with coal, each propelled by its men. We entered, pushing an empty to-tze before us as a guide to keep us in the centre of the passage and out of the water-channels excavated on either side. The object of so carefully closing the entrance was, they told me, to retain the fresh air that was being so laboriously pumped in. We progressed slowly through the slush, having to give way for each laden to-tze bound out, by removing our empty carriage bodily off the rails so as to let the other one keep its course. At length we reached the head of the tunnel, at a spot where transverse galleries branch off right and left, while facing us sat in pitch darkness a solitary fanner, turning the wheel, whereby the air of the tunnel was pumped into the gallery to the left, which again was closed by double doors similar to those which guard the main entrance. To the right were abandoned galleries, now impassable owing to the caving in of the roofs. Passing through the doors on our left, we scrambled along the low passage, necessitating constant stooping, for nearly 500 yards, when we came upon the present workings. We here turned off to the right along the seam, which appeared to be about three feet thick, and inclined to the horizon at an angle of not more than twenty-five degrees. The miners were hewing sideways with a single-headed pick; a short distance down water had been reached, and was being painfully kept down at its present level with bamboo pumps. The air seemed quite fresh, but the cramped position induced me to beat a speedy retreat to the outer air. Here, having enjoyed the warm bath which all the miners take on coming off their shift, and having dressed in the presence of an admiring crowd, we sat down to an enjoyable breakfast. At the meal, washed down with warm, cheap, and not unpalatable wine, the owner and lessee anxiously discussed the possibility of introducing steam pumping machinery. At nine o'clock we again mounted our sturdy little nags and commenced the steep descent. It was a most lovely morning, and as the path followed down a small ravine, entirely shaded by the overhanging foliage, with the roar of the tiny waterfalls at our feet, the ride was most exhilarating. Breaks in the foliage exhibited glimpses of the smiling valleys we had traversed on the previous day, framed in a ring of blue mountains in the distance. About halfway down we came upon a little mat shed, erected in a small clearing, in which was ensconced the accountant and the clerk of the works of the new mine which was being opened. A pressing invitation to rest and take tea was followed by an offer to conduct us to the works. These had been in progress now some six months, and had resulted in a tunnel similar to that leading to Tung's mine, having been driven about forty feet into the mountain. Two men were at work quarrying the hard sandstone, their progress being at the rate of about seven inches a day: they expected to reach the coal-seams in about seven years. The handsome scale upon which these works are laid down forms a striking contrast to the miserable burrows of the mines in the Hu-peh province which I had visited on my voyage up the Yang-tse, and, like everything else in Szechuan, gives one a favourable impression of the exceptional well-being of this province. The great and, apparently for Chinese, unnecessary height of eight feet, is given to the tunnels solely for the sake of ventilation.

According to Richthofen, the coal-measures underlying the sandstone which forms the surface of the Szechuan plateau are among the most extensive in the world. They are worked wherever the strata have been tilted up by the elevation of the numerous ranges that cross the plateau in a north-easterly and south-westerly direction, and so made accessible. In these, simple horizontal adits enable the coal to be attacked with comparative ease. The frequent rivers have cut through these ranges, forming gorges and exposing perfect sections of the different strata, amidst which the coal is embedded.

We now continued our route to Shih chia-liang, where we had arranged to take the boat for Chung-king. The road was a ten-inch-wide flagged path built for the accommodation of the coal-porters, strings of whom we met returning to the mine with empty baskets, and who, warned by the jingling bells on our ponies' collars, stood promptly aside to let us pass. Suddenly my companion ordered me to turn up a steep path on the left, which led to the farmstead of Lin chia kou, the Lin family gap, a level terrace formed in a ravine, up to which we ascended by a handsome flight of steps. This turned out to be the farm at which Tung's attacking party had assembled a few years before, and it was to protect our present host from the consequences of his unlucky manslaughter at the fight above described that the Tungs had to expend 4000 taels. Our host was a fine specimen of a Western Chinaman of the farming class—a tall, well-built man, of quiet dignified bearing, as great a contrast in appearance to the trading Chinaman as is the typical British farmer to the London cit. The farm buildings, substantially built and of two stories, occupied three sides of a triangle, the open courtyard overlooking a splendidly fertile valley reaching down to the river and watered by a noisy brook, utilized, as usual, to irrigate the paddy-fields which occupied the more open ground. Above rose bamboo groves and pine forests to the mountain's top. The poppy, which here forms the winter crop of the bean and maize lands, was just ripe for gathering, and a close examination of the capsules showed them to be scored with the four-bladed knife, from the wounds made by which the opium was now slowly exuding, so much so that, walking through the fields, my white clothes were all stained with the brown juice. I had many discussions on the subject of opium cultivation, the enormous extent of which in the western provinces strikes every traveller with amazement. It is distressing to find the English name everywhere associated with the forcible introduction of this beneficent and at the same time pernicious drug. Of course it is useless to tell Chinamen that opium must have been used in China long before the old East India Company introduced it. The Portuguese were the first to bring opium from India to sell in China, and it is certain that they would not have brought it, had they not found a ready sale for it. The opium-pipe is most surely a Chinese invention, for it is absolutely unknown in any other land. As for its pernicious effects, I look upon the money and time wasted upon it as far worse than its direct effects on health. In China, where the wages of a working man barely suffice to keep body and soul together, the money spent on opium is withdrawn from his daily food; hence the half-starved appearance of opium-smokers among the poor, and the cruel destitution their families often suffer —much as with the gin-drinking poor at home; but how many opium-smokers, in easy circumstances, does one meet with seriously injured by the drug? I have met but a very few such myself, during a forty years' stay in the country and extensive intercourse with natives of every class. To the well-nourished Chinaman, his evening pipes are more a pastime, a means of passing the time pleasantly in a state of placid inactivity dear to the Oriental; while the merchant conducts many of his best bargains over the pipe, much as negotiations are often conducted over a bottle of wine at home. To this class the waste of time over the pipe is not such a serious objection as it undoubtedly is to the official body. The work of a conscientious mandarin in China is most arduous, and it is almost impossible for the best-intentioned and most energetic official to overtake the arrears of work, especially in the troublous times of war, rebellion, and famine, with which for the past fifty years the empire has been unceasingly afflicted.

With undefined duties; with executive and judicial, and at times even military functions strangely intermingled, a Chinese mandarin is dependent on his subordinates at the best of times; but when he succumbs to the opium-pipe, and spends more than half his time on the opium-couch, rapacity and misgovernment go on unchecked. The fault is in the system, which allows a man notoriously incapable to remain at his post. Such men are said to possess the "Yin" or passionate craving for the drug, a vice analogous to dipsomania with ourselves. In the absence of the "Yin," all Chinamen will tell you that opium-smoking is a harmless though foolish pastime. As to eradicating the vice by edict, it would amount to a social revolution, such as in the history of the world has never yet been carried out. Even attempts to stay its cultivation, which have been tried by well-meaning but impracticable philanthropists, who are to be found in China as in the West, have all proved futile. As my former host at Lin chai kou informed me, himself a non-smoker, if it were forbidden to collect the drug, his winter crop of poppy would still pay him for its other products, such as the oil produced from the seed, the lye used in dying, produced from the ash of the stalk, and the heavy crop of leaves which goes to feed the pigs which every Chinaman keeps. Nor, with the Chinese system of applying all the town manure to the fields, does the crop exhaust the ground or render the summer crop of maize any less prolific. Opium seldom appears planted on the level paddy-fields, but commonly on declivities too steep to grow much else with profit. Still it would be best abandoned altogether.

Tobacco is another very important product, the quality of the Szechuan tobacco being far superior to that of any other of the eighteen provinces. It is curious to a foreigner accustomed only to the smoking of the coast provinces, where a Lilliputian bowl is filled for each inhalation, and the burning ash is perpetually being knocked out on the floor—not a little to the annoyance of the neat-minded Western—to see a totally different method here adopted. The leaf is carried in a pouch (filling and wrapper separate), and a short cigar made up on each occasion, which is leisurely smoked in a pipe. The tobacco is of excellent flavour, and costs about fourpence a pound.

Our host had expected us to stay a night with him, and was not a little put out upon my representing that I must positively be in Chung-king that day. The fact was, day after day was slipping away, and I feared I might not reach Hankow in time for the tea-season if I failed to impress my native friends with my impatience to leave. So, notwithstanding the blood-stains in the courtyard of the unfortunate porker that had been ·slaughtered the night before in our honour, and to which our host appealed most pitifully, I regretfully took leave, having partaken only of sweetmeats, cake, and wine.

Threading our way down the narrow, winding path, which led among the banks of one of the countless ravines by which the land is split up, its soft sandstone sides decorated with a luxuriant growth of ferns and creepers, we safely reached the small village, combining fort and ferry-station, of Shih chia-liang. The little village has one narrow, paved street, and its houses are built on a sloping ledge, the only piece of level ground at the mouth of the gully being occupied by the coal depôt. Here some 200 tons were stored under lock and key, awaiting sale and shipment down-stream to Chung-king. The water being now low, a steep descent of about a hundred feet leads down to the river-bank, where a few coal-barges were being loaded, with streams of porters coming in coal-laden, and others carrying the coal down to the river, the weight of each load being carefully checked in both instances by the omnipresent steelyard. The place had the busy and well-to-do aspect which seems to characterize Szechuan villages. Meanwhile a boat had been chartered to convey us down-stream to Chung-king, our ponies returning with their mafus by a short cut on the opposite bank. It was a pretty sight to see the clever way in which these little ponies ascended the narrow landing plank and jumped down into the hold of the ferry-boat, not the least alarmed by the roaring of the rapid at the foot of which Shih chia-liang is situated. These Kwei-chow ponies are renowned throughout all Western China; they are probably, for their size, the most powerful animals in the world.

All Szechuan rivers are torrents in the rainy season, and journeys by them seem to be measured more by the amount of water traversed in ascending them than by the actual amount of ground gone over; thus I was informed that the journey before us was only ninety li, say twenty-five miles, while the upward voyage is reckoned at 120 li. The li is no definite measure, and varies perpetually from place to place; 250 to a degree of latitude is a convenient standard generally adopted by foreign travellers, which gives 3·62 li to the statute mile—a fairly correct average in Szechuan (in Yünnan the li is longer).

The name of this, the only affluent from the north of any size met with from the Han upwards—a distance of 800 miles—is, according to the maps, the "Chia-ling ho;" but here it is called the "Lin chiang ho," or river of Lin-chiang, a place situated some distance higher up. From the spot where we now embarked, we could look up to the gorge, by which the stream forces its way through the range, the lower slopes of which we had just descended. The gorge is steep and narrow, with a rapid at its base precisely like the Yang-tse gorges in miniature, and would well repay a visit. The gorge is called the "Kwan-yin hsia" (Kwan-yin is the Goddess of Mercy, and holds in the Buddhist worship a position analogous to that of the Virgin Mary in Europe), and its upper continuation, the "Wên t'ang hsia" ("Warm Spring Gorge"). In it is a temple with mineral baths, efficacious in skin diseases—with which more than half the population seem afflicted. This gorge opens up the coal-seam in which are the coal-workings I had just visited. Here the coal is lowered down directly into barges at the foot of the cliff, by baskets running on bamboo lines leading from the pit's mouth.

We glided swiftly down the stream, our boatmen doing little more than keep the boat in the centre of the current, clear of the eddies and ·rocks at the side. We were in company with a small fleet of antediluvian-looking vessels laden to the water's edge with drugs from the borders of Kansu —rhubarb and liquorice-root. These boats are built of rough planks, pegged together with tacks of bamboo; they are only constructed for the downward voyage; arrived in Chung-king, they are broken up, and their planking sold for house-building. It is curiously Chinese to entrust such valuable produce to such frail craft.

The beauty of the scenery is indescribable. The ravine through which the river flows offers a fresh picture at every turn. The winter crops are all ripe for harvest, and every slope is cultivated to the summit; the red, perpendicular cliffs which rise up in every direction are alone left bare, and form a rich contrast to the surrounding vegetation. In these cliffs are the square openings of the caves that formed the homes of the aboriginal inhabitants of the country, looking like the port-holes of a rock fortress. The present inhabitants take but little interest in, and know still less about, these curious vestiges of the past. They can only tell you that they belonged to the Man-tze, or "savages." More recently they have served as the home of the "Man yin," or "savages of darkness," being the locality to which, until latterly, the loose women of Chung-king were strictly relegated by the authorities. The scaffolding, by which these caves were formerly rendered accessible, has disappeared, and to explore them now a supply of ropes and ladders would be needful, which, unfortunately, I had no time to provide. Mr. Baber has sent an elaborate account of them to the Geographical

Society, but he is able to come to no conclusion as to who constructed them. Like all the Szechuan rivers, the Siao ho forms a succession of pools and rapids, its bed being curiously obstructed in places by reefs of rock which the water has not yet succeeded in disintegrating. Thus, a few miles above Chung-king is the stone gate (Shih men), a ledge of hard sandstone rising some twenty feet above the present winter level, and through which the river flows in a rapid current by four narrow, winding channels. These, as long as the rocks are visible above the water, are easily navigable; but in summer, when the river is in flood and the rocks are hidden, the passage is perilous in the extreme. Every spot has its legend, and if I were to relate all that I learnt on my voyage up and down, I fear this account would never be brought to a conclusion. All who have a slight acquaintance with the history of China are aware that, during the troublous times that preceded the fall of the Ming dynasty, in the early part of the seventeenth century, the province of Szechuan was almost depopulated by the ferocious rebel—"Chang-hsien-chung," Chang the Loyal (!). The province was re-peopled by immigrants from Hukwang and Kiangsi, to whom land was allotted on exceptionally favourable terms—terms which have been faithfully observed to this day, the land-tax being nominal in amount, and considerably less than that imposed on any other of the eighteen provinces, while its soil is among the most fertile in the empire. During the rebellion of Chang the Loyal, a popular official of Chung-king, named Tung, drowned himself in the Siao ho, and his body was changed into a rock, which still obstructs the navigation a short distance above the stone gate. Near by is the "Shih ma ho" ("Stone Horse Temple"), opposite which stands a stone horse wanting in feet. He represents an unfortunate animal that was in the habit of straying at night and eating the crops (in China there are no fences). The cruel country people amputated his feet, and, as they thought, put an end to his wanderings; but Buddha, defender of every breathing thing, turned him into stone on the spot, and on dark nights the horse resumes his fleshly form and still continues his depredations. Higher up we traversed another group of rocklets, which the river has not yet succeeded in eroding entirely, known as the " Chiu shih kang," or " ninety jars," each one of which is filled with silver, secreted there by the inhabitants before their massacre, which would repay a public-spirited surveyor who would clear them from the channel. Beguiled by many such yarns, we sped rapidly on, and reached Chung-king at sunset. During these interesting colloquies, my Chinese companions had reclined gracefully in the boat upon a red blanket of foreign manufacture, the advantages of which over the ordinary native wadded quilt they extolled highly. Unlike on the latter, the fleas could not leap on its woolly surface, and were hence easily caught and destroyed, as ocular demonstration showed.

Our boat took ground under the overhanging battlements of the north gate, to which we ascended by a steep climb of nearly three hundred filthy steps, and, almost groping our way through the dimly-lighted streets, at length reached home in time for a welcome supper. I was anxious to know how our ponies would fare in the dark over the rocky roads, but was told to have no care, for they were accustomed to travel by night; and "had they not, like all horses, 'night eyes' in their fetlocks?"

The river, which during my fortnight's stay had gradually risen ten feet, and covered the greater portion of the shingle beds opposite the city, next day suddenly fell six feet, and gave another respite to the extensive " bamboo " town which grows up under the walls and along the water's edge in the winter season. On this day I visited the Shansi Guildhall —a handsome, spacious, highly decorated building, situated just within the wall, and facing the picturesque hills on the opposite bank. The view from the terrace between the hall and the city wall, and on a level with the embrasures in the latter, is thus magnificent; but nothing of it is seen from the interior of the building, which is, as usual, entirely enclosed in four lofty walls. A dinner and theatrical performance was in progress, and lively groups of eight surrounded the tables with which the courtyards were filled. I kept myself out of sight behind the colossal, gilded josses that occupy the daïs at the upper end, not wishing to join in the feast nor to cause the commotion which my unexpected appearance would have created. There is much in the present aspect and uses of these guilds in China, as, indeed, in many other things, to remind one of the condition of our own country in the Middle Ages.

The same contrast between the glory and magnificence of the public institutions and the comparative squalor of the homes; the exclusion of the fair sex from their festal meetings; * the richness of the costumes and the dirt hidden beneath them; the universal interest with which all public festivities, religious as well as secular, are regarded; the rigid thrift observed in private combined with a magnificent lavishness in public; the settlement of all trade disputes by the guild, and the shunning of all laws and lawyers; the rules laid down by the guilds obeyed unquestioned, and the unwritten etiquette of business no less strictly observed; the liberal subscriptions and legacies given to the guilds, and the way in which these institutions are the first to be called upon for funds in times of calamity and distress— mark the resemblance between East and West in different

* In London this is a modern development.

ages. Szechuan is specially worthy of study in this respect, its customs being unalloyed with outside ideas. It has, too, of late years been more free from political disturbances than any other province, although its history is not free from the periodical convulsions that in times gone by have afflicted the West no less than the East. The trade control of the Chinese guilds is still a living power, and, as far as I have seen, one invariably exercised for the good of its members and the honour of the craft. I could even wish at times that our city companies still exercised some supervision over the trades which in name they represent. Here, the grievance of the individual becomes the concern of the guild, and he is thus protected alike from unjust exactions by officials and the often no less tyrannical procedure of powerful monopolies. The wealthy foreign firms established along the coasts have to reckon with them, and hence the somewhat jealous eye with which they are regarded; but their action on the whole is undoubtedly beneficial as much in upholding fair dealing amongst their members as in protecting them from outside injustice. More than one instance of their power has been shown at the river-ports within the last twelve months. A large steamer of two thousand tons, belonging to the China Navigation Company, was wrecked in the Yang-tse, and became a total loss. The shippers, entirely Chinese, claimed from the company the value of their shipments, and the fear of "taboo" compelled the company to make them good. It should not be forgotten, in connection with this now established custom in China, that in the same way, where our own Government charters vessels or ships stores by them, it, by the simple device of striking a pen through the arbitrary excepting clauses of the bill of lading, holds the owners responsible "for neglect of master or crew," and, in the event of loss or damage, the

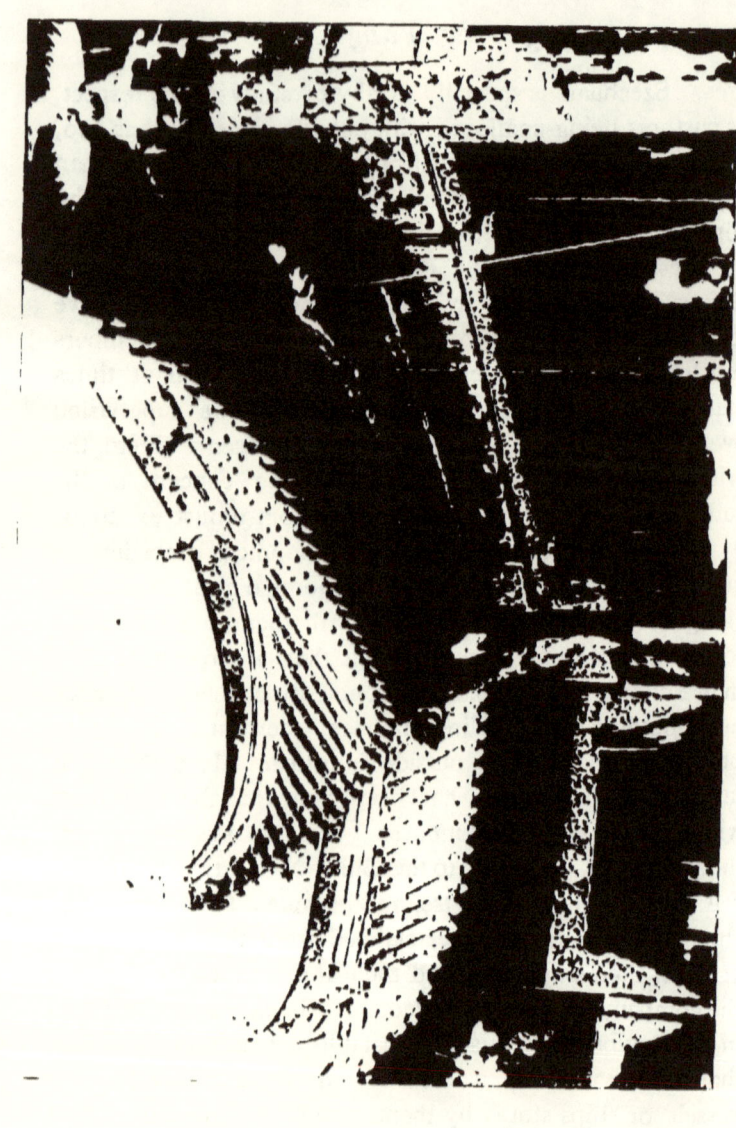

Court in Hukwang Guildhall, Chung-king.

To face p. 202

owner has to pay, as in the case of the steamer wrecked off the Cape during the last Zulu War. With us, it is true, the insurance is supposed to protect the ship from losses such as these; but there are many risks which no insurance covers, and against these an individual is helpless, in the face of the excepting clauses which exonerate the shipmaster from any care of his goods, and to which he is bound to subscribe; butwhat only a Government can do at home is in China effected by a guild. The other instance was the determination of the Hankow Tea-guild, in the spring of 1883, to put a stop to the unfair system of weighing which had long prevailed at that port. A notice to all the foreign buyers was simply sent round by the chairman of the guild, to the effect that henceforth exact weights would be insisted upon, and a long prevailing injustice was forthwith abolished.

One fine day I hired one of the cabs of Chung-king, a sedan-chair, stands of which are to be found at almost every street corner, and set out for the west gate, to reach which it was necessary for me to traverse nearly the whole breadth of the city, about two miles, but seemingly much more, owing to the constant ascents, many of the staircases being cut out of the solid rock. The city is, in fact, divided into the upper and lower city, the "Shang pan cheng," and the "Hsia pan cheng," the former being built on a sandstone bluff which rises about a hundred feet above the latter, and is generally too steep to admit of any houses being built on its precipitous sides. The business hongs and the principal yamens are in the lower city; the missionary establishments, the pleasure gardens, and the foreign consulates in the upper; and from this upper city a succession of distant and beautiful views is obtainable. The chair fare for any distance within the walls is twenty-five cash, equal to one penny of our money, and, wonderful to relate, the coolies demand no more from a Chinese-speaking, and hence civilized, barbarian than from a native. I thus usually took a chair through the city, in order to avoid the crowd, as far as the gate, being able to walk through the country in perfect freedom. Leaving the west gate, the road falls to a narrow ravine, rising again beyond over the grave-covered hills, which, crescent-like, extend across between the two rivers, and wall in the city in its rear. In the ravines are situated the crematoria, in which the waste paper of the city is solemnly committed to the flames. These crematoria are elaborate places, comprising a walled enclosure, in which is a garden and a cottage for the superintendent of the ceremonies, besides the square pagoda-shaped tower some fifty feet high, in which the paper is offered up. The Chinese character is esteemed too sacred for any paper on which it has been inscribed to be allowed to descend to base uses: hence the formation of benevolent societies, who maintain a corps of colporteurs whose business it is to make periodical house-to-house visitations, and collect every scrap of writing-paper which has been thrown aside. These colporteurs are further armed with a pair of bamboo tongs, with which to seize any fragments that have been unwittingly neglected amidst the garbage of the streets. Thus we see, what is also noticeable in other lands, more given to superstition than to science, a great amount of labour devoted to a superstitious object which would be better spent on scavenging.

My goal on the present occasion was a country house situated on the banks of Siao ho, about two miles out of town. The place is celebrated for its flower-garden, and is a resort for dinner-parties. The path winds through the hills in a gradual descent, until a walled enclosure, situated a quarter of a mile back from the river-bank, is reached. I was accompanied only by a coolie as guide. We knocked at the door, which was opened by a woman, and entered a courtyard filled with orange-trees in pots. A range of buildings looking on to courtyards filled with flowering shrubs in pots occupied the enclosure, and were thus capable of affording accommodation to separate parties. I sat down in one of the pavilions, where tea was served by some young girls, daughters of the proprietress, who, with their mother, their cousins, and their aunts, crowded round and overwhelmed me with questions. There was a pleasing absence of that painful shyness which precludes all intercourse with respectable women on the part of a foreigner in other parts of China, with, at the same time, no lack of true modesty. It appeared that the proprietress was a widow, her husband having died a short time previously, leaving her with a large family of daughters, and little beyond this property to depend upon. Her endeavour to earn a living by letting out the place to picnic parties from the city had not been over-successful. Times were bad in Szechuan, as elsewhere, and the wealthy trading classes were economizing—the same lament that I heard from the Taoists at Lao-chun grotto. But, unlike these, the old lady, far from being clamorous for money, resolutely declined payment for her tea. She wanted to sell the property, however, and tried to persuade me to give a thousand tiao (£200) for it. How different is this "Zuvorkommenheit" to the sulky reception a foreigner meets with upon attempting to negotiate for anything of the kind in the neighbourhood of the open ports! Having enjoyed the tea and the rest after the hot walk, I descended to the bank of the river, which here forms a "t'o," or pool, where the current is slack and the water wide and deep—a seductive spot for a bath, which I was prompt to utilize. A small but silent crowd collected on the bank, and I was undisturbed by any rude remark, and, after dressing, sat down on the bank to admire the scenery. An old gentleman offered me his pipe, and descanted on the dangers of the river, now flowing so tranquilly at our feet, when swollen by the autumn floods. A walk back to the city along the riverbank, now on a well-turfed sandbank, now scrambling with the aid of rock-cut steps over a jutting promontory, ended a pleasant outing, and produced an appetite for the somewhat insipid dishes of an ordinary native dinner.

Mine host appeared early on the morning of April 25th with his little daughter, whom he had brought down to the hong from his home in the upper town to see a Taoist show, which was to pass our door, in the street of the White Elephant. She was a little *chétive* thing of ten years, but from her size looking much younger, and so pale that I asked her father whether there was anything the matter with her. He said, " No; but that she was suffering from her feet," as all growing girls upon whom this frightful practice is imposed necessarily must do. Hers were bandaged up until they looked more like those of a doll than the feet of a human being, and the poor child never attempted to walk without holding on to some one's hand, and was always carried up and down the flights of steps which led from one courtyard to the other. My host, like other Chinamen with whom I have conversed on the subject, agreed that it was a pity for the children that such a custom existed; but that when they were grown up, should their feet have been left alone, no one would regret the fact more bitterly than the girls themselves. In short, it is the fashion; and any family setting their faces against it would be socially ostracized, and would be debarred from all decent matches for its

Country seat of the Yuen Family, outside Chung-king.

To face p. 202.

daughters. With the exception of the boatwomen in the south (the "Han-shui mei," or salt-water girls), and the aboriginal tribes in the west, as also perhaps a few beggars and outcasts, all the women of China, poor as well as rich, are crippled in this barbarous fashion. Ancient custom appears to have reconciled the people to the habit, and to have hardened the hearts of parents to the sufferings entailed on their children by it. So few Englishmen ever have an opportunity of mixing intimately with the natives and seeing anything of their family life—and then only on rare occasions—that the terrible evils attending this abominable practice seldom come home to one, and by those living at the open ports it is hardly noticed, the women destined to associate with foreigners being specially brought up in a natural manner. Undistorted feet are odious in the eyes of the Chinese, and are associated with all that is vile. Is it not possible that this enfeeblement of the mothers through countless generations has had its effect in stunting the mental growth of the Chinese as a nation? The Chinese are great Nature-worshippers, and their dread of acting in discord with Nature is shown in their superstitious regard for "Feng-shui." In a country where the monsoons blow with the regularity that they exhibit in China, the doctrine of the evil influences attending the north wind, and the absolute necessity of a southern exposure, are founded on a true observance of nature, and are worthy of close imitation by the foreigners whose lot is cast here. In a country, too, whose staff of life is dependent on irrigated fields, interference with the watercourses is rightly guarded by a religious dread of interference with the earth-dragon. But man has a double environment, with both sides of which, in order to be happy, he must try to live in accord, though the two are often incompatible. The Chinese have laboured as successfully as most peoples to place themselves in accord with their *natural* surroundings; but, as in the West, though in a less degree, the forces of their *social* surroundings have proved too strong for them. In a case like this, *force majeure* is needed to break through the bonds of custom, and I verily believe that, when our troops were masters of Pekin, had we had the courage to usurp the dragon throne, and had issued an edict prohibiting henceforth the mutilation of the children's feet, the command would have been obeyed, sullenly perhaps at first, but afterwards thankfully. Such a proceeding, though possibly not warrantable on other grounds, would, in the cause of humanity, have been perfectly justifiable, and precedent for such despotic edicts exists in more than one instance in Chinese history. The Manchus, as is well known, not only introduced the pigtail, but enforced the use of narrow sleeves, with the cuffs cut like horses' hoofs, on a reluctant people; and at this day the flowing dress of the Mings is seen nowhere but on the stage and in the dress of the Buddhist priesthood. Wu san-koei, the conqueror of Yunan under the first emperor of the present dynasty, found there was such an unintelligible mass of outlandish dialects, that he ordered the people, on pain of death, to learn Pekingese; and to this day travellers in this remote province are struck with wonder at the purity of the language spoken there. The Chinese are a law-abiding people, eminently respectful to constituted authority, and patient acceptors of accomplished facts. Their rebellions, really less frequent than they seem when viewed through the perspective of their long history, seem invariably to have been the outcome of local oppressions or of unrelieved famines, and never simply pure uprisings against an alien dynasty. The club-feet question is one on which it is impossible for any person who has lived amongst the

Chinese not to feel strongly, and thus to be led to grope for a probably unattainable remedy.*

In contrast with the slender, listless appearance of young Chinese girls, was the robust, sturdy look of a Manchu family whose acquaintance I made at the Kung-kwan or Ya-mên, in Chung-king, maintained for the reception of travelling officials. The father was a hale old man, hardly distinguishable from a well-to-do Chinaman, but his daughters were the picture of health, and full of vivacity; the difference was so striking, that before I noticed their feet, I was struck with their unusually healthy look and easy manners. It is curious that, owing probably to this distinction, the Manchus have, unlike all previous conquerors of the country, never freely intermarried with the natives; they are still physically superior, though apparently still intellectually inferior, and they appear to have lost the conspicuous energy that enabled a handful of foreigners to overrun the country two centuries ago. They seem to be gifted with a dogged bravery, but, even to a greater extent than the Chinese themselves, to be wanting in initiative. Possibly this is due to the fact that they are, to all intents and purposes, pensioners of the State. Their numbers are too few to cause much jealousy in the native Chinese, who see them thus specially favoured. They form the nominal garrisons of the principal cities, as in the days immediately succeeding the conquest; but they live in a quarter apart, as they and their families have done for generations, without intermingling with the rest of the people. They are forbidden to hold land, and do not trade, and lead a life of indolence on the pittance doled out to them.

* There is now an influential European society throughout China (organized by Mrs. Little) to oppose this evil practice, and innumerable Chinese societies formed in imitation of it. Three viceroys have already condemned the practice, and numbers of little girls are already growing up with natural feet, not to speak of grown women, who have unbound.

Their military exercises, with bows and arrows, are of the feeblest nature, and I have never yet seen a Manchu regiment armed with muskets! A fixed number of posts in the administration are specially reserved for them, as they would succumb were they dependent for employment upon success in the competitive examinations with the more active-minded Chinese. The mutual jealousy of the Chinese mandarins, who hold, as it is, all the highest posts in the provinces, coupled with their conservative dislike to change, alone at the present day retains the Manchus on the throne. What would happen, were an energetic emperor like Kangshi to arise and attempt to take the governing power really into his own hands, no one can tell, any more than they can prophesy what is to be the end of the contest between the decaying civilization of the foremost empire of the East and the aggressive civilization of the West, now hammering at its gates.

A Cantonese merchant, named Chen, had invited me to dine with him in a garden in the lower city. He promised me a dinner cooked in European style; having lived in Shanghai and Canton, he was supposed to comprehend the wants of the barbarian appetite. On arriving, I was introduced to two Cantonese mandarins who were reclining on the dais at the head of the guest-hall, whiling away the time with the unfragrant drug. Shortly afterwards the rest of the party arrived, and we sat down to the round table in the centre, seven in all. The dinner proved, unfortunately, a most decided failure; the strange meats were unacceptable to the other guests, and, in order to show due appreciation of my host's hospitality, I had to make up for my fellow-guests' indifference by setting to as best I could. As it was a very hot day, I asked leave to remove my coat, after the Chinese fashion, and set to with a will. Certainly if anything were needed to convince the company of their superior native refinement, as compared with our barbaric methods of eating, this feast was enough. In lieu of the chicken being neatly cut up, and stewed in a delicate sauce, all ready for serving to the mouth with the elegant chopsticks, a rough, plain boiled fowl was set on the table, with no carving-knife to dissect it with. Each guest had been provided with a miniature ivory-handled knife and a two-pronged fork, and after much effort we succeeded in gnawing at fragments of the carcase, unaccompanied with bread or vegetables. Then came a leg of mutton roasted "rare," not bad in itself, but without potatoes and bread somewhat unpalatable. Fortunately, we had some Chinese dishes to finish up with, and a cup of fragrant tea with which to wash down the heterogeneous repast. After experience of this meal I began to think myself less a victim than I did before, in being generally restricted in my travels to a Chinese cuisine pure and simple. Dinner over, we adjourned to another court, in which a local artist had made ready to photograph us in a group. The man was a Cantonese, who had been brought from Shanghai by some English traveller, whose name I could not succeed in deciphering from his Chinese version, and who had brought him thus far to photograph the scenery *en route*. The man had settled in Chung-king, and was apparently doing a thriving business. The group was successfully taken, and forms an interesting record of my visit. I may here mention that I heard the photographer expatiating to the mandarins, his fellow-countrymen, upon the benefit he had derived from consulting Dr. Edwards, of the China Inland Mission in this city, for ophthalmia, from which he had been long suffering, and of which he was now cured: he dwelt upon the fact of the doctor's receiving no payment ("yi ko chien pu yao"), but the idea of becoming a Christian seemed never to have entered his mind. The man was well off, and could well afford to pay for his treatment. After this, I said adieu to my kind host and his two mandarin friends, who held office in Chêng-tu, the provincial capital, and returned home to pass the evening in semi-obscurity as usual. No wonder that the Chinese, with no new books and no newspapers to amuse them, gradually take to passing their evenings over the social pipe. As with our lower classes, who are addicted to the public-houses from much the same causes, if the Chinese are to be weaned from the opium-pipe, they must be provided with amusements and more exciting occupations, such as the admission of Western enterprises can alone afford.

CHAPTER X.

THE DOWNWARD VOYAGE.

Adieux—A crowded boat—Change to a salt-junk—A strange manœuvre—A day on the rocks—Sham tea—Equipage of the junk—The gorges once more—Mooring for the night—Delays—Change to a wupan—Pirates—Fêng Tu.

IT was now nearing the end of April, and the time for my departure had come. I called to make my adieux to the members of the China Inland Mission, who have a staff of five or six members in this city. The China Inland or Taylor Mission is the most active of all the Protestant societies in China, and the only one that had, at that date, followed the example of the Catholics in adopting the native dress. They lead hard lives, and work on a most ungrateful soil; but as they believe themselves to be simply carrying out the commands of their Master, and leave the results to Him, the fact that there are so few genuine Protestant converts in China does not appear to trouble them. In fact, seeing that one of the few *bonâ fide* converts to Protestantism devastated thirteen out of the eighteen provinces in his endeavours to Christianize his fellow-countrymen a little more rapidly than the missionaries were doing, the Chinese may deem it fortunate that not more enthusiastic converts are made. "Hung shiu chuen," the Tai-ping king, accepted the example and teachings of the old Jewish captains in all their literal ghastliness, and slew the idolators without mercy. Sixteen years of desperate fighting (1848-64) passed away before his bandit hordes were broken up, and his capital, Nanking, given to the flames, in which he and all his household perished. Nearly twenty years have now elapsed, and the still desolate appearance of this, the southern capital, remains a witness and a warning. It is practically impossible to convert a Chinaman to Christianity, and leave him still a faithful member of his family, and a loyal subject to the powers that be. Confucianism is so interwoven with family observances and political doctrines, that if the one is overthrown the rest follow. "I come not to bring peace, but a sword," has been but too truly exemplified in this country, and nothing but the weakness of the Chinese enables them to tolerate missionaries as they do. "Take away your opium and your missionaries," Prince Kung is reported to have said in taking leave of Sir Rutherford Alcock. An instructive comment upon this is the fact that few foreigners in China ever employ a Christian or an opium-smoker if they can help it. It is not too generally known that a practical people like the Dutch, who hold the larger portion of the Malay race under their rule, forbid propagandism entirely, throughout the whole extent of their vast territories. We cannot, then, wonder at the Chinese desiring to do the like, and in common justice should allow the Government free action in a question of internal economy like this—especially where, under extra-territoriality, each individual mission is allowed free rein to its idiosyncracies, and the Chinese officials responsible for order, find it impossible to control the resulting *imperia in imperio*.

After endless delays, and constant urging on my part, it had been at length arranged that we should make our start down river on the morrow. Room had been engaged in a small boat carrying a light freight, and with good luck we might hope to be back in Ichang in a week's time. A farewell dinner was given me in the evening by a piece-goods hong with whom I had arranged some business, the hour, as customary, being four o'clock. We sat down, a mixed party of sixteen; a party of eight at each of the two square tables, including two Mohammedans, of whom there are a goodly number scattered throughout the West of China. The "Hui hui" (literally, "returners") are not recognizable from the other Chinese, in whose customs and worship they freely join; but they are rigid abstainers from swine's flesh, and in consequence at our to-day's feast beef was substituted.

The last day of April had now come, and after breakfast at ten o'clock, the customary hour, we managed to effect a start. We set out on foot to the Tai-ping gate, accompanied by a train of friends who had assembled to see us off. At the foot of the long staircase of 220 steps, which leads down from the gate to the river, and is of the respectable width of fully twenty feet, a small cargo boat was in waiting, with our luggage, to convey us on board our river-going junk, which was moored ready laden a short distance up the Kia-ling or Siao river, in which safe anchorage the vessels loading general cargo lie, the marvellous natural harbour in the main river, situated just below Kiang-peh ting, being appropriated by the huge, almost unmanageable salt-junks. Descending the stream past the city walls, a few minutes brought us to the mouth of the Siao river, up against the current of which a short pull soon put us alongside our craft. She turned out to be a shen po tze, a little larger than that in which I had ascended, with the difference on the present occasion of her being fully laden and apparently offering no accommodation for passengers whatever. The forehold, which is decked with loose planks, their edges resting on narrow waterways, gives accommodation to the crew and their stores, and contains the rice-boiler and the kitchen, which is only opened at and immediately before the meal hours, when, with the wind ahead, volumes of acrid smoke stream through the opened cabin to the great delectation of the hungry passengers. The stern accommodates the skipper, who is usually the owner, and therein the little cargo he usually carries as a private venture is stowed. On the present occasion our vessel was laden with ducks' feathers, destined for sale in Shanghai, and eventually, probably, for Mincing Lane. These feathers were packed in huge bales of bamboo matting, and reached to within three feet of the roof. Aft a small depression had been left, just affording squatting-room for our party of three round a dwarf table at meal-times. Seeing that, unlike the voyage up, on the downstream journey there is no opportunity of quitting the boat, except at night, and that I was anxious, too, to see something of the scenery going down, I at once made up my mind that this vessel was impracticable. Chinese supercargoes are perfectly content with such accommodation; they ask nothing better than to enjoy an earthly Nirvana for a week, free from anxiety and undisturbed by anything but the periodical call to meals. However, I waited to see what my friends would say, knowing that there was no use in protesting too soon, and that there was no likelihood of our getting away that day. Sure enough, after scrambling through the boat with no little difficulty, they all set upon the unfortunate man who had been entrusted with the engaging of our passages, and roundly abused him. The passage was cried off, and it was decided to look out for something better. As it would be impossible to find private accommodation elsewhere that afternoon, and as I firmly withstood the proposal to return on shore, with the prospect of having to say all our adieux over again two days hence, we remained in our boat, squatting on the top of our luggage, while a young fellow from the hong was sent to see whether he could procure us room in a salt-junk, of which, at this season, the one most favourable for the navigation, a fleet of five or six sail daily. After three weary hours' sitting in the sun, the time being passed by an interchange of pipes, and the consumption of some of the packets of cakes and sweetmeats with which kind friends had speeded my departure, our "runner" returned. He had found places for us in a salt-junk sailing the next morning, and as it was now sunset we all adjourned.

Below the mouth of the Kia-ling ho, and abreast of the city of Kiang-peh ting,* which, as I have previously described, forms practically the northern suburb of Chung-king, the river widens out, and a long ledge of rocks stretches up and down, forming a barrier between the rapid current of the main stream, and a lake-like expanse between it and the steep hills on the left bank. Here the salt-junks are moored in tiers, their bows to the shore. Approaching by the stern, we scrambled over the high gunwale aft, and entered the skipper's cabin, on the floor of which, being the raised main-deck, we at once spread our quilts, and shortly afterwards went supperless to bed. The fare down, a distance of eight days, had been agreed upon at sixteen dollars for the three of us, including a portion of the sailors' plain boiled rice three times a day, "trimmings," if wanted, having to be provided by ourselves. Upon the floor of this cabin slept also the pilot, a fine, tall, well-built Chinaman, with a handsome oval face, dignified in manners,

* This city has just been captured by the anti-missionary rebel, Yü Mantse, who is said to be now (October, 1898) besieging Chung-king itself.

and evidently imbued with a sense of the dignity of his calling; immediately behind, and in a small cabin partitioned off from the rest, slept the skipper with his wife and two children; the cabin-boy was apportioned to our division. We were to start at daylight.

Sure enough at early dawn the following morning I was awoke by the skipper, who in a gruff voice requested us to hurry up and get our beds out of the way, without delay. Though not particularly gratified at being thus rudely disturbed in my morning's slumbers, I was consoled by the thought that now at last we were really off, and that the harassing delays of the last few days were at an end. Every hour was of importance, as I had just eight days to catch the Ichang steamer to Hankow: this vessel makes the round trip in about ten days, and if I missed this voyage I should be inevitably too late for the Hankow tea season, which opens about the 12th of May. Imagine, then, my astonishment when, still half awake, we were hurried over the side into a large sampan, and at length given to understand that we were to return to the shore. My men having all the arrangements in their hands, and, they urging me to submit, I remained passive, awaiting explanations later. I found we were being rowed across the basin to the rocks in the centre of the river. All I could make out, as long as the boatmen were present, was that the skipper did not wish to be seen starting with a foreigner on board. The true inwardness of the matter I afterwards discovered to be this. Salt is a Government monopoly throughout the empire, and privileged licensed merchants are alone allowed to deal in it; the salt-junks all carry an official flag, and sail in a certain routine and on fixed days; owing to the value of their cargo and the danger of the navigation, they are not allowed to take passengers down-stream, lest the crew, and especially the pilot, should be disturbed by them. Now, the official inspectors were due with the junk's clearance, shortly after daylight, and hence our skipper's anxiety to get rid of us.

This reef, which shuts off the still-water harbour of Lien-uc tung from the roaring current, and the channel beyond, in which is no anchorage, is known as the "Liang-toh;" it is about a third of a mile in extent, and varies in width from twenty to a hundred yards. It evidently forms part of a hard sandstone ledge, through which the river has cut and is still cutting its way, the opposite (right) bank being lined with a terrace of precisely similar formation which projects horizontally from the low steep range, which here, as on the right bank, forms the immediate shore of the river in summer, when all these rocks are entirely out of sight. At the present moment the reef was almost covered with a long street of substantially built bamboo-frame and mat-walled houses which had been gradually erected last winter, as the falling stream successively exposed the needful foundations, the highest of which were now not more than fifteen feet above the present level. The water had already covered the more low-lying portions, and owing to the recent rise, several houses from which the contents were now being hastily removed were standing in the water; of these the mat walls and bamboo frames were being gradually removed and transported to the opposite shore. No doubt during the winter a good trade is done here with the large junk population, which justifies the unusually spacious erections of this temporary town. We strolled on into a roomy tea-shop, and, having bought a few "torillas" from an itinerant pastry-cook, sat down to Chota hazari. A porcelain cup, containing a few green tea-leaves, was set before each of us, boiling water poured in, and the cover put on as usual, and lastly a huge earthenware jug of hot water was set in the middle of the table, from which we could replenish at leisure: all this luxury, including the liberty, of which we freely availed ourselves, of dawdling, Chinese fashion, as many hours as we liked over the repast, for the sum of five copper cash. I am sorry to say, however, that I found the tea, which had a lovely, transparent green appearance, so bitter as to be undrinkable, and I had to content myself with hot water, instead of the refreshing cup to which, after our early rise, I had been looking forward with most pleasant anticipation. "Cha" in China denotes any infusion of herbs (we ourselves go so far as to say beef-tea), and was probably used to mean an infusion of any kind, many centuries before tea proper was discovered. Certainly my tea at the Liang-toh did not contain a single leaf of *Thea sinensis;* they were apparently all young spring willow leaves dried in the sun. I rambled about for two or three hours, waiting for our dilatory skipper to send for us, and thus had a fine opportunity of examining the rocky islet upon which we were abandoned. Its rugged outlines had been rounded off by the water, although in places the ascents were so steep that short staircases had been neatly cut in the rock. The whole surface was honeycombed with perpendicular cylindrical holes, as though bored out by a mighty auger, from a few inches to several feet in depth, and of equally varied diameters. In truth, a host of mighty augers had been at work, and the tools were still *in situ,* now lying idle at the bottom of the pits, but only waiting for the untiring hand of nature, in the shape of the now rising flood, to again set them in motion. The tools had been brought from a distance, as though specially appropriated for the work of clearing away these destructive reefs, and consisted of boulders of porphyry and gneiss washed down from the Tibetan mountains. In many places, where the auger-holes, as one may well call them, approached the water's edge, their sides had been broken in, and thus the hard rock was being rapidly disintegrated. This process is being carried on throughout the whole river-bed, from Tibet all the way to the great plain of Hukwang, which is being steadily filled up with so much of the detritus as does not find its way still lower down to the delta of the Great River in Kiangsu. My Chinamen, seeing me poking about and fishing up the boulders from the bottom of the basins, most of which contained a pool of stagnant and by no means fragrant water, of course imagined I was looking for gold; they received an attempted explanation of the phenomena, that were so interesting to me, with an air of absolute incredulity. It is as hard to lead a Chinaman to believe that natural phenomena are due to natural causes, and not due to mysterious polytheistic agencies, as it is in the West to convince a devout believer in witchcraft of the non-existence, or rather non-interference, of the supernatural in current mundane affairs. Whether the old philosophers of China ever had any real insight into the workings of nature, such as is credited to them by their enthusiastic admirers, I entirely doubt; but certain it is, that at the present day Fêng-shui, although a delightful superstition, greatly interferes with progress, and prevents the search for real remedies for the many ills from which humanity, and Chinese humanity especially, is still cruelly suffering. This living and travelling for any length of time with such unsympathetic creatures as the ordinary Chinaman, is exasperating to a degree, and I do not wonder at those Europeans who have cast their lot in the interior of China appearing eccentric, to say the least, to their fellow-countrymen, when they again emerge into real civilization. For it is not as though one were living with savages : the Chinaman has all the outward manifestations of a refined civilization, and hence the greater disappointment when you do pierce the crust. The only way to travel here with any profit is to conceal your real feelings and appear to sympathize with all their comical beliefs : this the Chinaman travelling in the West does to perfection, every Chinese child being an actor by nature. Thus our few Chinese visitors in Europe have acquired a reputation for acuteness far beyond their merits, and it is curious to see, in the rare instances where, as in their published journals, the veil has been lifted, how trivial are their ideas, and how totally they fail to grasp the grand truths which lie at the bottom of Western progress. Hence the disappointment we experience at the absence of all influence in favour of Western ideas, displayed by returned Chinamen, diplomats no less than merchants.

The sun was now blazing forth out of a cloudless sky, and the reflection of its rays from the bare rocks drove me back to the glad shelter of the tea-shop, until at ten o'clock, after nearly five hours' waiting, our boat arrived. The junk meanwhile had got under way, and was slowly creeping through the still waters of the pool, looking, with her low deck and dozen sweeps on either side, like a huge centipede. We soon caught her up in the sampan, and, when we got on board, found her drifting down-stream at the rate of five miles an hour—drifting, I say rightly, for though we had no less than sixty men toiling at the sweeps, their united efforts did no more than keep the head of the heavily laden craft pointed down-stream. On the down trip the junks, large and small, unstep their masts, and lash them alongside ; this feature, together with the high deck-houses aft, culminating in the lofty stern, gives them an ungainly look. The

Salt Junk, about 70 Tons, with Screw-oars or "Yulees" alongside, moored near Entrance to Ichang Gorge, bound down River, Mast lashed alongside.

To face p. 222.

mats which cover in the fore part, when the crew are sleeping on the deck at night, or when the rain is too heavy to proceed, are piled up on these houses, while farther aft everything is covered with the coils of the enormous tow-lines required for the voyage up. Our main motive power consisted of four huge sweeps, each worked by eight men. These were composed of young fir-trees unbarked, the thicker end, over a foot in diameter, being in-board, with a short plank lashed to the head in guise of paddle. Another similar sweep, also some forty feet long, projected directly over the bows, its paddle cutting the water in advance. This, in conjunction with the huge barn-door of a rudder, served to guide the lumbering craft safely through the rocks and rapids of our course. In addition to these, two lateral yuloes (sculls worked by a screw motion), also manned by half a dozen men each, were attached to the sides forward of the oars. These colossal sweeps are called by the Chinese "che," or "wheel," in contradistinction to the usual word for oar, "jao." Our progress *through the water* was extremely slow, the men pulling the sweeps laboriously though steadily at the rate of eleven strokes to the minute. The junk advanced five to six feet each stroke, giving a speed of 1200 yards to the hour. In short, with good local knowledge such as the pilots possess, and by taking the right channel in good time, nothing more is required than to keep steerage-way on the vessel, to enable her to avoid the whirlpools, and to pass down the rapids in safety. The pay of each boatman for the down journey, which, according to the state of the water, occupies from eight to ten days, is 300 cash, besides three meals of rice daily, with eight ounces of pork each, three times on the voyage. For the voyage up, which occupies thirty to forty days, the pay is 800 to 1000 cash (about three shillings). Compare this with the pay which the same coolie would get if on board a foreign steamer—at least eight dollars a month, his rice costing two dollars—with the toils of a galley-slave exchanged for almost nominal labour. Steamers on this part of the Yang-tse would naturally be regarded with some jealousy; but if, as they should do, they employed local labour, and did not bring more strangers from other provinces than were necessary to teach the new hands their work, opposition would soon be disarmed. I was constantly asked when we were going to begin running steamers, and it shows how little heart for untried enterprises foreigners in China now possess, that (in 1883) seven years should have elapsed since the right to run steamers on the Upper Yang-tse was acquired, under the Chefoo Convention, without any attempt to take advantage of the privilege having been made.

Soon after noon we, to my great disgust, brought up alongside the bank in the "t'o" or lake-like expanse of comparatively smooth water at the mouth of the "Tung lo hsia," or "Brass Gong" Gorge, which, like all the gorges, seems to turn off sharply at right angles to the river's previous course through a cleft in the hills, the entrance to which is entirely hidden until you are directly opposite to it. Here, ten miles below the city, is the first barrier, and the salt cargo had to be again checked. Meanwhile, the laggards of our crew, who had failed to join in Chung-king, were to come up with us here. There was no village at this station, nothing but a roomy bamboo house for the Customs officers, with the customary smart gunboat in attendance. We were delayed here four hours in the hot sun, with nothing to do but write up my journal and watch little boys on the bank making and launching sailing-rafts of reeds, ingenious models of the bamboo rafts in use on the mountain streams throughout all China. We at last unmoored, and drifted into the Gong

Gorge. The general course of the river between Ichang and Chung-king, a distance, following its windings, of nearly 500 miles, is east. by north, Chung-king being in north latitude 29° 33′, and east longitude 107° 2′; Ichang is in north latitude 30° 41′, and in east longitude 111° 53′, there being thus a difference of sixty-eight geographical miles in latitude, and of 267 miles in longitude between the two places. According to the "Hsing Chuan pieh yao" (in pigeon-English, "Walkee Szechuan must want-jee"), or vade mecum of Admiral Ho, the distance between Ichang and Pahsien (Chung-king) is 1800 li. This, at three and a half li to the mile, would give 514 statute miles, which probably is not much in excess of the actual distance traversed; the true distance, of course, never will be known until an exact chart, on the same scale as that of the Lower Yang-tse drawn up by our naval surveyors, has been published. Blakiston's, though admirable as far as it goes, and a marvellous monument of rapid work executed under most disadvantageous conditions, is on too small a scale to show all the windings and abrupt twists that the river really makes. The longer reaches run south-west and north-east, parallel to the prevailing direction of the mountain ranges; but where these are cut through, as they are in the constantly recurring gorges, it is always at right angles to their axes, and in these the prevailing course of the river is consequently north-west and south-east. Hence the succession of sharp, picturesque turns, with their accompanying whirlpools and rapids.

The Gong Gorge, so-named from the stone image of a brass gong, said to be apparent on the right cliff, and from a brass drum on the left, is cut, as usual, through a limestone elevation, which has raised up the coal-measures, into which tunnels run from the face of the cliff. The cliffs themselves seem to rise in a succession of steep steps, which yield

Q

ledges just large enough for the support of a luxuriant vegetation of cedar and bamboo. In the mouth of a small lateral ravine, but perched high up on a rocky pinnacle, I noticed a snug farmhouse; otherwise the gorge seemed deserted, and constituted a wild break in the generally continuous cultivation and smiling farms of the Szechuan country. I do not estimate these hills at over twelve or fifteen hundred feet above the river, which is here fully half a mile wide. Everything about the Yang-tse Gorges is on such a large scale that estimates of distances are not easily formed; that careful observer, Blakiston, in one or two cases in which the heights he gives have since been checked by actual measurement, is found to have under-estimated them by fully one-third. From the deck of our junk it appeared as though we were the sole occupants of the gorge; only on close inspection could I discover the upward-bound junks toiling along close under the shore, and it required a good field-glass to make out the gangs of trackers scrambling over the rocky tow-path ahead of them. How swiftly we seemed to sweep by! in a few minutes gliding by a rocky point that had occupied us nearly as many hours in ascending. Yet, although we were not making more than six knots over the ground, it was all too fast to enjoy the scenery, and I was glad that I had already had the opportunity of studying it at leisure on my way up. In these days of steam, how few places one has the opportunity of thoroughly enjoying! Notwithstanding the many discomforts of Chinese travel, one is, to my thinking, more than compensated by its absence of hurry, at least in such regions as these, where every yard is of interest, and a new picture opens out at every mile. A fine waterfall tumbles over the cliff on the right bank, but its murmur is lost in the noise of the rapid, by which the seemingly still waters of the gorge are discharged into the next reach. Passing this and the "Yeh lo-tze," or "Wild Mule," we brought up, shortly before sunset, in the "Ue tsui t'o," or "Fish-mouth pool," having made sixty li, or about eighteen miles, in less than four hours' travel. The rise in the river had tamed down the "Wild Mule," which was by no means as formidable an obstacle as it was when we came up; as is always the case, when the river is in flood, the water was of a rich chocolate colour, and in a tumbler looked almost as thick as a *bonâ fide* cup of that inestimable beverage. Millions of tons of Tibetan soil are thus carried down every summer, and go to raise the many yet unfilled depressions of the great Hukwang plain, the finer particles being carried even as far as the open estuary, a distance of two thousand five hundred miles.

The selecting a mooring-ground for one of these big junks is an important matter. In the first place, the water must be deep enough to ensure that the vessel, which is always tied up close under the bank, will not touch the ground in the event of a fall of six or eight feet occurring in the night; then there must be a good current at the spot, in order to keep the water out of the leaks, yet not a current so strong as to risk her breaking adrift. Upon rounding-to, preparatory to taking up a berth for the night, the diver plunges on shore with a line, which he makes fast to a stake in the ground, after which one of the massive young fir trees, or "che," is extended from the bows to the bank as a shore, while another is shoved out from the stern, both being firmly lashed to "bitts" on deck, as well as to stakes driven into the bank. Supper is then served to all hands, the crew squatting in groups of eight or ten round the rice-tubs; and immediately the meal is over, the mats are extended all along the forward deck, and the crew, mostly naked, and packed as close as herrings, are quickly wrapped in slumber —a few, perhaps one in ten, devoting an hour or more, before turning in, to the fascinating drug. We meanwhile are similarly occupied, the two cabins and helm-house aft, in which also the weary pilot spreads his bed, being filled with passengers. I now observe the wisdom of the rule which forbids these large cargo-junks from taking passengers. As we sat and talked and smoked, the high voice of the skipper's wife resounding through all the din, I noticed the unfortunate pilot turning over and over in his bed anxiously trying to sleep. It was nearly eleven before our lights were out, and then the tiny lamp of a couple of opium-smokers, merchants bound to Hankow like ourselves, was still burning on the bed facing my own. The pilot never leaves the helm for a moment while the vessel is under way, except for his meals, which, together with those of the men, are taken in easy spots where the junk may be allowed to drift, on which occasions the skipper temporarily takes his place. His pay for the voyage to Shasze is twelve dollars. The skipper is usually part owner, and his duties appear to consist mainly in urging the crew to greater exertions in the dangerous places. Although the crew had a head man specially for this purpose, a true *farceur* who behaves like a maniac, yet the skipper found it necessary to second him in his antics. Our captain was a tallish, spare, active, erect man of about five and fifty, with considerable ." side," as became the captain of one of the largest class of vessels on these dangerous waters, and who showed as much condescension in pointing out, or rather in answering my questions about the places of interest, as might the captain of a Cunarder. I got to sleep at last, although with everything closed it was uncomfortably warm, and when I awoke the next morning we were already under way.

The men rise at earliest dawn, now five o'clock, clear away the mats, which are stowed on the deck-houses aft, and are served with their hot breakfast before getting under way. Half an hour afterwards we entered on the "Wen-tang hsia," or "Warm pool gorge," which opens on the long reach of Mutung. This is one of the long reaches which run parallel with the prevailing ranges, that is, south-west and north-east. The river flows in a steep ravine, and urges its way by numerous channels through a maze of rocks, now rising some fifteen feet above the water, but in summer entirely covered, at which time the navigation is attended with no little danger. At this season the main channel is plainly marked, and is of ample width, nowhere less than a hundred yards; but seen end on from the low deck, and foreshortened, the maze appears at first sight impassable. This reach ends in the rapid of the Double Dragon ("Soang lung tan"), and brings us to the industrious mat-making village of "Lo chi," so named from a dangerous rock opposite, the "Lo chi," or "Dripping Stone." We passed Lo chi at 8.30, and at 9.15 arrived in the "Shan-pei t'o," or "Fan back reach," having made, according to the native itinerary, thirty li, or eight miles in three-quarters of an hour—the real distance being probably five miles. The "Shan pei t'o" is behind the "Fan rock," and facing it is the "Fan cliff," a nasty point for upward-bound junks to round; below this, on the south bank, is the "Koan yin miau," one of the numerous temples to the Goddess of Mercy that one finds scattered throughout the empire, and especially in the south; then past the "San kiang tsao," or "Race of the three rivers," to the picturesque old city of "Chang sho" ("longevity"). Here one of my companions, a native of Chung-king, informed me he had been two years at a boarding-school, the first time I ever heard of the existence of such an institution in China. Chang-show hsien is said by the itinerary to be thirty li from Shan pei t'o, a distance which occupies us exactly an hour. But if I proceed to enumerate all the rapids and rocks of the river, of which the "Gazetteer" gives over a thousand between Chung-king and Ichang, I shall never get to my journey's end. In fact, we hurried past them at such a rate that it was quite impossible to keep pace with the numerous places of interest on either bank. Many spots that I had missed on the way up displayed greater prominence on the downward voyage, and many a picturesque scene, that had become indelibly impressed on my memory in the tedious ascent, now escaped with a passing glance. We no sooner arrived at a rapid than we were shot past it, and had no time to realize the danger, which, though apparently less than in the ascent, is in reality far more serious. At the rapid of Wang-chia tan, just above Chang-show, a big salt-junk, which had sailed from Chung-king the morning previous to our own departure, lay stranded on the boulders of a large cape of shingle, which extends along the south bank, and so narrows the channel as to form a small rapid; others come to grief on the rocks or in the whirlpools, and go down bodily. With these lumbering craft a quick helm and perfect discipline are necessary, and above all taking the right channel in good time, so as to avoid the eddies, in which, if the junk is once caught, she becomes unmanageable. There is no anchoring anywhere, and no anchors are carried. As on the upward voyage, so now, everything possible to excite the crew was done; on approaching a rapid, four guns were fired out of a curious four-barrelled piece, the tubes strengthened by iron rings welded on, with a wooden handle by which the cabin-boy, upon whom devolved this duty, held it on the bulwarks. The gang-master danced from oar to oar, his weight having apparently no effect whatever upon the huge tree-stems as he leapt from one to the other. Gesticulating and shouting at the top of his voice, he belaboured the bare backs of the men with his rattan, and thus succeeded possibly in bringing up our speed at the critical points to a mile an hour; then the skipper would take his turn in urging the unfortunate "tui jao tih" (oarsmen) to exert themselves to the utmost; meanwhile the men themselves shout like demons, and stamp on the loose deck boards as fast as they can move their feet. An onlooker suddenly set down here would imagine pandemonium set loose. I went to the door of the foremost cabin, looking out on the deck, and gazed on the strange scene; my smiles (they were all facing me at the time, rowing, for a change, with their backs to the bow) set the men off laughing and shouting still louder, when the surly skipper beckoned to me to go in again, and upon my afterwards demanding an explanation, told me that my presence disturbed the men. I believe myself, however, that my being there cheered and amused them, and made them work all the harder. Blakiston tells us that he will ever hold in pleasant memory the intrepid *voyageurs*, as he calls them, of the Upper Yang-tse: most assuredly a more cruelly worked or more poorly paid, and withal a better-tempered set of fellows are not to be met with the whole world over. Dirty and ill-paid, mostly covered from head to foot with itch-sores, and treated like dogs, they work with a will, and are always ready for a joke. During the whole of my trip, I, in my ridiculous foreign dress, never heard an uncivil word from one of them; and, as I have related in my account of the upward journey, on more than one occasion, when rambling along the shore I found myself unexpectedly caught in a tight place, they good-naturedly came to my assistance. With all this hurly-burly, the progress of the junk through the water could only be detected by throwing a biscuit over the side and carefully watching its slow recession. No wonder, then, as the Chinese say, one junk in ten gets stranded, and one in twenty totally lost each voyage.

We drifted rapidly on; past the "Hwang-ue ling," or "Herring Mountain," and the rock-strewn reach of the "Shih chia te," "Stone family pool," the "Tranquil rock," the "Scholar's rapid," the "Fire-wind rapid," and into the "Scissors gorge," a picturesque wooden glen some ten miles above Fu-chow; thence past the hamlet of "Sai Feng tu," literally, "Rival Feng-tu," the celebrated home of the ruler of Hades, through the "Black Dragon gorge," and the narrows of the "Tortoise gate," and at length by the mouth of the "Dragon King," we emerged in the reach at the foot of which stands the important city of Fu-chow. It was now three o'clock, and the usual afternoon up-river breeze, so invaluable to ascending junks, had set in; but this same breeze was fatal to our further progress that day, and much to my chagrin, I shortly afterwards found the junk's head swung round and a berth for the night, in a spot on the right bank combining all *desiderata*, taken up. With their weak motive power, a very slight breeze interferes with the steering, and as, in this complicated navigation, there is danger in being caught a hair's breadth out of the proper course, a head wind, in all but the straight, clear reaches which are very few and far between, compels the downward-bound junks to anchor, or rather, seeing that anchoring is unknown in the Upper Yang-tse, to tie up to the bank in the manner described above. On this occasion we had immediately before us the dangerous right-angled turn which the river takes at Fu-chow, whereby, and also owing to the influx of the waters of the Chung-tan ho, now in flood, one of the worst whirlpools in the river is created. The rocks and the extensive sandbank directly opposite the town, upon which I noticed so many of the queer "twisted stern" junks peculiar to this place hauled up for repair, and the new ones being built, were now entirely submerged, with nothing but the curls of the whirlpools to mark the dangerous banks, which nearly extend to mid-stream. A curious characteristic of the two main affluents (and the sole navigable ones) of the Yang-tse between Chung-king and Hankow—the stream that drains the Tung-ting Lake, and this the Chung-tan ho—is that they flow in a line continuous with the course of the river below them, and appear to the ascending traveller to be the main stream itself, the river proper turning aside at right angles to its branches. At these points naturally a fierce "chow-chow" water exists, and where, as opposite Fu-chow, the land is bold and steep-to, a frowning cliff forms the point, and entirely conceals the channel, by which the traveller has to ascend, from view. The city of Fu-chow is built in the angle of the two rivers, and, rising from the water up to the steep slope of the wooded hill at its back, looks down proudly on the long ravine below, and forms a conspicuous object in the distance for hours before it is reached in the toilsome ascent. Every one of these mountain cities yields a striking and distinct picture, once seen never to be forgotten, and they would well repay the visit of an artist competent to portray them. Some such are represented in Garnier's splendid work on the exploration of the Mei-kong, and nowhere else that I know of; the wild water in the foreground, and the weird Chinese architecture, in such perfect harmony with the general landscape, form an *ensemble* as unique as it is artistic.

The spot at which we were moored is known as the "Li chêng yuen," or "Garden of undeflected gain." In mooring here, our pilot had unconsciously followed the instructions given in Admiral Ho's recently published itinerary, who, in speaking of this place, writes, " Upon arriving at Li chêng yuen, when the water is high, this is a good place to moor; should an up-wind be met with, sudden and fierce as a herd of swine, this is the time to stop; if the Fu-chow small river is in flood, it is usually impossible to proceed. At low-water time, with an up-river wind, it is also right to stop here and avoid it."

We landed and walked along the rocky shore to the city. We found the people in the suburb below the walls busily engaged in removing their houses out of the reach of the stealthily approaching flood. Entering a huge bamboo-walled godown, from which we observed steam to be issuing, we found that the building was one of the Government salt depôts, from which all the salt bales had been removed, and that the frugal-minded godown-keepers were now boiling down the sweepings and the upper stratum of the earthen floor and evaporating from them a fine jet-coloured salt. So valuable does the Government monopoly render this indispensable and usually cheap article, that although produced in the immediate neighbourhood, and even, as we saw on the way up, in the river-bed itself, salt is retailed in Szechuan at fifty cash a catty, equal to twopence a pound. In Hankow, situated midway between the " salina " of Yang-chow and the salt-wells of Szechuan, the price has risen to eighty cash, while descending the river still farther to Shanghai, which derives its supply from the neighbouring Chusan Islands, where, with the enormous junk trade, smuggling largely prevails, we find the price fallen to twenty-eight cash, or little over a penny per pound. On the other hand, in districts comparatively remote from the main lines of communication, and where the small traffic is not conducive to smuggling, the price at once increases enormously. In Hwui-chow foo, the centre of the celebrated Fu-chow tea districts, I found the price, when travelling there in 1864, to be 180 cash the catty, equal to ninepence the pound. Four years previously in Yen-chow foo, 100 miles to the south-west, the exigencies of the then raging rebellion had so advanced the *likin* or transit and *octroi* dues, that this high price was again doubled. How far this artificially high price of salt is responsible for the repulsive prevalence of skin disease, I leave it to be imagined. One effect it has, and that is to cause a large import of seaweed from the Japan Islands. Seaweed prepared in one of many fashions is eaten at almost every dinner-table in China; certainly I was present at no meal in Chung-king at which this condiment was not served. The salt gabelle is, however, one of the few important sources of revenue in the empire, and the salt commissioner in each province takes rank after the governor. A junk found smuggling salt is confiscated on the spot, and the unfortunate hulk of such an offender may occasionally be seen exposed on the bank, alongside a custom-house station, its body sawn completely in two, a witness of the inexorability of the Chinese "dazio."

Fu-chow, though an important centre of junk navigation, is of comparatively small extent, and it did not take us long to find our way through the dirty suburb to the city gate. The walls are thick and low, not over twenty feet high including the battlements; the archway of the gate would not admit a mounted horseman. The main street contains some good shops, and is thronged with traffic, through which women, bearing loads of dust-coal on their backs packed in the picturesque pei-lo of the country, jostle their way. I tried here again to purchase one of these "back baskets" peculiar to the gorge country, and which afford such a pleasing change from the eternal carrying-pole of the Chinese coolie, but in vain. No porter would part with one, and there were no shops for their sale; like most of the articles in common use in China, they are all manufactured away in the homes of the peasantry as necessity requires, and no capital is allowed to remain locked up in stock. The pei-lo are somewhat conical-shaped baskets with expanding mouths, neatly woven out of split bamboo, the shoulder-straps being of the same material, the whole fitting comfortably on the back and enabling heavy weights, up to 250 pounds, to be carried with a minimum of fatigue. Children are also largely carried in them, snugly packed in an erect position. I tried likewise to obtain a model of the extraordinary "wai pi-ku" junk used on the Kung-tan river, and induced the proprietor of a picture-shop, owned by a relative of my Chung-king companion, to undertake the commission, advancing him five dollars for the purpose. I afterwards strolled along the top of the wall, the only promenade in a Chinese town where every one of the five senses is not perpetually offended, and regaled myself with the magnificent view up the valley of the Kung-tan. This, the east wall, is built on the edge of a cliff which falls away perpendicularly to the margin of the rushing stream below; the sand-flats, together with the bamboo town and adjacent junk fleet which existed here on our voyage up, having entirely disappeared. Half of the city enclosure seemed, as usual, to be occupied with public buildings, temples, gardens, and literary monuments, whose red walls and coloured tile roofs give these cities, especially when built on a steep slope, such a gay appearance from a distance. The buildings were mostly in bad repair, and, as everywhere in these degenerate days, little used, the fine courtyards being overgrown with grass and weeds.

I tried here to find a small boat to take us on to Ichang

at once, and I was tired of the constant delays of our salt junk, and we were promised still further detentions at the Li-kin stations lower down. I was willing, too, to lose fifteen dollars to escape living another fifteen days in such close quarters with my fellow-passengers, while the privacy of a small boat would be more conducive to quiet observation of the rapids and the keeping up of my journal and sketch-book. But nothing suitable was obtainable, and we returned in the dusk to supper and another night on our salt-junk. Going ashore afterwards for a stroll with my cheroot, I entered into conversation with some of the junk-men belonging to vessels that had come down during my absence and moored near us for the night. They told me that with the up-river wind sure to prevail at this season, and the inevitable delay at the Kwei-kwan barrier, the salt-junks would not get down in less than ten days, while a "wupan" would do the journey in five. One of these had recently passed down, and would certainly moor for the night at Fu-chow; she was empty, and I should probably be able to engage her. These "wupans," or, as they are here called, "wu pa'rh" (literally, five planks: the common "sampans" or open boats of the ports being "three planks"), are the sampans of the Upper Yang-tse; they are larger and have more freeboard, and they carry a square, classically cut lug, which, together with the mast, is stowed away for the down-ward voyage. These wu pa'rh act as tenders to the big upward-bound junks—carry their tow-lines ashore, and transport their crews from bank to bank at the crossings. Although not affording much accommodation, they are eminently safe boats to travel by, their crews being familiar with every rock and eddy, while, if they do touch, their tough but elastic bottoms of hardwood (li-mu, a kind of oak) bound off again, where a laden junk comes to total grief. They are not procurable for the upward voyage, being all engaged as tenders, nor would they prove desirable for a lengthened sojourn, an arched mat amidships forming the sole protection from the weather; but for the short run down-stream, they are most handy. I have much wanted to engage one of these originally at Chung-king, but my Chinamen would not hear of it. However, I now insisted upon my companion going down to Fu-chow in the dark, and endeavouring to procure the boat. I then turned in, hoping for the best. While spreading my pu-kai (bedding of cotton quilt), one of my fellow-passengers, who slept in the next compartment, begged me to turn my bed round, and sleep with my head against the panel that divided us. As his motive was "Fêng-shui," the religion of China, I assented with a good grace. I knew it was consonant with the proprieties to sleep head to head and feet to feet, but I was not aware before that the rule applied to the occupants of adjoining cabins. My attendant, with whom I afterwards discussed the matter, remarked that Chinamen regarded propriety under all circumstances. I retorted, "Where is the propriety of observing a trifle like this, when the more urgent propriety of allowing the pilot to get a quiet night's rest is entirely disregarded?"

Next morning I was awoke from my first sleep at one a.m. by the splash of oars alongside—a welcome sound, which told me that the wupan had been secured. My friend had settled everything, and we were to start at dawn. The wupan, with its crew of six men, including the laota, who was assisted by his wife, had been hired for fifteen dollars, under guarantee to land us in Ichang in five days' time.

Our luggage and stores having been transported to the wupan, we were off again at six o'clock, and the sun had not risen ere we were round the point, and rapidly descending

Trackers hauling Junk up the Shin t'an, or New Rapid.

[*To face p.* 238.

the reach towards Fêng-tu. At this point, some 300 feet above the water, is erected the tomb of Cho-hwang, the tutor of the Emperor Tow-kwang, who ordered this fine tomb to be erected for his præceptor in his native province.

The fine weather, which had been continuous for the past two months, now at last began to break up, the prayers for rain, the fasts, and the closing of the south gates of the cities, which we had observed on our upward voyage, having been at length successful. A thick mist enveloped the summits of the hills on either side, giving breadth to the view, but promising an uncomfortable voyage in our small, ill-protected vessel. A strong head wind set in, and our crew, who had hitherto been content to let the boat drift with the current, had now to work hard at the oars in order to keep headway on her. A short, broad junk, with a long, high-roofed house, manned by a dozen rowers protected under a mat awning, well named a " pa wo'rh," or " creeping nest," that had so far kept company with us, was now compelled to bring up ; the ascending junks moored under the rocky bank were almost invisible, and we seemed to have the mighty stream—here three-quarters of a mile wide—all to ourselves. The rain now came down heavily, and the men, unprovided with the coir rain-coats which are worn on the lower river, had to come aft and couch under the mats for shelter. Meanwhile we drifted on, spinning round in the eddies in a manner that rendered me at last quite giddy. We continued this until noon, when, on approaching the dangerous reefs above Fêng-tu, we were forced at last to moor to the bank. A noticeable feature of the " Chuan river," already mentioned, is that, no matter how hard it blows, a sea is never raised, the ceaseless eddies and the ascending and descending columns of water breaking up each ripple as soon as it is formed.

Between the cities of Fu-chow and Fêng-tu, a distance of thirty-five miles, the itinerary gives a list of nine rapids and five races (tsao), in addition to an enumeration of sixteen rocks, to be carefully rounded in the ascent. In truth, there is no tranquil water anywhere in the river from Ichang upwards; it is one long, seething cauldron, which only accurate local knowledge and constant practice enable the hardy Szechuan boatmen to traverse in safety. The spot where we now moored, with our head and stern attached to loose boulders on the bank, was called the "Tsao͑ mên hsia," or "Furnace Gate Gorge," the picturesque reach immediately above Fêng-tu, as wild a spot as any on the river. The cliffs on either bank rise almost vertically for six or seven hundred feet, while behind rise conical peaks twice or three times that height, their summits now hidden in the clouds. On narrow ledges in the limestone rock, at spots one would deem barely accessible to monkeys, minute patches of barley, now being harvested, are visible; here, too, as throughout Szechuan, many of the crests are surmounted by stone battlements, built as refuges from the many wandering hordes of rebels and of unpaid troops by which this province, no less than its neighbours, has been periodically devastated. It is curious still to see painted up on the rocks here and there, in big white letters, the words, "Ho tao pu ching," *i.e.* "Waterway not clear." This does not, as might be imagined, allude to the numerous rocks, whose presence, indeed, is almost self-evident without any such notice, but to the river-pirates and petty water-thieves who still infest nearly all the inland water-courses of China, notwithstanding the numerous revenue and police cruisers constantly patrolling them. To these four words are usually added four more characters, meaning, "Small boats should anchor early." At eleven o'clock the weather cleared, although a fresh up-river breeze was still blowing. We pushed out from the shore, and drifted down the formidable "Tsan pei tan," or "Silkworm Back Rapid,"—so-called from the formation of the rock by which it is produced—and spinning through the boiling waters, taking two complete turns in the whirlpool below, which our Lao-ta informed us were *de rigueur* at this spot, we swept past Fêng-tu at four o'clock, doing in a couple of hours a distance which occupied a day on the way up. The maze of reefs, through which we then threaded our way with such painful toil, were now mostly covered, with only the roar of the surging water to indicate their presence. The danger was now much greater, none but a skilful pilot, able to take the right channel in time, being able to pass in safety. To one not familiar with the place, the danger of being swept on a rock and dashed in pieces seems appalling; only for a few moments, however. Scarcely has one had time to realize the peril, than he finds himself tranquilly drifting in the smooth water below. We passed the twin city of Fêng-tu—the one on the hill-slope, with its imposing walls enclosing a vast empty space; the other a busy trading-mart, squeezed in between the river-bank and the foot of the steep hills behind.

Below Fêng-tu is a long reach three-quarters of a mile in width, and seven or eight miles long, which terminates in one of the numerous cross ranges through which the river breaks its way, turning off suddenly at right angles, until, the obstructing range past, it takes another sharp turn in the opposite direction, and resumes its original course of E.N.E. The valley here, as throughout the whole distance above Ichang, is no wider than the river-bed. Here the left bank is also steep, with room for a few scanty patches of barley on narrow ledges here and there. The right bank, however, is composed of softer material, and its more gentle undulations admit of a rich cultivation.

R

CHAPTER XI.

HANKOW.

Return to Ichang—Hankow—Changes in the river—Lifeboats—Accidents—The "awakening" of China—Pliny on the Chinese.

THE last day of our downward journey now lay before us. The wild country of the "Yao-tsa Ho," and the long zigzag reaches of the Ichang Gorge, alone lay between us and the return to "Western civilization," as represented by the advanced guard of foreigners residing in Ichang. As we slid down rapid after rapid in the hourly increasing current, it was difficult to realize the arduous struggle we had sustained with each projecting rock in our toilsome ascent. We moored for the last night at Hwang ling Miao, the point in the upward journey that porphyry and granitic rocks are first met with; and going ashore for a stroll before sunset, I had my last look at the wild valley, with its scattered piles of huge rocks illuminated by the setting sun. This valley forms an exception to the continuous ranges of calcareous and sedimentary rocks through which the river cuts its way in its course from P'ing-shan, the highest navigable spot to the plains of Hu-peh, a distance of 800 miles. The range out of which this valley has been cut, and of which Hwang ling Miao marks the eastern termination, would seem to form the axial centre of elevation of the whole of this mountain district. On its flanks, to the east and to the west, lie the gently tilted strata of sedimentary rocks, through which the channel flows in clean-cut gorges. Here, on the other hand, the water has disintegrated the crystalline material, and left the less soluble rocks strewn around in colossal fragments. Through and past these gigantic stone-heaps the river threads its way, and, at points where the water is not visible, the valley floor exhibits nothing but a vast expanse of barren, broken rocks, while the slopes beyond are gleaming in their rich spring verdure. Tedious work it is for the ascending junks, as the unfortunate trackers toil painfully over the successive headlands composed of angular rock fragments. Numerous lifeboats are stationed here, as in all the dangerous parts of the river.

Hurrying down through the Ichang Gorge, the scenery as we approached the city seemed tame to a degree, after the grand country we had just been traversing. The only interesting object is the "Ko tao shan," "Mount of the Taoist (hermit) Ko," which, seen from this aspect, looked like a perfect pyramid, of the same shape and size as that of Cheops. It is this pyramid which forms the bane of the Ichang Fêng-shui, and which the good people of Ichang are now spending myriads of taels to counteract.

The river, now in early May, had risen sufficiently to allow of the steamer *Kiangtung*, of the China Merchants' Company, making her first voyage of the season, and in her I returned to Hankow, making in thirty-six hours the voyage which had occupied nearly a month in the ascent. Below Ichang the river was nearly bank-full, and the roofs of the houses were just visible behind the big embankments, much reminding one of Holland and of Dutch scenery generally.

Hankow, at which my voyage terminated, is situated 600 nautical miles from the mouth, and the river here is nearly a mile wide, the depth of water such that the largest ocean-steamers come up every summer to load tea. This great inland mart is built on a mud-flat situated at the point of junction of the great 'Han river, which is navigable some five hundred miles to the north-west, and the Yang-tse. The name Hankow means "Han mouth." This spot is the centre of a great plain of alluvium, interspersed with steep, rocky, island-like hills, and from the summit of one of these, which is situated in Han-yang—as the town on the opposite side of the Han is called—a fine view is to be had over the three united cities of Wuchang, Hanyang, and Hankow. The celebrated Abbé Huc, who passed through long before the country had been depopulated by the great rebellion, credits the three towns together with a population of 5,000,000. To-day possibly the whole may amount to 1,000,000—certainly not more. The spot is said to owe its prosperity to its curiously auspicious site. Here the dragon, the snake, and the tortoise are all represented, and join in perfect harmony to perfect the Fêng-shui. North of the river, the steep hill of Hanyang forms the tortoise, a projecting rock, which juts out into the river at its foot, being the head. On the head of the tortoise is built a handsome three-storied temple, which serves to fix the tortoise to the spot, where his protruding nose arrests the downward current, making a backwater below it, and thus obviating the possibly too rapid removal of the wealth brought down from above. On the opposite shore the folds of a gigantic snake may be traced twisting in graceful curves through the walled city of Wuchang; his tail rests on the level ground beyond the south wall, and is retained there by a pagoda placed on its tip; his snout protrudes slightly into the river in a rocky point, which faces the tortoise head, and has likewise its corresponding eddy behind it. This rock had its surmounting pavilion, the famous Hoa Hoa Lo, a substantial four-storied tower standing on a forest of high wooden pillars, and said to date from the Ming dynasty. Lamentable to narrate, this tower, the most conspicuous and picturesque object in the view across the river from the English bund, was (in 1884) utterly destroyed by fire, and this untoward disturbance of the snake will, it is feared, produce results disastrous to the three cities. Already, in the following winter, an enormous sandbank, over a mile in length, rose up in a few days, and the deep water off the Hankow bund suddenly became dry land. This land extended nearly halfway across the river, and was rapidly covered with temporary shops for the supply of the wants of the passing junk population, while the foreign steamers, which had previously discharged their cargoes alongside the bund (a fine stone quay fifty feet in height), had to anchor half a mile away. Fortunately for the port, however, this bank was cut away again by the current in the following year. The river water being so highly charged with sedimentary matter, it is only necessary to put some impediment in the way of the current, such as will produce still water, to insure a deposition of the silt, which in a short time will assume vast dimensions. In this instance, a freshet in the Han, meeting the main stream at right angles, acted as a dam, and caused this bank to form below it.

The Yang-tse lifeboats are the only honest Government organization I have ever met with in China. They were set out in their present form, and stationed at each dangerous spot all the way from Ichang to Chung-king, by one "Admiral" Ho, who has his head-quarters at Ichang, and is responsible for the police of the great waterway, and the protection of the numerous travellers on it from its many dangers. Of these, in his well-arranged, illustrated "Yang-tse Pilot," or, as it is literally entitled, "Vade mecum to Szechuan," Admiral Ho enumerates about a thousand, and adds directions how they may best be avoided. The lifeboat service was recently (in 1883) instrumental in rescuing one of our consuls, Mr. Christopher Gardner, who was wrecked in the Ching T'an; and it is a pity that our Government did not give the indefatigable boatmen there stationed some official acknowledgment of their action, as I believe it would have been highly valued. The sailors only receive about sixpence a day wages, but are rewarded by 1000 cash for every life saved, and by 800 cash for every corpse—irrespective whether it be male or female—so the lifeboat regulations state. The boats are very strongly built, of great beam, and, with their varnished sides and gaily uniformed crew, are remarkably smart-looking. They are constantly cruising round and round—up the eddies and down the rapids, keenly on the look-out for a disaster.

Although accidents are not infrequent, yet in proportion to the vast traffic their number can hardly be deemed excessive. Careful inquiries, made during my residence at Ichang, have led me to the conclusion that the loss of junks and merchandise in the rapids between Ichang and Chungking amounts to about four per cent. of the value of the traffic.* This includes the damage by water to goods afterwards salved, which form by far the larger proportion of the losses. The loss of life is not large, as the junks, after striking a rock, generally succeed in safely reaching

* The new rapid at Yünyang (formed by a landslip in September, 1896) has since doubled this risk.

the shore in the tranquil bights below the rapids. Of the value of accurate statistics, the Chinese have not the slightest idea, and hence it is impossible to speak accurately on this or any other point in China where numbers are in any way concerned. However, one thing is certain—there is no insurance among the Chinese, so that the losses, when they do occur, are often ruinous. Hence there is little doubt that steamers would be welcomed by the merchants, and that, were a line once running to Chung-king, the uninsurable junks would be gradually abandoned; then, with reduced freights, and the regularity of steam, the Szechuan people would ship to the east their varied and inexhaustible supplies of produce in largely increased quantity, thus enabling them materially to augment their purchases of foreign manufactures in return. The junks would soon find compensation in the increased traffic that steamers on the main river would bring to its numerous and extensive affluents. This has proved itself in a remarkable manner on the Lower Yang-tse. Since Hankow was thrown open to steamers in 1860, the direct traffic has increased until now it employs a daily steamer of 2000 tons, and nine-tenths of the traffic between that port and Shanghai is now carried on by steam; yet there are more junks on the river than ever. These are engaged in transhipping produce landed by the steamers at the seven river ports—to which steamers are at present confined—to remoter districts, accessible by means of the numerous lakes and large river systems communicating with the Yang-tse.

Judging by recent articles in the London press, it seems to be believed at home that the Chinese are turning over a new leaf, and welcoming Western progress. My own experience is that the desire of the officials to avail themselves of our superior mechanical appliances is confined to implements of war. " Let us avail ourselves of our enforced intercourse with the barbarians in order to keep them out!" is the burden of the great patriot, Tseng Kwo-Fan's memorial to the throne, submitted shortly before his death. This is but natural: with half a dozen hungry nations knocking at their doors, and the fate of Turkey and Egypt before them, the Chinese are at their wits' ends to devise a means to retain their antiquated civilization whole and uncontaminated from the upstart barbarian. It is a hopeless task, but one cannot help sympathizing with them. Their talent, in the shape of natural resources as great as those of the United States, lies buried and undeveloped, and they will be forced to give an account of it. Tseng Kwo-Fan has been canonized, and the temple built by the Emperor in honour of his names stands on a hill in Wu-chang, the scene of his labours in the flesh. The Marquis Tseng, late ambassador in England, was his eldest son. Railways, which we are all so anxiously waiting for, have been commenced tentatively with their own resources; but the large networks, now planned, are to be carried out with the aid of foreign experience, and with foreign capital. The destruction of the little railroad that ran from Shanghai to Woosung, in 1874, is an instance of the dogged resistance the officials make to any innovation too forcibly pressed upon them. The Chinese people themselves were delighted with this experimental railway of ten miles length, which united Shanghai to its port of Woosung, and the trains were crowded as long as they were allowed to run.* The local authorities had of course given their consent, but the central Government had never been consulted. Sir Thomas Wade, unwisely in my opinion, allowed the Peking officials to purchase the line,

* This line has now (October, 1898) been rebuilt, and its opening just reported.

thinking they would then work it themselves. He did not understand the Chinese. No sooner bought, than the line was pulled up and thrown into the sea, and Shanghai, the commercial capital of China—built up as it has been by foreign enterprise—is still dependent upon house-boats and a few steam-launches for communication with its port of Woosung, distant by water fourteen miles. The road (of nine miles) on which the rails were laid, and which for a time was used for a driving road, has been allowed to decay, and communication has again reverted to the old footpaths. A crucial test of the feeling in the Chinese bureaucracy, in the face of foreign innovations, is exhibited in their attitude towards the Shanghai Waterworks. Alongside the magnificent foreign settlement of Shanghai, with its fine, wide, well-kept streets, its grand quays and avenues of shade-trees, its water, gas and electric light, stands the inexpressibly dirty native city. The natives themselves fully appreciate the difference, for, notwithstanding the high municipal taxation and the despotic foreign rule of the "settlement," they have flocked in to the land set apart for foreigners in such numbers (about 250,000) that their presence has become a nuisance to all of the European residents, except to the landowners, whose rents have enormously increased in consequence. Meanwhile, the high Chinese officials, to whom the contrast is a bitter eyesore, sulk behind their crumbling walls; and when the Waterworks Company apply for leave to confer the boon of a pure water supply on the native city, will have none of it until such time as they shall be able to do the work themselves and in their own way.

I have not space to enter on a disquisition on the motives, many worthy of respect, which induce this thorough-going conservatism. On the river, they dread the army of trackers being thrown out of work; while their traditional objection to mining, and indeed to every industry but agriculture, prevents the superabundant population finding employment in the many new enterprises which steam communication would inevitably open up, were the restrictions that now forbid all enterprises of the kind freely removed.

I have often twitted the Chinese officials at Ichang upon our having to import the coal for our steamers all the way from Japan and 1000 miles up the Yang-tse river, when Ichang lies upon the border of the largest and easiest accessible coal-field in the world (Richthofen). Yet such is the fact. No foreigner is allowed to have anything to do with mines, and even the natives are discouraged from mining on a large scale owing to the dread the mandarins have to any assemblage of unruly men, such as miners are supposed to be. Thus the mineral wealth of the great West lies undeveloped, while thousands of able-bodied men go about begging their bread. Nor are there any signs of a change in the immediate future. Were it otherwise, the masses, who earn a bare subsistence by serving as beasts of burden, would have more elevating occupations opened out for them, and might be earning decent wages, while adding to the general prosperity of their native land.

Returned once more to the comforts and amenities of our European civilization after a three months' absence amongst the Chinese proper, I was mostly struck by the total absence of all change, and by the intense stagnation of this peculiar people. Such as the Ser Marco Polo describes them, such are they to-day. Indeed, we may go back ten centuries further—to the time of Pliny—and find them described by the same characteristics; and for this reason I will conclude by quoting Pliny's words, which are as much to the point now as they were on the day they were written (Pliny, "Ammian." i. 23, c. 6) :—

Pliny's Account of China 251

"Seres mites quidem, sed et ipsis feris persimiles, cœtus reliquorum mortalium fugiunt, commercia expectant.

"Agunt ipsi quietius Seres, armorum semper et prœliorum expertes, utque hominibus sedatis et placidis otium est voluptabile, nulli finitimorum molesti.

"Cœli apud eos jocunda, salubrisque temperies, æris facies munda, leniumque ventorum commodissimus flatus : et abunde silvæ sublucidæ, a quibus arborum fetus aquarum asperginibus crebris velut quædam vellera molientes, ex lanugine et liquore mixtam subilitatem tenerrimam pectunt, nentesque subtemina conficiunt sericum, ad usus antehac nobilium, nunc etiam infimorum sine ulla discretione proficiens.

"Nec minus celebres tenuissimis lanis, quas ex arboribus suæ regiones collectas, conficiendis pretiosis vestibus in omnes terræ partes mittere solebant."

"The Chinese, though of mild disposition, yet having something of the brute nature, avoid intercourse with other mortals, but yet are ready to trade and barter.

"The Chinese live quietly, always keeping clear of arms and warfare, and as peaceful and quiet men are fond of repose, they cause their neighbours no trouble.

"They have a pleasant, healthy climate ; a clear atmosphere ; gentle, favourable winds ; in very many places dusky woods (of mulberry-trees), from which, working the fleecy produce of the trees with frequent sprinklings of water, they comb off a very delicate and fine substance—a mixture of the down and moisture—and sprinkling the thread of it they make silk, which was formerly only used by the nobles, but now by the lowest classes without any distinction.

"Nor are they less celebrated for a most delicate wool (cotton), which they collect from the trees in their own country, and send to all parts of the world to be made into costly garments."

Excepting in the account of the manufacture of silk, about which the ancients held very hazy notions, it is remarkable to find them in possession of so much accurate knowledge of this remote nation. Their peculiar aversion to war and love of ease notwithstanding, the Chinese have suffered more disastrously from internal convulsions and disastrous wars than almost any people in history. Their history seems to prove the fact that, for nations as for individuals, the worst way to obtain peace and quietness is to ostensibly seek it.

As an instance of their unwarlike (and Christian) disposition, and of their devotion to appearances above everything, Captain Hall, of the famous *Nemesis*, the first steamer that rounded the Cape, tells a good story of our first war with China, in 1839. Told off to take a fort below Canton, he moored his ship off the place until the Chinese commandant came off in his barge to call on the strange fire-ship. In his silks and satins he was assisted up the gangway and taken to the captain's room; the portly Chinaman turned out to be an ex-compradore who had been given the post as a potential barbarian tamer, or, at least, familiar with his wiles. Upon the British captain giving him the unpleasing information that the ship had been sent to demand the surrender of the fort, or, failing this, to capture it by force, the Chinese commandant remarked that if he surrendered he would lose his head. The captain replied expressing his sorrow to be compelled in that case to open fire at daylight next morning. The Chinaman calmly replied: "All right; you along my belong good flen; you no puttee pillee, my no puttee pillee; bimeby you come ashore, my pay you fort; so fashion no lose face, no spoilem man." * And the fort was honestly handed over on the following day.

* "All right, you are my good friend; neither side need shot their guns; then you land and I will surrender the fort; thus appearances will be saved and no one hurt."

City of Chung-king, built on Rocky Peninsula at Junction of Kia-ling River, from the North and Yang-tse:
View taken from South Bank of Yang-tse.

[*To face p.* 232.

CHAPTER XII.

THE PHYSIOGRAPHY OF THE YANG-TSE VALLEY.

Length and fall—Advance of the delta—Direction of river's course—The gorges and rapids—Absence of roads—Coal-fields—The flora and fauna—Mineral wealth.

THE Yang-tse River, which is known to the Chinese as the "Kiang," *i.e.* "The River" *par excellence*, the "Chang Kiang," or the "Long River," and more commonly still as the "Ta Kiang," or "Great River," has a course of about 3000 miles in length. It traverses the country from west to east, and may be said to divide the Chinese Empire into two nearly equal portions,—eight provinces being situated on its left bank, with the same number on the south: two only, Ngan-hui and Kiang-su, lying partly on both banks. For two-thirds of this distance, it runs through mountain land in a continuous ravine, the valley being nowhere wider than the river-bed. In the lower portion of its course, which forms the remaining third of the distance, the valley widens out, and the stream flows through an alluvial plain, following generally the southern boundary of the valley, except where it forces its way athwart the limestone range, which forms the division between the provinces of Hu-peh and Kiang-si, above the port of Kiu-kiang, past the vertical cliffs called Split Hill and Cock's Head in our

English charts, until it emerges into its delta proper at Kiang-yin, 110 miles above the mouth of its estuary at Yang-tse Cape. The stream leaves the mountains at the Ichang Gorge, 960 nautical miles from its mouth; and some fifty miles below this point the boulders and gravel of the Upper River give place to banks of soft alluvium, the outline of which varies every season, notwithstanding the gigantic embankments with which it is sought to retain the stream in its channel. These begin a short distance above the great emporium of Shasze, situated in the midst of the Hu-peh plain, eighty-three miles below Ichang. This, by the way, is one of the important towns, with which we were debarred from trading, although it is regularly passed by our steamers on their voyages between the so-called open ports, until the Japanese forced it open, in reality as well as in name, by the Simonoseki treaty. Shasze has at least ten times the trade of Ichang. Here we find the river, at the time of its summer floods, running with a six-knot current at a level of ten or fifteen feet above that of the surrounding country, the great dyke on the north bank being continuous nearly to Hankow; while owing to the decay of the embankments the south bank is open to the floods as far as the eye can reach, a vast inland sea is then formed, which mingles its waters with those of the Tung-ting Lake proper, from which its outline is indistinguishable. From this point downwards the fall in the bed is comparatively slight.

A comparison of three years' simultaneous barometrical readings at Chung-king (in Szechuan) and Sikawei (the Jesuit observatory near Shanghai), and the *résumé* of some 4000 observations enumerated in Mr. Baber's paper on the subject, exhibit the almost incredibly small difference of level between the two places of 630 feet. Now, as the average rate of the current down the rapids, which, large and small, obstruct the river throughout the whole distance of nearly 500 nautical miles between Chung-king and Ichang, is not less than five knots, a fall of twelve inches to the mile between these two places cannot be considered excessive. This would give a total of 500 as the fall for these 500 miles, leaving only 130 feet for the 960 miles between Ichang and the sea. The great fall in the river-bed is, as is only natural, in the upper half of its course, where the stream rushes as an unnavigable mountain torrent through the defiles of the almost impenetrable ranges of Western Szechuan and Thibet, and where Mr. Baber estimates the fall at not less than six feet to the mile. The average speed of the comparatively more tranquil lower half of the river's current, say from Ping-shan, the city situated at the head of the present junk navigation, some 1700 nautical miles from the sea, is still, as Captain Blakiston points out, double that of the Nile and Amazon, and three times that of the Ganges.

The volume of water brought down per second, as measured by the same observer, is, at Ichang in June, 675,800 cubic feet: that at Hankow at the same period, according to Dr. Guppy, of H.M.S. *Hornet*, being nearly 1,000,000 cubic feet, the increase being due to the influx from the Tung-ting Lake, and from the Han River, the only true affluents between these two points. Compared with these figures, it is curious to note that the water discharged into the sea by the old familiar Thames is estimated at 2300 cubic feet per second. Reducing the figures given by Captain Blakiston for Ichang in June, to the average of the whole year, on the basis of Dr. Guppy's monthly observations in Hankow, we find the discharge at the former port to be actually 560,000 feet per second for the whole year round, which would make the volume of water at Ichang,

960 miles from the sea, just 244 times that of the Thames at London.

The comparison of the sediment, annually brought down by the respective rivers at these two points, is as 2,000,000 cubic feet to 5,000,000,000, or as 1 to 2500. Taking the drainage area of the Yang-tse at 600,000 square miles, and estimating the sediment discharge as above, both Captain Blakiston's and Dr. Guppy's figures give a rate of subaerial denudation for the whole catchment basin, of about one foot in 3000 years. Estimating four-fifths of this amount of sediment as employed in raising the banks and filling up the expanse of its inferior valley while inundated by the summer floods, the remaining one-fifth is sufficient to create annually a fresh island in the Pacific one mile square, and fifty fathoms deep. The rapid rate at which the coast-line is gaining on the ocean, startling ocular evidence of which is presented to every old resident of Shanghai, is thus not surprising. In the very near future the innumerable rocky islands, which fringe the coast, and which now stand out of the shallow muddy waters of the estuary, will look down upon embanked paddy fields, precisely as the hills inland from Shanghai now stand out from the fields, which have been raised by the same process in recent geological times.

It seems to me a matter of no doubt, that in quite recent times the Yang-tse River, upon leaving the mountains, discharged its waters into the ocean through a series of lakes, the remains of which still occupy a considerable portion of the valley in winter, and which in summer are enlarged by the floods to almost their original surface area. The first of these lakes is comprised within the boundaries of the present province of Hu-peh, and at the highest floods, which occur every eighth or tenth year, making sport of the numberless huge embankments, the whole country is covered to the depth of several feet; a vast inland sea is formed in the centre of China, a few tree-tops, and roofs of houses still standing, alone breaking the boundless water horizon. When we see that each summer nearly half an inch of sediment is deposited, and the level of the surrounding country raised each year to that extent, we cannot help being struck with the fact that there must have been a vast lake bottom to fill,—seeing that the soil set free by the erosion of the Szechuan watercourses to a level many hundred feet below that of the original plain has failed even now entirely to fill it up. Another striking fact is the very recent formation of the existing landscape. In short—*China, the oldest country politically, is geologically one of the newest.* This fact applies more especially to Central and Northern China, within which were comprised, until recently, the limits of the Chinese Empire. A few years more, geologically speaking, and this and the other lake basins will be entirely filled, and the whole sediment brought down will be available for promoting the advance of the coast-line, an advance even now so rapid that within the lifetime of men now living Shanghai threatens to be left an inland city unapproachable by tidal waters. This first lake is formed by the damming-up of the river seawards by the Wusuch range of hills, and is drained into the next lower basins, that of the Nganhui province, by a comparatively confined channel through which the river flows with a rapid current—much as the Detroit River drains Lake Huron into Lake Erie.

The next lake bed, I take to be represented by the plain north of Kiukiang, and the valley west of Nganking together with the Poyang Lake region: this is again bounded seawards by a cross range, through which the river has burst its way, in the narrow winding rock-infested channel known

s

as "Hen point." Below this, again, we have the wide plain, of which Wu-hu forms the centre, the eastern outlet of which is through the gate of "the Pillars." We then come to Nanking, to the south of which now stretches a large alluvial plain, the lower portion of which is still, for a considerable period of the year, below the level of the river, and which apparently formerly, in connection with the Tai-Hu ("Great Lake") of Kiangnan, formed part of the ancient estuary of the Yang-tse, at the time when the river here turned southward and debouched into the Hang-chow Bay. At present we find these ancient lakes practically filled up, being ourselves only just in time to see the finishing touches given by the annual summer floods to the land that now occupies their site. Formerly the bulk of the sediment was arrested in these lakes, and the turn of the delta had not yet come. At the same time, however, we have no reason to expect that, as the banks become thus rapidly raised, the floods will soon cease altogether, natural as this result would at first sight seem to be: for the bed of the river must be rising simultaneously in the ratio of its extension seawards, and thus higher banks are constantly needed.

Marco Polo, 600 years ago, in his chapter on the "Great River Kian," says, "It is in some places ten miles wide, in others eight, in others six, and it is more than 100 days' journey in length from one end to the other,—it seems, indeed, more like a sea than a river." Now if, as is probable, Marco visited the river during the summer floods, there is no exaggeration whatever in these statements, and it is curious to find Colonel Yule criticizing this passage as exaggerated, and giving as a probable explanation, the suggestion that Marco's expressions about the river were accompanied by a mental reference to the term "Dalai," the sea, which the Mongols appear to have given to the river.

We thus ascend by a series of wide steps, well described by the Chinese as "Men-ka'rh," or thresholds, and over each of which flows one of the famous rapids—"effrayantes cataractes," as they are termed by the worthy Père Amand David, the celebrated naturalist—but at the same time rapids amenable to steam power in the opinion of the few other Europeans who have ascended them. These steps lead us by way of the great gorges, cut through the limestone ranges, which bound Szechuan on the east and shut in its basin from the wide plain of "Hukwang" (Hu-peh), the province of "Broad Lakes," which begins in the level country immediately below Ichang.

If we turn to a map of Indo-China, we are at once struck with a peculiarity in the Yang-tse, as distinguished from the other great rivers, which, together with it, take their rise in the eastern edge of the Thibetan plateau. Four rivers, the Yang-tse, the Salween, the Meikong, and the Irrawaddy, here start seawards. All four in the early part of their courses flow together in deep parallel ravines running north and south, but the three latter alone continue to follow the prevailing lay of the mountain ranges, and persevere in their southward course to the Indian Ocean and Cochin China Sea. The Yang-tse or the Murui-Ussu (Blue Water), as the river is designated by the Thibetans, and which is called lower down, where it flows through Western Szechuan, "Kin-sha Kiang," *i.e.* "Gold-dust River" by the Chinese,— behaves differently. After accompanying its less vigorous neighbours down through nearly ten degrees of latitude, upon reaching the vicinity of Talifu in Yünnan, it suddenly recurves northward, abandons its associates, and strikes out a course of its own, athwart transverse rows of mountain barriers, which fail to turn it aside from its steady progress to the Eastern Sea. Owing to the circumstance of its course being thus mainly in a direction transverse to the higher ranges traversed by it, we find its channel thence down to the point of its emergence in the plains of Hu-peh, to be a series of zigzags, consisting of a succession of reaches running at right angles to each other alternately S.W. and N.E., and N.W. and S.E. In the former it runs in comparatively open ravines, parallel to the radial axes of the mountains enclosing it; in the latter it breaks through them in the magnificent clefts of the gorges. The strata in these latter are for the most part horizontal, or only slightly inclined, and it would appear that they are in part natural splits in the rock, and in part gorges, formed purely by erosion like that below the falls of Niagara. In some of the gorges, and these spots naturally afford the most striking views, the split takes a sharp rectangular turn such as is only likely to occur in horizontal strata with vertical cleavage, the absence of more extended denudation being very striking and giving, I should say, unmistakable proof of their comparatively recent origin. The confused mountain mass, which separates Hu-peh from Szechuan, commences a short distance below Ichang, and extends to the city of Kwei-chow, a distance of nearly 150 miles from east to west. The radial axis of elevation appears to be a mass of igneous rock, chiefly gneiss, traversed by dykes of porphyry in vertical strata. These rocks have not been cut through, but have been decomposed by the water, and their *débris* now tower in Brobdingnagian stone-heaps, filling up the desert-looking valley, which breaks the continuity of the grand limestone gorges of Ichang and Nui-kan (Lukan of Blakiston). The difficult piece of river, which rushes on amidst these rock-piles, is known to the native boatmen as the "Yao-tsa Ho." This basin of the Yao-tsa Ho is to-day a wide depression, filled with low scattered rock-piles, in the midst of a surrounding mass of lofty precipitous limestone mountains which lie on its flanks at a very gentle inclination. These extend eastwards to the mouth of the Ichang gorge, dipping under the sandstone and coarse conglomerate which form the outlying spurs of the range. The city of Ichang stands upon this conglomerate, which, with its superincumbent sandstone, dips in its turn under, and is lost in the alluvial plain, which begins about fifty miles further down. West of the "Yao-tsa Ho" basin we again traverse the limestone until, on the other side, it meets and is lost under the new red sandstone plateau of Szechuan. As we ascend the river further, we meet, however, with fresh cross ranges of the same limestone formation, upon the flanks of which the inexhaustible coal seams of the province lie conveniently tilted.

Above and beyond Kwei-chow fu we enter the red basin of Richthofen, where the river traverses the vast new sandstone formation of Eastern Szechuan in a ravine cut down 1000 feet or more below the surface. Here, owing to the softer nature of the rock, the rapids are less violent, although we have always a fierce current to contend against. These conditions prevail until we reach the fork of the Yang-tse at Su-chow,* where on the one hand we meet the "Kin-sha" River, flowing as a mountain torrent through inaccessible gorges, and on the other the "Min," which, though the smaller stream, appears to be regarded by the Chinese as the true "Kiang"—probably in view of its greater navigability, while the Kin-sha sweeps round the Mountains of the Sun, inhabited by the wild Lolo tribes, and is useless for traffic. By the fork of the Min River we ascend in light-draft boats

* Not to be confounded with Soochow, near Shanghai.

to the unique plateau of Chêng-tu, the political capital of the province. This plateau is our next step up from Chung-king, and lies another 600 feet higher. Beyond this plain, famous for its fertility and elaborate system of irrigation, which spreads in a north-westerly and south-westerly direction, ninety miles in length by forty in width, the mountains on the west (the nearest conspicuous peak of which is the famous, sacred, temple-covered O-shan, or Mount Omi) rise rapidly to a height of 22,000 feet and upwards, and form the eastern bulwarks of the great Thibetan plateau beyond. This alluvial plain of Chêng-tu, through which now flows a network of clear streams with gravelly beds, appears once to have been a lake whose basin was gradually filled with the boulders and coarser detritus from these western mountains. Below this we have evidence of the great inland sea, that probably in tertiary times occupied the now rugged country of Eastern Szechuan, and in which the coal measures with the superincumbent sandstones, of which the surface is now composed, were deposited. At a subsequent period, as the land rose, the surface of the former sea-bed must have been gradually exposed to denudation, and the channels of the present rivers began to be cut out; and if, as seems probable, a dam then existed on the eastern borders of the sea, it had not been broken through, nor had the gorges through which the water subsequently escaped seawards then been opened. Through and across this sandstone plain run, at wide intervals, a succession of parallel ranges of limestone mountains, all tending more or less in a north-north-east and south-south-west direction, and rising to a height of two to three thousand feet above the sea, forming the "cross ranges" through which the Yang-tse and its affluents now break their way in a series of magnificent gorges. The intervening plateaux, originally level, except where tilted up against the flanks of these "cross ranges," have since been worn away by erosion into a fantastically rugged landscape, recalling the picturesque scenery of the Saxon Switzerland, but on a grander scale. Every stream, large and small, has cut its way down and flows in a steep ravine. Hence the land-roads are nothing but the usual narrow footpaths broken by a succession of ascending and descending stone staircases, up and down which the sturdy little Kwei-chow ponies scamper with astonishing nonchalance. It is in spots where these sandstone cliffs overhang the streams, that we find the numerous square porthole-looking entrances to the dwellings of the aboriginal inhabitants of the country, who are spoken of by the modern inhabitants of the province as "Mantse." Coal underlies the whole formation, and is exposed at the surface in the gorges of the Yang-tse and its affluents, where these cut through the cross ranges. It is largely mined by the primitive Chinese methods, and forms the staple fuel of the country; the junks at the upper waters all have their brick chimney, and at meal times, when vomiting the soft-coal-smoke, have all the appearance of primitive steamers.

The limestone mountains of the great gorges are equally cut by ravines splitting them up in every direction. Each little stream has cut out its gorge, often more picturesque, though perhaps less imposing, than those of the Great River with its rocks and rapids. Up these side glens there is no other path than the bed of the stream, which has to be perpetually crossed and recrossed on slippery stepping-stones. The vegetation is most luxuriant, the country being well-watered, and the limestone *débris* affording a most favourable soil. Apart from the ferns, which, as might be expected, are found in endless variety, flowering plants, many of which have hitherto been credited alone to Japan, cover the rocks in dazzling profusion. A few of the most common to be met with in a day's walk up any of the glens are : camellia, rose, larkspur, Chinese daisy (*Boltonia Indica*), begonia, sunflower, virgin lily, bignonia, wistaria, lavender, gardenia, honeysuckle, yellow jasmine, orange lily, besides many others equally beautiful, which have no common English names. The cottage gardens abound with pomegranates, loquats, peaches, plums, orange and other fruit-trees. On the higher slopes, above the precipices, we find glorious woods of walnut and chestnut-trees, while the useful tallow-tree, with its beautiful tinted foliage and exuberant scented blossom, grows everywhere. This tree is the *Excalcaria Sebifera* of Mueller, and is known in Szechuan as the " Chuan tse" shu (tree), and in Hu-peh as the " Mu tse" shu.

Fine forest-trees universal in Szechuan, and which are to be found surrounding almost every village, are :—

"Nan mu" (Wood of the South) or literally, "South wood," a red hard-wood, used for the pillars of houses, *Persea namu oliv.*, now referred to the genus machilus.

"T'an mu," yielding a close-grained hard-wood employed for rammers, in the ubiquitous oil-presses, probably a species of *Dalbergia*. (For this and the following botanical names I am indebted to Dr. Henry, of the Imperial Maritime Customs, an indefatigable observer.)

" Chou mu," an oak with white wood.

"Li mu," a kind of oak, very tough and elastic, the planking of which is much sought after for boats navigating these rock-infested streams.

"Sung mu" (*Pinus massoniana*).

" Peh mu " (*Cupressus funebris*).

"Sha mu" (*Cunninghames sinensis*), a tree of great beauty and excellent for planking.

Then we have three kinds of "Tung" tree—all widely spread.

"Wu t'ung" (*Sterculia platinifolia*).

"Pao t'ung" (*Paulonia imperialis*).

And lastly, the

"T'ung tse" (*Aleurites cordata M.*). This is the celebrated wood-oil tree, the produce of which is in use all over China for houses, boats, and furniture, and a most excellent oil it is. The junk-men employ nothing else on their vessels but a coating of this oil, rubbed on by the hand at the annual overhaul in the dry winter season, and thus preserve them free from rot and fit for use for literally an indefinite period. *This tree is well worth the attention of the Indian authorities*, and ought long ere this to have been introduced into British India. It must not be confounded with the

"Ch'i shu" (*Rhus vernifera*), the likewise most valuable varnish-tree.

The commonest tree, seen everywhere along the banks of the Great River and its subsidiary streams, is the "Liu shu" of Hu-peh, or the "Ma liu" of Szechuan, often translated by foreigners "willow-tree," which it is not, but *Pterocarpa stenoptera*.

Two soap-trees are remarkable as furnishing an article of export to Eastern China in the shape of the seed-pods, which, after being dried in the sun, are used just as they are, in lieu of cakes of soap, for washing. There are two principal varieties, viz. :—

1. The commoner—short red pods and very fine delicate acacia-like foliage (*Gymnocladus sinensis*).

2. With long, flat, black pods (*Gleditschia sinensis*).

Evergreens of all kinds abound, as might be expected in 30° northern latitude. I will only mention the "Hoang kŏ," which, with its exuberant dark-green foliage, is a great ornament to the country, and a magnificent shade-tree to the tired traveller. It is in special favour as a decoration to shrines. It is known to botanists as *Ficus infectoria*. It is of the fig genus, but a casual observer might easily mistake it for a banyan. As an adornment to shrines its place is taken up in Hu-peh by the "Tung-ch'ing" (*Xylosma japonica S. and Z.*), a laurel-like tree, with rich scented blossom. Nor must I omit the holly, and the "La shu" (*Ligustrum lucidum*) among my list of common evergreens.

With so rich a flora, and such abundance of flowers and fruit, a corresponding richness in the insect world and in the fauna generally might be expected. I must refer those more specially interested to Amand David, and go on simply enumerating what struck me most as a passing traveller. Gorgeous butterflies; fireflies, the most brilliant I have ever seen; small birds innumerable, notwithstanding the numerous kites and eagles (in Chinese, "Ai ying," cliff hawk), the commonest of which are the golden oriole (*Urocina sinensis*), and the blue jays and the ubiquitous swallows. Two kinds of little rock-tits with red tails—one of them with a white top-knot, hop about the rocks by the water's edge. Back in the mountains are the golden (who seldom come below 5000 feet), the silver, and Reeves' pheasants, the former of which I only saw exhibited in cages for sale, while the latter's tail feathers are used everywhere to decorate hats on the stage. These Reeves' pheasants especially affect the conglomerate mountains opposite Ichang, where several have been bagged by European sportsmen. Thrushes and minas are also common, and the cormorant, which, as well as the tame otter, is everywhere employed in fishing. Of mammalia one sees little beyond the domesticated ox, pig, goat, and dog—the latter as great a nuisance to the stranger in Szechuan as he is elsewhere. One hears much of the leopards which come down from the mountains in the night, and rob the pigstyes;

and of the monkeys, flocks of which attack the maize-patches on the high hill-slopes in the early dawn. The more precipitous peaks are the home of the "Shan-yang" (mountain-goat), a sort of chamois: one or two specimens have been shot by adventurous sportsmen, but none have yet been bagged.

The fish in Szechuan are small, scarce, and consequently dear. The rapid sand-laden currents and rocky beds of the rivers are unfavourable to their growth, and in this respect, as in many others, the Upper Yang-tse presents a marked contrast to the Lower River. The distinction is sharply drawn at the foot of the Ichang Gorge. While in the Upper River no large fish are known to exist, here in the Ichang reach, shoals of porpoises may be daily seen disporting themselves in the clear water, which is the characteristic of the rainless winter months; immense sturgeon are occasionally caught, and, as is well known, the river swarms with fish of every description, up to saurians even; small alligators (*Alligator sinensis*) infest the lower reaches and the adjoining creeks, being occasionally caught in the Wang-pu off the Shanghai settlement.

As for the cereals and economical productions of Szechuan, are they not described at length in the voluminous reports from our consular residents, buried in those little-read, but most valuable productions, the Blue-books? Suffice it to say that nearly every food-crop, including sugar and not excepting opium, flourishes in Szechuan, besides an inexhaustible supply of drugs, huge junk-loads of which are despatched from Chung-king throughout the season, to enrich the drug stores and destroy the stomachs of their customers, the dyspeptic, well-to-do classes. From the millet-straw is plaited the finest straw braid in the world. Tobacco of excellent flavour, though strong, is grown everywhere; it is rolled up like cigars and smoked in pipes, every smoker carrying the wrapper and fillings in his pouch. With the exception of cotton, everything that grows in Eastern China grows better in Szechuan: its mountains may be regarded as the easternmost prolongation of the Himalayas, and certainly its tea partakes very decidedly of the Assam character.

Szechuan possesses an area almost exactly equivalent to that of France; an even superior climate; a far larger population, equally industrious and thrifty; a land delightfully *accidentée*, and cultivatable to its highest slopes. Many volumes might be written on the productions of this splendid province, but the exigencies of space have compelled me to limit myself to this rapid sketch.

The mineral wealth of the country is as varied as it is extensive. The whole copper supply of the empire has to run the gauntlet of the Yang-tse rapids. Discouraged though they be by the officials, we yet find iron-mines worked on a small scale, at intervals along the river's course between Wu-shan and Wan-hsien, a distance of a hundred miles. The iron is brought down in the minute bars affected by the native trade, by numerous small affluents on the left bank at and between these two places. The sandstones of Szechuan are largely impregnated with iron, the washings from which give the red colour to the summer floods in the Hankow plain. These floods, which reach their culminating point each year on or about August 1, seem clearly attributable to the monsoon rains, and not mainly, as it is often stated, to the melting of the Thibetan snows. On the other hand, that mountainous region undoubtedly furnishes the golden sands of which a fresh layer is deposited each summer, and carefully washed for on the sandbanks, laid dry each winter—as far east as the Tung-ting Lake—and soon the rich matrix thus indicated beyond, may prove another California in the world-supply of the yellow metal.

The outline sketch will show how much has still to be observed in this wide region. China, though partially ransacked by many explorers, is still but little appreciated by scientific writers in Europe, as is evident from the way its teachings are ignored in the common generalizations of science. It was left for Richthofen to show, by his examination of the great *loess* country of the north-west, the possibility of ærial influences modifying the earth's surface in a way that was hitherto thought to be only possibe to water. Another instructive field of study is opened by the recurring droughts with which the province of Shansi, once the granary of the empire, in now afflicted. The change that is going on before our eyes in the Yellow River, second only in size and importance to the Yang-tse itself, is another problem which upsets many of our preconceived notions in hydrography. Here we have a vast river, historically of far greater interest than the Yang-tse, flowing along a bed considerably higher than that of the country it should naturally drain—a river that little more than thirty years ago shifted its mouth to a point 300 miles northward, and in one summer deserted the Yellow Sea for the Gulf of Pechili, silting up the Port of Tientsin, and rapidly converting the gulf into an agricultural plain. Railway projectors talk glibly of railways in every direction, and draw their "air" lines with equal facility across the crumbling loess terraces of the north and the unbroken series of precipitous mountains and deep-cut gorges of the west. Yet who knows how far our Western railways unmodified will answer in such a country?

Not alone physical problems, but others, social, political, and ethical, present themselves upon a closer study of the condition and of the past history of this vast land. Such a study, carried on by unprejudiced minds, will undoubtedly produce results which would modify many of our commonly accepted generalizations on these subjects. The belief, for instance, that order, justice, and a high state of civilization is the monopoly of Christian nations, ceases to be held upon a close study of this people on the spot. Yet the good people of Europe and America are not deterred in their endeavours to plant our Western habits and beliefs in a soil utterly unsuited to them, believing apparently that the uprooting of a system so firmly rooted in the past, and so thoroughly suited to the genius of the present is only a question of men and money. With eighteen provinces in China proper, each as large and as populous as a European kingdom, the field of observation affords room for yet countless explorers, not alone in every branch of physical science, but equally in historical, ethical, ethnographical and linguistic studies. . We have here a nation whose civilization, contemporary with that of Nineveh and Babylon, has survived, by the accident of its isolation, for the edification of the critical nineteenth century. Let us study it carefully. When we rightly understand and thoroughly appreciate this interesting survival from antiquity, may we not possibly gain from it some hints towards the solution of many of the grave ethical problems now confronting us in the West? This civilization, totally independent, both in its origin and in its development, must have lessons to teach us, no less than our civilization has for the Chinese. What will be the ultimate result of the intermingling of the two we cannot yet tell. Hitherto the Chinese seem anxious only to profit by our superior attainments in the arts of war, the object, if not the result of which, is to keep nations apart. Let us hope that the end will be to bring them together, and that the day is not far distant when, in the expressive words of the Chinese classic—

"Above is fulfilled the decree of heaven, and below the laws of earth, and in the midst the harmony of man joins in."

Compare Shakespeare—

"Right and Wrong,
Between whose jarring discord Justice reigns."

CHAPTER XIII.

THE NEW "GLORIOUS" RAPID.

The great landslide—Earthquake phenomena—Steps taken to modify the rapid—Need of Admiralty survey.

The New Rapid above Yun-yang.—This, the latest freak of the Great River, is one of the most remarkable natural phenomena that I have ever had occasion to investigate. In appearance like the effect of a great earthquake, the phenomenon is really due solely to the action of water. When I first visited the spot, two months after the occurrence, the lines of disturbance were still as fresh as on the day they were formed, and I had a fine opportunity of examining the hills and clefts as nature had left them. On a subsequent visit, a year later, the industrious agriculturists were hard at work levelling the land, rebuilding their farms, and generally obliterating the early landmarks. Still, even then the traces of the great landslide were distinctly visible, especially in the sundering of the roads traversing the displaced land, which were all broken short off where they touched the chasm formed between the landslip and the unmoved ground, the sundered portions still running in their original directions, but some hundred yards lower down the valley.

In the year 1896, during the months of August and September, rain fell continuously day and night, and created widespread damage throughout the province. The harvest of rice had been a bountiful one, but the crop was largely destroyed by mildew, and a disastrous famine throughout Szechuan and in Western Hu-peh resulted. On the mountain slopes in this latter district, as well as in Eastern Szechuan, hundreds of square miles of arable land were washed bodily down off the steeper slopes, leaving nothing but bare rock: this, added to the fact that much of the best land in Western China is given up to the beneficent and noxious poppy, and so abstracted from cereals, led to a repetition of the famine in the following year; indeed, owing to the absence of easy inter-communication, there is now rarely a season in which some district of the rich province of Szechuan is not a victim to famine with its attendant loss of life, pestilence, and riots. This "glorious" rapid is situated in the district of Yun-yang, in Szechuan, and about thirty miles west of the city of that name, described in page 98. The name of the spot is Lung ching Wan, or Dragon's Ford Bay; the new landslip, the cause of the rapid, is on the left or north bank of the river, in longitude 109° 16' east, and latitude 30° 54' north. Mr. Consul Bourne, from whose description in the *Geographical Magazine*, August, 1897, I take the above figures, says of it—

"The current in the middle is very fast, and on either bank huge waves are thrown up by the water dashing against the rocks below. As our eyes fell upon it for the first time, a large Szechuan junk, coming down stream, struck a rock in the trough of the waves and was a wreck in three minutes. . . . A hundred junks and a thousand lives have been already (December, 1896) lost, we are told. . . . About five hundred junks were lying at the rapid when we passed, the cargo on which may be roughly valued at £800,000."

The landslip took place on the nights of the 28th and 29th of September, 1896. The river valley is here three to four miles wide, and is bounded by precipitous mountains rising to about twelve hundred feet; between these and the present river-bed lie undulating foot-hills, formed in ancient times from the detritus of the cliffs behind; these rise to a height of three to four hundred feet, and are a pleasing feature in the foreground as one travels up the Great River; the land is very fertile, and is covered with farmhouses, and villages nestled in woods of walnut and fruit-trees, interspersed with bamboo groves, while vari-coloured crops cover the slopes and the wide-spreading banian adorns the summits. The river bottom is composed of a hard grey sandstone in which the river has scooped out a gigantic ditch which forms the channel of the stream at low water. At the time of high water, during the summer floods, this ditch is obliterated; its rock walls, now rising sixty feet above the water, are all submerged in twenty or thirty feet of water, and the width and volume of the river are increased tenfold. It was over this rock-edge that the slide of foot-hills which broke bodily away from the vertical cliffs of its parent mountain, poured its mass of detritus, comprising large angular fragments of hard sandstone rock, with intervening stiff clay, into the bay which formerly occupied the spot, building up a lofty projecting spit which suddenly narrowed the river from about four hundred to one hundred and fifty yards; in one night converting a tranquil reach into a furious rapid, with a fall of ten feet in the distance of one hundred yards. A reef of now (February) half-submerged rocks extends diagonally across the channel from the right bank, two-thirds of the way towards the newly formed point, greatly adding to the danger and the fury of the rapid.

The area of land set in motion is about half a mile in frontage by one mile in depth: a chasm filled with enormous rock fragments separates the firm land at the rear from the land that has slipped forward. The cause of the slide appears to have been the washing out of the earth beneath this hill of detritus at a point beneath where it rested upon impermeable rock. Thus undermined, a subsidence took place, and the whole mass then slid bodily forward in the direction of the river: arrived at the solid bank, the land seems to have been forced upward by the pressure from behind, as we see by the position of the displaced farmhouses, and notably a stone oil-mill, the walls of which now stand inclined inland at an angle of thirty to forty degrees. The slide occurred in the night of the twenty-third day of the eighth moon; the occupants of the various farms scattered over the surface were warned by ominous rumblings and crackings the day before, and so had time to clear out: not so the inhabitants of a valley just above, through which, on the same south bank, flows an affluent of the Yang-tse called the Siao Ho. Here a navigable river was entirely dammed across, and the navigation now goes no farther than the foot of the landslide; it is here arrested by a wall two hundred feet high, over which the river descends in a grand waterfall from the lake that has formed behind. Sixty souls, the population of a farmhouse on the bank, lie buried in the *débris*. But although the landslip produced no fatal injury on land, it was otherwise on the water: several junks, ignorant of the existence of the rapid, rowing down stream, were caught in it before they had time to make any preparations to descend, and so were swamped unexpectedly, with the total loss of their crews: now an inscription on the cliff a mile above the rapid warns descending junks that "a new vicious rapid has sprung up." At the time of my first visit, in 1897, the mandarin in charge of the rapid informed me that over one thousand lives had been lost; I myself saw a small boat engulfed and one large salt-junk with sixty rowers caught in the whirlpool below. This occurred at noon as she was descending the rapid, of course lightened of her cargo; and it was just sunset when I saw her at last get free. There was no danger as long as daylight lasted, with an empty junk, high out of water and well manned; but it was an extraordinary sight to watch how the "Dragon in the Rapid" baffled the persistent efforts of the crew to escape from the vicious circle that held them in its watery grip. Safety lies in descending the rapid in the centre, where the compression has arched the water and piled it up high above the eddies on each side; to hit this centre a descending junk has to steer between a gap in the reef over which the water now falls before it forms the rapid. This reef was harmless originally, as the main body of the river lay to the north of it; now the new landslide has pushed up to this reef, and over and through it the whole river now passes.

During the first winter after the formation of the rapid in the month of February, when the water is at its lowest, the Chinese attempted to improve the channel by digging away the point. The salt guild of Lu-chow, whose junks had been the greatest sufferers, gained permission from the Szechuan Viceroy to do what they could with manual labour only, and some two thousand workmen were employed in breaking up the rock masses into manageable pieces, and in then transporting the broken-up material into the whirlpool bay below. This method, slow and sure, suited the Chinese; but the point was not appreciably reduced before the spring rise in the river arrested the work. It was an interesting sight to see the busy ant-hive swarming on the point, the masons in red and navvies in yellow turbans. These managed to get through a good deal of work, although without dynamite they were unable to clear away the rock below the water level. A triangle, or to speak more accurately, a conic section, measuring roughly 450 by 150 by 50 feet, was removed, adding fifty yards to the width of the channel when the river should have overflowed the excavation. Three thousand pounds was the sum allotted to the work, which was being expended at the rate of thirty pounds per diem in wages. The Viceroy's alleged reason for prohibiting the use of dynamite was, that in Yun-yang resides the Fêng-shui, or Guardian Angel of Chêng-tu, the provincial capital, and that an explosion here would destroy his ya-men there. Some years ago a careless boatman lit a fire on a rock in mid-river above Wan-hien: this rock is the Fêng-shui of Pao-ning-fu in north-east Szechuan: the result was the destruction of the city of Pao-ning by fire that very same night.

When, in the spring of this year, we passed up in the "Leechuen," we found no less than 327 junks laid up in the reach below the rapid, either waiting their turn to ascend, or transhipping their cargo to fresh junks above. All boats that venture to pass the rapid have to strip even to their fittings, so as to make them as light as possible;—that is until the summer rise obliterates the fall. Coming from Yun-yang city, and rounding the point which opens up this wide reach, we could have imagined ourselves entering some wide fiord with a picturesque landlocked harbour crowded with traffic. Gangs of heavily laden coolies were groaning under bales of yarn and Manchester goods as they laboured along, up and down the steep improvised paths over the rocks on either shore. The rapid was at its fiercest, and the huge breakers below the smooth tongue reminded one forcibly of the rapids of the Niagara river below the falls. But now, at last, serious efforts were being made to effect a permanent cure in this new obstruction. During the preceding summer, the Imperial Maritime Customs had obtained the concurrence of the two Viceroys concerned—Hu-peh and Szechuan—to the employment of dynamite, and we were delighted to find a deputation, lent by Sir Robert Hart from the lighthouse service, hard at work. This deputation consisted of Messrs. Tyler, Gray Donald, and Myers, with some two thousand coolies working under their directions. In the economical way in which public works are carried out in impoverished China, these gentlemen had a very limited sum placed at their disposal, were short of dynamite and electric material, and supplied only with inferior local made gunpowder. Yet much had been already accomplished; great excavations had been made in the point which grows higher and higher, and wider, as the work advances. Much of the mid-reef had been removed, and with the *débris* from the cutting away of the right bank, a road was being built up for trackers under the cliff that lines the south shore; but their job is far from finished.

Mr. Tyler, who had necessarily made a prolonged stay on the spot, kindly furnished me with the following figures, which are most valuable in enabling the reader to form an accurate conception of the size of the river and the dimensions of the new obstruction to its flow:—

Volume of water passing the rapid in winter, at time of lowest water level	111,000 cubic feet per second.
Volume in summer, estimated at	1,110,000 ,, ,,
Winter level section	25,366 square feet.
Summer level section	419,093 ,,
Width at rapid	500 feet.
Width at section	959 ,,
Summer rise in water level (1897, often-more)	140 ,,
Agricultural land displaced by landslide	80 acres.
Height of "foot-hill" displaced above river	450 feet.
Mean velocity three feet below surface	5·48 knots.
Height of fall at head of rapid	6½ feet.

The work of cutting away the cliff ceased in April, leaving two million cubic yards of rock and earth to be still removed, before the rapid can be rendered positively safe for winter traffic: so far (May, 1898) only 80,000 cubic yards have been removed, so that the bulk of the work has still to be done, and to do it will occupy the engineers further two or three winters. As the rapid now is, so our friends told us, scarcely a day passes that a junk is not swamped with loss of life. Men falling into the water are sucked under instantly —snapped up, the Chinese say, by the Dragon who formed the rapid. The loss to trade may be estimated as a new tax of five per cent. upon all cargoes imported into Szechuan, half of this amount being loss in interest by the delay which merchants have to suffer. Steam would make light of the difficulties which so impede the junks in the high-water season. Being tracked from the shore, they are unable to keep clear of the rocks which infest the inshore channels. A steamer would then keep clear of the shore and steam on in deep water; she would find the rapids smoothed over and practically non-existent. The main junk traffic is in winter, when the rapids are at their worst; but, when towing in the intervening reaches, is easier, and the prevailing north-east monsoon provides a steady up-river breeze. The gorges are almost impassable to junks in summer, owing to the absence of towing-paths past the overhanging precipices, and the prevalence of calms. In a light passenger junk last summer, some friends of ours were just two months in covering the five hundred miles from Ichang to Chung-king. What with the loss in time, the often total loss of goods, the water damage which scarce a single junk escapes, the risk to life and limb, the loss in interest and the absence of insurance, the wonder is, not that the trade is no greater, but that it exists at all. A well-managed line of steamers on this grand but dangerous river will be as great a boon to the Chinese as it is a bugbear to the officials, with whose "squeezes" it threatens to interfere.

A large heterogeneous crowd is now collected round the banks of the New Rapid, engaged in the portage round the falls, and in road-making, etc. There must be at least ten thousand people squatting in the villages of wooden shanties and straw huts, which have been rapidly run up, and will all have to be removed as the river rises, and again replaced in winter. The movement is something extraordinary; crowds of coolies, soldiers, sailors, innkeepers, passengers, carrying their valuables round the rapid and struggling under their burdens, remind one of a fair and the traffic at a big railway-station combined. To keep all this population in order, to settle disputes, arrest thieves and order the traffic, which Chinese officials do in a rough-and-ready but practical way, a Deputy Magistrate has been appointed from Yun-yang; he lives in a temporary ya-men with walls of matting, and has been thrice burnt out. Little rain falls in winter, and once a hut catches fire the whole place goes. He was a young man, and anxious to learn; he gave me an excellent dinner, and told me some of his experiences and troubles. One dispute, on arrival was, To whom did the land belong upon which the village stands;—to the man who originally owned the site, or to the man whose fields were now superimposed on the first by the landslide? In true Solomonic fashion he solved the quarrel by dividing the land between the two litigants. The Chinese further say that the mandarin also interrogated the Dragon as to why he had wrought this evil. The reply was, "I do my Dragon business, you do your mandarin business."

Twenty-two years have elapsed since, by the Chefoo Convention negotiated between Sir Thomas Wade and Li Hung Chang, the port of Chung-king was nominally opened to British trade. Throughout that period constant suggestions have been made that the British Admiralty should survey the river. To a China resident it seems a simple thing to detach, say, a torpedo-catcher from the large squadron in China waters, and send her to do the work. It would be an instructive expedition to officers lying idle in Hong-kong, and a pleasant outing for the men employed; the winter climate of Mid-China is cool and rainless. Admirals interviewed and impressed with the boon such survey will be to would-be navigators, reply that the order must come from the Foreign Office. Thus the Foreign Office is the obstacle, and will apparently remain so until this department of our Government is reorganized, and an influential official appointed who shall give *continuous attention* to Far Eastern affairs. It goes without saying that all work done on the Upper Yang-tse goes towards spreading our influence in that region—a region which we now profess to regard as our special "sphere of influence." How long will it remain our sphere, if no steps are taken, either by our Government or by British capitalists, to survey and develop its resources, warn off intruders, and make the occupation really effective? We have precedents in the Russian occupation of Manchuria, in the German occupation of Shantung, and in the French expeditions to Yünnan. There is thus no time to be lost if our sphere of influence is ever to be more than "You ming wu sze"— a name without a reality.

Pavilion in Garden of "White Emperor's City," on Cliff at Mouth of Below Gorge. *To face p. 282.*

CHAPTER XIV.

FIRST ASCENT BY STEAM.

Feasibility of steam navigation in Szechuan—Account of the first ascent of the Yang-tse rapids by steam in 1898—Remarks.

IN posing the question of running steamers to Chung-king, I wrote in 1887, in the original edition of this book, words which are equally applicable to the position of affairs to-day:—

"The navigability of the Upper Yang-tse by steam has often "been called in question, and assuredly any one who has care-"fully perused the preceding journal will agree that it is no easy "matter. At the same time I am decidedly of opinion that, if "the necessary conditions are fulfilled, there is no insuperable "difficulty in the way. These conditions are: A powerful "steamer, easily handled, and of a draught of water not exceed-"ing that of the present junks. In looking myself into the "matter, I found that nearly all the junk losses occur in the "upward voyage; scraping along the rocky shore, with often "insufficient towing power, they are unable to contend with the "powerful eddies, and are thrown against the rocks, when holes "are quickly knocked into their weak, untimbered sides. A "steamer, keeping clear of the shore, would not be exposed to "these risks, and where necessary she could feel her way up as

"slowly as she liked. Her danger would be in coming down.
"Now, if we look at the junks on the downward voyage, we
"find that, with only just sufficient power on board to give them
"steerage way, they have no difficulty in keeping in the middle
"of the channel, where there is at all seasons plenty of water
"for light-draft vessels, as well as plenty of room; consequently
"a steamer of the same draft, following in the wake of the junks,
"can hardly fail to go right, and as time went on, the captain of
"a steamer would learn the river, and proceed with greater con-
"fidence. Competent pilots take the junks down each dangerous
"rapid; they have landmarks by which they know the depth of
"the water on every dangerous rock, as the level of the water
"varies from day to day, and the cumbersome junks are steered
"down by them in perfect safety. Most of the accidents coming
"*down* stream occur to the small boats, whose masters think
"they can safely dispense with a local pilot. Of course, a
"steamer, to succeed, must be specially constructed for the
"work; and to the fact that no such steamer has as yet been
"procurable in Chinese and Japanese waters must be attributed
"the neglect to make the experiment, conditionally sanctioned
"in the Convention of Chefoo. This Convention, made by Sir
"Thomas Wade with Li Hung Chang, as long ago as 1876,
"stipulates that arrangements for the opening of the port of
"Chung-king to foreign trade may be taken into consideration,
"as soon as steamers have succeeded in ascending the river so
"far. The wording of the Convention is involved enough to
"satisfy the professional pride of the most thorough-going
"diplomatist, containing as it does the seeds of a quarrel ready
"to hand, for either of the high contracting parties to take up
"at any time. The clause affecting the Upper River is a notable
"instance of not allowing a boy to enter the water until he has
"learnt to swim. Doubtless, when a suitable steamer is pre-
"pared to ascend, pressure will be brought to bear on the
"Chinese to gain the necessary permission to try the experiment;
"but there can be little doubt but that the Peking authorities
"will shelter themselves behind the ambiguous clauses of the
"Treaty as long as they can, so as to avoid giving their
"consent."

It was not long after penning these words that I endeavoured to back my views and translate them into action. I succeeded in getting a few well-wishers to subscribe the necessary capital to build an experimental steamer. The *Kuling*, a stern-wheeler of about five hundred tons burthen, was built on the Clyde, put together in Shanghai, and taken to Ichang in 1889 with the view of ascending to Chung-king, and so getting the place opened to foreign trade as a treaty port; but I reckoned without my host in the shape of the British Government and their then representative in China, Sir John Walsham. These refused to coerce the Chinese Government in any way, and so the *Kuling* was eventually sold and the scheme abandoned. The prime mover in the opposition was the then Viceroy of Szechuan, backed by his father-in-law, Li Hung Chang, whom the Japanese war had then not yet unmasked. The Chinese palmed off the most frivolous objections on good Sir John, whose home instructions apparently compelled him to let the Chinese interpret the Chefoo Convention in their own way, and so postpone the opening of Chung-king *sine die*. Nothing could be more fatuous, in the opinion of British residents in China, than the conduct of our Government towards the Chinese since their defeat in 1860. Our Foreign Office officials seem to be untaught by history, and so seldom profit by past experience in their dealings with China. It is interesting to read how, more than a century and a half ago, Commodore Anson, in his famous voyage round the world with one ship, the *Centurion*, succeeded by firmness in gaining his point with the Chinese of his day. The Canton Viceroy put him off by endless delays and excuses, Anson wanting only to refit and revictual. At last Anson went up alone to Canton city, and insisted upon seeing the Viceroy himself, telling the Chinese that, if he did not return in safety, his ship had orders to come up and look for him. Needless to say that he got all he wanted without firing a shot.

How applicable are the words in the following extracts from "Anson's Voyage round the World" (London, 1748) to the situation to-day!

"And yet this populous, this rich and extensive country, so pompously celebrated for its refined wisdom and policy, was conquered about an age since by a handful of Tartars; and even now by the cowardice of its inhabitants and the want of proper military regulations, it continues exposed, not only to the attempts of any potent state, but to the ravages of every petty invader" (p. 414).

And how entreaties are of no avail, but threats omnipotent!

"Mr. Anson told him the next day that if he longer refused to grant the permit (to revictual at Canton) he would man and arm his own boats to carry him thither, asking the Hoppo at the same time, who he imagined would dare to oppose him. The threat immediately brought about what his entreaties had laboured for in vain" (p. 365).

"That if by the delay of supplying him with provisions, his men should be reduced to the necessity of turning cannibals and preying upon their own species, it was easy to be foreseen that they would prefer the plump well-fed Chinese to their own emaciated shipmates" (p. 362).

The matter of the Upper Yang-tse navigation thus remained in abeyance until the successful Japanese war of 1895 overthrew the barriers of Chinese conservatism by main force. At the conclusion of the war the Japanese were able to stipulate for the formal opening of Chung-king to steamers, and the clause was embodied in the Treaty of Simonoseki. This clause must have been a bitter pill for Li Hung Chang to swallow, he being the plenipotentiary who signed the treaty on behalf of the Chinese Government. By this treaty, under the favoured nation clause, the Upper Yang-tse became open to the world, and I consequently applied to our minister in Peking to ask if he would support me in the event of my again having a steamer built for the purpose. Sir Claude Macdonald, our present minister, a man of action, unlike the kindly gentlemen who preceded him in sleepy Peking, encouraged me by all means to proceed, and promised energetic support. I thus ordered a twin-screw steamer to be built in Shanghai, fifty-five feet long and ten feet beam, with which to experiment in the rapids. The boat was built, with a teak hull, by the Shanghai Engineering Company, steamed nine knots, and proved herself an excellent little vessel for the work. I should have much preferred a larger and more powerful vessel; but, as the risk was all my own this time, and insurance unobtainable, I had to cut my coat according to my cloth. I set out from Shanghai on the 15th of January, 1898, and, including delays at the various treaty ports on the way, spent three weeks in ascending the 970 miles to Ichang, the then limit of steam navigation on the river. Arrived at Ichang, the Chinese Governor of the port sent officers on board, and also to the Consul there, Mr. Holland, to propose the discussion of regulations for preventing collisions, etc., and so delay our departure. Having spent six months, a whole winter, over futile discussions ten years before, we refused to reopen the question, Mr. Holland wisely declining even to see the "deputy" who called upon him; he simply wrote to the Governor that the steamer would start on the 15th of February, with or without his permission, but that the vessel would delay a week, so as to give him time to advise his brother officials up river of our intended voyage, which he declared to be necessary. Hereupon the opposition vanished like magic: it was the old story of Chinese cobwebs dispersed by a show of firmness.

So, on the 15th of February we set out upon the first steam voyage to Chung-king, an ascent of 500 feet in 500 miles, broken, so the Chinese "Gazetteer" states, into thirteen big rapids and seventy-two minor ones. The Governor had sent as an escort a gunboat and a lifeboat; these we had to take in tow, in addition to our own tender carrying six tons of spare coal, and a spare crew of ten men to help on occasion, in case the local trackers at the big rapids should refuse their aid. This was no imaginary danger, for my own crew of men from the coast, sailors and engineers, had all tried to desert on several occasions, as stories of the danger ahead were impressed upon them. They had signed on for six months to me as registered captain, yet I had to use a mixture of force and persuasion to keep them to their posts. At length, at noon, the start was made, the whole foreign community of Ichang accompanying us a few miles up the river, and giving us a last cheer as they shoved off in their boat which we had towed up. We had now in tow three vessels—our own tender, a flat-bottomed sailing barge nearly as big as ourselves; the Chinese gunboat of similar build, with a small cannon in the bows, and a smart crew of twelve Hu-Nan "braves;" and the lifeboat manned by six uniformed sailors. These vessels are stationed all along the dangerous Upper River, are well disciplined, and effectual in keeping down piracy and in saving life and property. We ran fast through the slack water of the Ichang Gorge, and seeing all clear, I handed over the helm for an interval to the native pilot and went below. He immediately ran into a ferry-boat full of

"We were the first that ever burst
Into that silent sea."
　　　　COLERIDGE'S *Ancient Mariner*.

To face p. 288.

passengers, and knocked the helmsman overboard. The man was fortunately rescued unhurt, and so a great danger to our progress averted, while I was warned not to leave the deck again while under way. We moored for the night, tying up to the bank at the entrance of the Yao-tsa-ho, the river of piled rocks, having made thirty miles in six hours. On the following day we negotiated with great ease the little races that run round the jutting-out points of this stretch of river, so difficult to junks to tow past for want of points of vantage for the trackers, and affording most precarious foothold. We got through the fierce Otter Rapid—a rapid with breaking waves, but with wide channels of deep water between the reefs—with much trouble and after repeated attempts, on one occasion swept bodily astern and broadside on to a high reef—which we just cleared by hastily changing our course and heading straight down river. At last we got through, and then followed up a long smooth reach with swift current, crossing and recrossing to pick out the easiest water, until we came to the Kung ling Rapid. This rapid has narrow winding channels amongst the rocks scattered across the river, so we tied up below it and engaged a T'an sze, or "rapid expert," to pilot us through. When the old man came on board and realized it was a steamer, which would go through without being towed, he tried to bolt and hide himself, and our attendant officials on the gunboat had to use much "persuasion" to induce him to stay. Eventually, he took up his position on the platform I had built for the bow-sweep projecting over the bows, and directed the steering by his arms with the greatest *aplomb* and certainty; the noise of the rapids renders shouting useless. From here on we steamed through the Niu-kan Gorge, its gigantic walls threatening to crush us in the fading light, and just

U

succeeded in tying up below the famous Shin tan, or "New Rapid," by dark, having steamed forty miles, including two rapids, in ten hours.

The Great Rapid of the Shin tan is at this season an actual waterfall, although when the water rises in May it disappears altogether; and we careered about in the big waves below until we crossed the river and tied up to the right shore immediately beneath the fall. Two tow-lines were attached, and with one hundred coolies straining at the lines, aided by our own steam, we were up in a few minutes. After waiting a long time in the deep, still water above the fall for our three consorts to be hauled up, we took on our tows again, and steamed through the Ping-shu Gorge with majestic ease; but in the more open valley at its head we encountered a fierce race over a boulder flat, in which the propellers seemed to get no grip, and we crawled along, making about one mile an hour until, at dusk, we tied up under a steep sand-bank on the left shore, having advanced only ten miles in as many hours.

On the following morning we entered one of the most confused and troublesome reaches of the river—that from the upper end of the Ping-shu Gorge, to past the walled city of Kwei-chow. Here a series of parallel reefs run across the river at right angles to its course. These reefs jut out from either shore a distance of about a hundred yards, in huge hard limestone masses rising about forty feet above the level of the water. These reefs appear to have been cut through by the river, but they still extend under water across its bed, and cause awkward cross currents and eddies which tried the power of our small steamer to the utmost; we had constantly to cross and recross the wide river, taking advantage of the eddies, and avoiding the rocks as best we could.

On one reef a large junk was sunk with her stern just visible: her crew had tied her to the shore with long bamboo hawsers, leaving only a small passage between her and the rocks, through which we had to steam, meeting the full force of the current in a narrow winding channel. We ultimately moored in a swift current opposite Kwei-chow, having taken nearly six hours to advance six miles. We had dropped our tows, who, fortunately, aided by a strong up-river breeze, did not detain us long. But in taking them on again for the smooth stretch of swift water from Kwei-chow to the foot of the Yeh-tan (rapid) a serious accident happened. The bamboo hawser of the gunboat became entangled in one of our propellers, and was twisted round it so firmly that we had to tie up to the shore again, and were delayed some hours before one of our willing crew dived down and hacked it clear with a sharp hatchet. At four in the afternoon we moored a mile below the Yeh-tan, where a heavy snowstorm compelled us to tie up for the night. I had much trouble all the way with these accompanying gunboats; but I did not like to offend them, this being the first steamer to invade their beats, otherwise many a time I should have cast them adrift. The life-boat, on the other hand, proved itself of the greatest use, having a very smart and well-disciplined crew, always ready to help us in any difficulty. At the Yeh-tan, which is a clean rapid, due to the narrowing of the river by a huge cone of dejection from a now dry affluent on the left bank, we had again to be towed. We lost nearly a whole day waiting our turn until the junks ahead of us had gone up and left us a clear way, for we failed in our attempt to steam round and get ahead of them, such was the force of the current. From above the Yeh-tan, past the city of Pa-tung, where great crowds of blue-coated people, including the magistrate and his suite, watched us steam by in silent astonishment, we steamed on until, in the evening of the following day, we came upon the rock-strewn rapids of the Niu-kou (ox head) and the Hêng liang (transverse ridge). We crept through these, running up in the eddies; then meeting the down current, which swept us back, we crossed rapidly to the opposite shore; then on again in the next eddy, until we at last got safely through. It was here, in the Hêng-liang-tźe, that we saw two large junks capsized: one had been towed ashore; one was floating on her side in the eddy as we passed up. Both these junks had been tracking up in the eddy, when, upon rounding the point and meeting the down current, they had suddenly taken a sheer and gone over before there had been time for the trackers to release the tow-lines. Warned by their disaster we attempted, by careful steering, to bring our stem head on to the current in good time; but, as it was, we rolled gunnel under, and, had we been tracked, must have infallibly capsized. Above these picturesque, but from the navigator's point of view nasty, places, we entered the great gorge of Wu-shan, Wu-shan-ta-hsia; and here we thoroughly enjoyed the triumph of steam, traversing its twenty miles, with our heavy tows, in about five hours. This long gorge is the crux of junk navigation, unless when a fair wind blows, as the cliff walls defy tracking, and it is impossible to row against the current: at its upper end is the city of Wu-shan, where we moored for the night. The next day saw us through the rapids of the "Kitten" and "Dismount from your horse," until at dusk we moored at the foot of the rapid which, at this season, flows over from the reservoir of the Bellows Gorge with considerable violence. It was here that, while steering inshore amidst the rocks, to avoid the current, we were swept back and touched a rock with our starboard propeller, badly bending two of the blades: these being made of bronze we, later on, at Chung-king, succeeded in hammering back into shape; but our speed for the remainder of our voyage was reduced by this accident to about six knots. Fortunately half our journey, counting by rapids, was over when, on the following morning, we tied up safely under the walls of the ancient city of Kwei-chow-fu.

We delayed two days at Kwei-chow-fu to give our Ningpo engineers a rest, and time to overhaul the engines, which had had a severe strain put upon them during the past week while keeping up full steam, 150 lbs., continuously. Crowds lined the shore where we lay—a great contrast in their quiet behaviour to the rude shouting and mud-throwing we had so often had to put up with at this place while travelling in native boats. All wanted to come on board, but we were compelled to restrict our visitors to those who presented cards; these we freely admitted, and our little saloon was at times inconveniently crowded.

From Kwei-chow-fu to the "Miao chi-tse," or "Temple stairs," we toiled, at our unfortunately reduced speed, through a succession of minor rapids, at the worst of which we had to cast off our tows and wait above for them to track themselves up, thus making in all only about eighteen miles in seven hours. For we moored at the Miao chi-tse early in the afternoon, the string of junks waiting to ascend showing that we should have to wait till the morning. It is remarkable how the rapids vary: this rapid was now running with greater force than the fierce Yeh-tan, a comparatively narrow slope of smooth water with big breaking waves below. We went up next morning with two tow-lines and 150 trackers. Owing to the unusual fact of the channel for junks towing up being in the middle of the river, here narrowed to about four hundred yards, I had a good opportunity of making a fair trial of the actual speed of the current. I had with me a Walker's patent log, which registers on the log itself, and not on the taffrail. In half an hour, during which we advanced about a quarter of a mile, it registered six nautical miles, making the speed of the current nearly twelve knots for a distance of a quarter of a mile, while the speed for the half mile lower down was probably seven to eight knots. From this we passed on to the Tung yang tse, a nasty looking cataract, but a less really formidable obstacle than its smooth-looking companion, the Miao chi-tse, past the city of Yun-yang, and on through a series of smooth rapids, rounding the innumerable projecting rocky points, to the foot of the celebrated New Rapid of Yun-yang, the culminating and most formidable hindrance to navigation on the whole river.

This rapid, the newest of all, and commonly called the Hsin t'an, or New Rapid simply, although its official name is the "Hing lung t'an," or "Glorious Rapid"—a euphemism to conciliate its guardian Dragon,—was formed as recently as 1896; so it is well entitled to its designation of new. Being in a separate province, that of Szechuan, its name does not clash with the old New Rapid, which is in Hu-peh, and dates from A.D. 1640. At least, so the Chinese say, but to our minds the nomenclature is most confusing. At this spot, up to the night of the 12th September, 1896, the river flowed in a wide tranquil reach; but on that fatal night, part of the foot-hills, about half a mile in width, broke loose from the mountains upon which they leant and advanced into the river, narrowing the channel at one stroke from about eight hundred to less than two hundred yards. The river was dammed up. A lake-like expanse was immediately formed above the landslip, the water from which burst into a similar expanse below in a frightful cataract, reminding one forcibly of the rapids of the Niagara River below the falls. Below this rapid we found 320 junks moored along both shores, some discharging their cargoes for transport to fresh junks above the rapid, others waiting their turn to ascend. We steamed up past them in the five-knot current, taking our place at the head of the line in preparation for our ascent on the following morning. It was a picturesque scene, the junks moored in a lake-like expanse surrounded by high mountains, and now gay with many lanterns, while numerous sampans plied across the river, ferrying passengers and supplies to the busy fleet. Next day we steamed up in the eddy below the falls and engaged a local pilot. Here a long discussion arose as to whether our little vessel could get up at all; for, in the channel close in shore, along the left bank, the only one safe to tow up at this season, there was said to be barely four feet of water. Our draft was three feet six inches, and, owing to the high waves, the four feet of water could not be depended upon throughout. We were advised to wait a month, until a few inches rise should ensure our safety. Determined, however, to risk the ascent, we lightened the boat by landing our coal and stores, and set out with three hundred men hauling on three main tow-lines ahead, with shorter lines carried ashore at right angles to the boat, acting as guys to prevent her taking a sheer, and so possibly breaking loose into mid-river, where she would inevitably have been swamped. Our engine staff again shied, but were ultimately placated by my tying our one lifebuoy round the body of the "chief," a middle-aged man, who controlled the two young firemen under him. At the start, one tow-line snapped off; but we got up successfully, the other two lines holding well, in twelve anxious minutes. In summer, as the water rises, the falls disappear, the rapid is changed into a race, and junks move up and down without serious difficulty. Arrived in the smooth water above we felt jubilant, believing that now this dangerous obstacle had been overcome, our reaching Chung-king was no longer a matter of doubt. In this we were somewhat premature; as will be seen later.

From the New Rapid to Wan Hien we steamed without difficulty through the race of the Eight Genii Gorge, having spent twelve days, including detentions, in covering the 250 miles of this, the first half of our voyage.

From Wan Hien onwards to Chung-king the valley widens out, the shores are less precipitous, and, although the walls, as well as the bed of the river, are still composed of rocks and huge banks of boulders, the current is easier and the numerous rapids are more manageable. Hence we accomplished this second stage of the journey in about half the time we had spent over the first stage. We got along better with our tows,—though once again fouling our propeller, owing to the carelessness of the gun-boat crew,— dropping them at rare intervals, mostly in shallow places where the clear water raced over a boulder bottom, the grinding of the boulders below being distinctly audible. Occasionally half a dozen men from our tender would have to jump ashore with a line and help us over a tight spot, often for a few yards only at a time. But for the accident to our propeller, this would not have been necessary. Then, again, our pumps got choked with sand, and necessitated constant stoppages. At times we despaired of ever reaching

Chung-king: we had often to lay up for repairs which our engine staff declared impossible. Then, our Japan coal finished, we had to depend on local coal. With this we could only raise ninety pounds of steam, and so were reduced to half speed; we managed to crawl along, however, making some forty miles daily, without serious accident until one evening when we struck a rock which all but wrecked the boat and our hopes together. We were in the Scissors Gorge, one of the many smaller gorges cut by the river at right angles through the cross limestone ranges that break up the sandstone plateau of Szechuan proper. It was dusk, we seemed to have struck some better coal, and were hurrying on to find a mooring-place, making about six knots over the ground in the still deep water of the gorge. Suddenly we bumped over a rock so sharp that it cut through the inch teak planking, broke two hardwood frames, and sent the water spouting up over the saloon floor. The vertical cliffs on either side precluded our at once beaching the boat: the only thing was to steam on to the end of the gorge. This we did, our attempts to stop the leak meanwhile barely succeeding in keeping the water from the fires. Fortunately, we soon spotted a little steep patch of sand in the moonlight, on to which we ran the boat: the men jumped ashore and quickly carried the anchor up the bank, and we made fast for the night. We worked the whole night through, stuffing cotton and white lead and tallow into the cracks; we nailed blankets down with planks over all, and by eight the next morning had stopped the leak sufficiently to be able to get under way again. Our pilot, who had proved very reliable so far, declared that this was a rock newly fallen from the mountains behind. In any case we should have cleared it, had we not been hugging the shore so as to avoid the current in mid-stream. When we beached the boat, the man disappeared, fearing punishment for his carelessness. He had been paid in advance. A more powerful steamer, keeping well out, would not be exposed to such an accident; the water in mid-stream in the gorges is immensely deep, and no newly fallen rock there could show up anywhere near the surface; a larger steamer, too, would be built in water-tight compartments like the junks, a precaution I had not thought necessary with our small boat. We stopped at the many large towns and cities which we passed in this populous region, and exchanged cards with the local officials, who, from politeness or curiosity, came to visit the boat. Great crowds surrounded us everywhere, often squeezing each other into the water in their anxiety to get a good view: we amused ourselves, at times, startling them with the whistle, when it was a curious sight to see a thousand hands suddenly go up to a thousand ears, while many of the more timid ran away altogether. As I had foretold to our minister ten years before, we met with no rudeness anywhere, but, on the contrary, with much intelligent admiration and inquiry.

At the "Coal" Gorge, fifty miles below Chung-king, so-called from its exposed coal seams into which adits are run whence an inferior surface coal is extracted, we again filled our bunkers; but, alas! we could make no headway with this coal, so we tied up to the shore and sent one of our crew overland to order a boat-load of the better coal obtainable in Chung-king. My Chinese there, with commendable promptitude, sent off a boat in the early morning, which reached us before noon on the following day: we then steamed on joyfully, passed up the difficult "Wild Mule" Rapid, took our tows through the beautiful "Gong" Gorge, and, on the evening of the 8th of March, moored alongside the Imperial Maritime

Customs station at Tang chia t'ŏ, ten miles below Chung-king, where we had been requested to wait by the Reception Committee arranged to welcome our arrival;—our troublesome but interesting voyage at last accomplished.

Early next morning, after we had cleaned ship and got out our bunting, the Reception Committee, with the greater portion of the British and American community in Chung-king, together with Chinese friends, some fifty in all, came in sight in house-boats covered with flags. These, including the ensigns of the British, American, and Japanese consuls, were transferred to the *Leechuen*, and we steamed on triumphantly after taking our friends on board. These gave us a rapturous welcome, our popular American doctor paying me the highest compliment in his power by assuring me that my enterprise had made me worthy of being an American. Upon reaching Chung-king, the Taotai (Governor) sent more gunboats, all gaily decorated, and at length, under a salute of cannon and a deluge of fire-crackers, we moored below the Chao tien mên, the " Gate that looks to Heaven," of the ancient city of Chung-king. Here an address of welcome was read and replied to, after which we steamed across to our permanent berth in the rock-formed harbour of Lung mên Hao—the lagoon of the Dragon Gate.

Our voyage from Ichang, a distance roughly estimated at 500 miles, had occupied eleven steaming days, or, including detentions, just three weeks altogether. It was a first experiment, which could not be hurried; it was, for necessary reasons, made at a season when the rapids were at their worst, and it was made with a vessel of insufficient power. Nevertheless my object was achieved, in demonstrating the possibility of navigating the Upper Yang-tse, and in drawing public attention to its necessity. When we consider that, as things now are, three months is an average time for goods to reach Chung-king from Shanghai, while six months is not uncommon, we realize what an impetus will be given to the trade of this rich province, once regular steam communication is established. That this will not have long to wait is now certain, and when it does come its promoters will reap a rich reward. Until some day superseded by a railway along the gorges, steamers on the river will command the cream of the immense carrying-trade now painfully served by fragile junks. The present army of wretched trackers will gradually be set free for more remunerative work as the mines are developed and new industries become established. Then will the pioneer voyage of the little *Leechuen* not have been made in vain.

APPENDIX

ADDRESS OF CONGRATULATION AND WELCOME

PRESENTED TO

ARCHIBALD J. LITTLE, ESQ., F.R.G.S.,

ON THE OCCASION OF HIS ARRIVAL WITH THE FIRST STEAMER IN THE PORT OF CHUNG-KING.

"Chung-king, 8th March, 1898.

"ARCHIBALD J. LITTLE, ESQ.
"DEAR SIR,
"We, the undersigned foreigners residing in the city of Chung-king, desire to offer you our hearty congratulations on this auspicious occasion, when we have the great gratification of welcoming your arrival here with the first steam-vessel to ascend the Upper Yang-tse.

"We desire to make this public acknowledgment of your unflagging perseverance, through many years, and praiseworthy determination to bring a steamer to this city, in spite of the obstacles which have been pronounced by some to be insurmountable, and we rejoice with you in the present accomplishment of the aim which you have had so long in view.

"We the more heartily do this because, in addition to the advantages which steam navigation on the Upper Yang-tse may bring to foreign residents in this great Western port, we believe eventually lasting benefits will also thereby accrue to the general native population in these interior provinces.

"We should therefore once more offer to yourself and to Mrs. Little, the sympathetic companion of your present successful voyage up-river, now so happily accomplished, our most hearty and united congratulations, with the expression of the hope that you may live many years to see great development in the steam navigation of the Upper Yang-tse, which you have always indefatigably advocated; while to yourself alone will always remain the honour of having brought the first steamer into the port of Chung-king."*

[Here follow the signatures of all (about sixty) the foreign residents in Chung-king.]

This was followed by congratulatory telegrams from the British Minister, from Consuls and others in different parts of the Empire, and from the "Ratepayers of Shanghai in Public Meeting assembled;" *i.e.* the Cosmopolitan Parliament of the Commercial Metropolis of China—the well-known "Model Settlement."

* Extract from the *North China Herald*, Shanghai, 11th April, 1898.

INDEX

ALCOCK, Sir Rutherford, 214
American Methodist Mission, Chung-king, 166, 171, 172
Anson, Commodore, in China (1748), 285, 286
"Ascent of the Golden Peak" (pass), 48, 49

BABER, Mr., 138, 181, 198, 254, 255
"Back baskets," used in Fu-chow, 235, 236
Banquet, a Chinese, 142, 143
Barton, Dr. Alfred, x.
Baskets, called Pei tsz, 119; called Pei-lo, 236
Battlements, built of stone, 240
"Bellows" Gorge, 81–83, 85, 89, 91, 292
Black Dragon Gorge, 232
Blacksmiths, town of, 108
Blakiston, Captain, travels in China, x., 32, 64, 89, 118, 137, 225, 226, 231
Boat, small, called Shen Potse, 29–31, 215
Boats; on the Kung t'an Hŏ River, 126, 127; laden with drugs from Kansu, 198. *See also* Junks

Bourne, Mr. Consul, 273, 274
Brass Gong Gorge, 132, 224, 225
Brine wells: Ta-ling city, 79; Kwei-chow, 85
British consular agents in Western China, 138
British trade with China, 3, 4, 7–10, 13, 14
Buddhas, of colossal stone, 133
Buddhist procession at Chung-king, 139
Buddhist temples, near Ichang, 42–44
"Bund" at Hankow, 16, 17

Cangues (wooden collars), 92
Canton guild gardens, Chung-king, 168
Catholic converts at Chung-king, 160
Cattle at Kao-chia chen market, 118
Cave of the Sage Lao-tse, 159, 160
Caves in Szechuan, 147; near Chung-king, 198
Cedar Garden (village), 75, 76
"Census" men, 109
Cereals in Szechuan, 267

"Cha" (tea), 186, 220
Chai-jen ("Ya-men runners"), 130
Chang, Mr., 17
Chang chung chien, rebellion of, 77
Chang-fei, temple dedicated to, 99, 100
Changkiang (Long River). *See* Yang-tse kiang
Chang-sho, city of, 125, 129, 229, 230
Chang-sing-tung Bank, Chung-king, 161, 162
Chao, manager of Native Bank, Chung-king, 161, 162
Chefoo Convention of 1876, viii., 135, 138, 281, 284
Chekiang province, population of, 12
Chen, a Cantonese merchant, 210
Cheng-tu-sêng, the capital of Szechuan province, 132, 140, 178
Chêng-tu, plain of, 262
Chia-ling ho, river, 197
Chiang-kow (River's Mouth) village, 32
Chiang-peh Ting, city of, 133
"Chien-tao" (Scissors Gorge), 129
Chi-fang (silk-weaving establishment), 180
Chili province, population of, 11
China, government of, 1, 2; revolutions in, 2, 3; population of, 3, 11, 12; British trade with, 3, 4, 7-10, 13, 14; coal-fields in, 5, 6; railroad construction in, 6, 7; cotton cultivation in, 10, 11; fishing in, 21; filthy streets of, 25; dogs in, 37, 38; dust-storms in, 38; otter fisheries in, 39; Feng-shui in, 41, 61, 62, 71; hospitality in, 45, 46; peasants in, 58; floods of 1870 in, 63; pagodas in Eastern, 71; official convoys in, 112, 113, 130; historical plays in, 116; gentleman's residence in, 141; a dinner-party in, 142, 143; religion ' of 'the people of, 145 (*see also* Fêng-shui); stonework in, 148; snakes and tortoises in, 148, 149; pastimes in, 157; inland postage in, 158, 159; saddles in, 176; foot-binding in, 186, 206-209; tea-drinking in, 186; Pliny's account of, 250-252; England and, in 1839, 252
China Express, the, 40
China Inland Mission at Chung-king, 158, 172, 211, 213; at Shasze, 29
China Merchants' Steam Navigation Co., 6, 243; wreck of a steamer of the, 202
Chinese boarding-school at Chang sho, 229
Chinese chess, 157
Chinese cities, filth of, 167, 168
Chinese guilds, 202, 203
Chinese residence, description of a, near Chung-king, 181-183
Chin fêng po, pass called, 48, 49
Ching Chiang (Clear River), 33
"Ching Kiang Sze" (Taoist temple), 60
Ching-tan, triple rapid of the, 61
"Chi-pa" (rapids), 51, 67, 71
Chiu shih kang (rocklets), 200
Cho-hwang, tomb of, 239
Chota hazari, 186, 219, 220

Index

Chuan Ho (River of Szechuan), 95, 239. *See* Yang-tse kiang
Chung-chow (city), 113, 114, 119; ancient site of, 110
Chung-king, a treaty port, 4, 5, 29; list of exports from, in 1867..8, 9; Customs station opened near, 132 *n*.; first view of, 133, 134; arrival at, 135–137; hongs at, 136; distance of, from the sea, 137 and *n*.; British consular agents in, 138; Buddhist procession at, 139; situation of, 149, 164; missions in, 154–156, 158, 165, 166, 172–4; native Banking Corporation at, 161, 162; walk along the foreshore of, 162–165; battlements of, 165; rising in 1885..166; dinner-parties at, 168; a walk through, 169–172; ponies of, 176; native guilds in, 201–203; cabs of, 203; division of, 203–204; the crematoria of, 204; suburban residence near, 204–206; a dinner cooked in European style at, 210, 211; farewell to, 214–217; barometrical readings at, 254, 255; opened to British trade, 281–286; voyage of s.s. *Lee-chuen* to, 287–300; address of welcome presented to Mr. Little by foreign residents in, 301–302
Chung-king Transport Co., 38
Chung-ku lo, temple called, 103
Chung-tan ho, river, 232, 233
Climate called Shui-tu (Water-earth), 33
Cloud-mist Mountain, 44–48
Clouded Sun City (Yun-yang hsien), 98–100

Club-feet question, the, 186, 206–209
Coalfields in China, 5, 6, 250, 263; near Chang-sho, 129; near Chung-king, belonging to the Tungs, 186–192, 196–198
Coal-baskets (to-tze), 190, 197, 198
Coal-dust, made into patent fuel, 68; at Kwei-chow, 90, 91
"Coal" Gorge, 131, 298
Cock's Head (cliff), 253
Confucius, the Sage Lao-tse a contemporary of, 160; the Chinese and, 173
Confucianism, 214
Cotton cultivation in China, 11
Cotton junk on the rocks, 56, 57
Crematoria of Chung-king, the, 204
Cross-beam rapid, 71
Customs, the, at Kwei-chow-fu 87, 88

DAVID, Père Amand, 155, 174, 259, 266
Despatch bearers, 112, 113, 130
Dinner-party, a Chinese, 142, 143; at Chung-king, 168; a dinner cooked in European style, 210, 211
"Dismount from your horse" rapid, 292
Dogs in China, 37, 38
Donald, Mr., 278
Double Dragon rapid, 229
Dragon Gate, lagoon of the, 299
"Dragon King," mouth of the, 232
Dragon King Cavern, 42–44
Dragon's Ford Bay, 273
Drought at Kwei-chow-fu, 90, 93

Drum and Bell Lodge (temple), 103
Dryanda Garden, 107
Ducks' feathers, vessel laden with, 216
Dust-storms, 38

EARTHENWARE factories at Yang tu chi, 116
Edwards, Dr., 211
Eight Genii Gorge, 296
England, trade with China, 3, 7–10, 13, 14; war with China in 1839, story of, 252
Entomology of Szechuan, 266
Exports, list of, from Chung-king in 1897..8, 9

"FAN back reach," 229
Fan Loch, 131
"Feng-hsiang" (Bellows Gorge), 81–83, 85, 89, 91, 292
Fêng-shui (or Geomancy) in China, 41, 61, 62, 71, 221, 238, 244; of Wan hsien, 104, 105; in Chung-king, 146–148, 151; of Chêng-tu, 277
Fêng-tu-Chêng, city of, 118–123, 239–241
Ferns, 263
Fire Smoke Rock, 75
Fire-wind rapid, 232
Fish in Szechuan, 267
Fishing in China, 21, 73; with otters, at Ichang, 39
Fish-mouth pool, 227
Five-Mountain Point, 113
Floods in China, 1870..63; Fêng-tu washed away, 122
Flora of Szechuan, 264–266
Flower-garden, a celebrated, near Chung-king, 204, 205

"Flowery Walls" (island), 110
Foochow, Kushan monastery in, 40
Foot-binding in China, 186, 206–209, and *n.*
"Foreign devil" term, unknown in Szechuan, 79
Forest trees in Szechuan, 264–266
"Four Streams" (Szechuan), 31
French Catholic establishment, Chung-king, 154–156
Fu-chow, city of, 33, 125, 126, 232–235, 240; temples at, 127
Fuh t'an (rapid), 108
Fukien province, population of, 12
Furnace Gate Gorge, 240
Fu-tu Kwan, 178

GANHUI province, population of, 12
Gardner, Mr. Christopher (Consul), 68, 246
Get-down-from-horse Rapid, 81
Glorious Rapid. *See* Yun-yang
God, various names for, 155, 156
Gold-washing in the Upper Yang-tse, 102
Gong Gorge, 224, 225, 298
"Goose-tail" rock, 83
Gordon, General, and the Tai-ping rebellion, 3
Gorge of the Eight Cliffs, 101, 102
Gorge of the Military Code, 61, 64, 290
Gorge of the River Temple, 60
Granite valley, near Nan-To, 55
"Grave-levelling law," the celebrated, 145
Gray, Mr., 278
Great River. *See* Yang-tse kiang
Guilds in China, 202, 203
Guppy, Dr., of H.M.S. *Hornet*, 255, 256

Index

HALL, Captain, of the *Nemesis*, 252
Hankow, city of, 18, 24, 25, 243-247; cotton mills in, 10; the "bund" at, 16, 17; price of salt in, 234
Han River, 18, 244, 255, 256
"Han-shui mei" (salt-water girls), 207
Hanyang, city of, 18, 19, 244
Hart, Sir Robert, 278
Hêng-liang-tse (rapid), 67, 71, 292
Henry, Dr., 51
Herring Mountain, 232
Hing lung t'an (Glorious Rapid), 294, 295
Ho, Admiral ("Vade mecum to Szechuan"), 234, 245, 246
"Hoa Hoa Chen" (Flowery Walls), 110
Hoa Hoa Lo, tower named, 245
"Hoang mao" hsia (Yellow Cat Gorge), 53
Ho-chow, city of, 140
Holland, Mr., 287
Honan province, population of, 12
Hong-kong, British imports to, 4, 8
Hongs (buildings) at Chung-king, 136
Hosie, Mr., 139
Hospitality, Chinese, 45, 46
Hotel bill at Chiu lèng po (pass), 49
"Ho yen shih" (Fire Smoke Rock), 75
"Hsia-ma tan" (rapid), 80, 81
Hsing-hsi-tang, Mr., 139
Hsin t'an (New Rapid), 294, 295
Huc, Abbé, 244
Hukwang plain, the, 227
Hunan province, population of, 12; timber from, 19
Hung sha chi (Red Sand Point), 103
Hung shiu chuen (fanatical leader), 76, 213; conversion of, 2
Hu-peh province, 256; population of, 12; lagoons, 21; plain of, 32; boundary of, 74; village of Nan Mu yu'rh in, 75, 76
"Hu-shu-tse" (rapid), 82
Hu-ya hsia (Tiger Teeth Gorge), 34, 35
Hwang ling Miao, 242, 243
"Hwang piao tsz'," (yellow paper), 105
Hwang Sheng Kang, rocky point called, 20
Hwang-ue ling (Herring Mountain), 232
Hwui-chow foo, 235

ICHANG, city of, 4, 5, 33, 36, 40, 49, 261; the approach to, 34, 35; foreign community of, 37, 38; trade of, 38; otter fisheries at, 39; temple near, 40, 41; rocks off, 48
Ichang Gorge, 44, 51, 53, 54, 243, 260, 288; quarries near, 53
Imperial Maritime Customs, 9, 10
Imports, British, to China, 3, 4, 7-10
Iron Coffin Gorge, 75
"Iron Threshold" (rapid), 117
I-tu, district city of, 33

JOSSES, near the city of Wan, 102
Junks from Szechuan on Yang-tse River, 52, 63, 94, 95, 106, 111, 112, 222-224; wreck of, 115,

Index

116; mooring-ground for, 227, 228; increase of traffic on Yang-tse, 247

KAIPING Coal Mining Co., 6
Kansu province, population of, 11; boats from, 198
Kao-chia chen, town of, 118
Kao-tsao, aquatic plant, 21
Kia-ling Ho (Small River), 133, 171, 181, 215, 217
Kiangnan, "Great Lake" of, 258
Kiang peh Ting, city of, 171, 215, 217, and *n*.
Kiangsi Guildhall, 153
Kiangsi province, 253; population of, 12; missions of, 174
Kiangsu province, population of, 12
Kiangtung, s.s., 243
King-Chow, city of, 27, 31
King ho kou, village called, 27
King River. *See* Yang-tse kiang
Kin-sha River, 261
Kitten Rapid, 81, 292
Kiukiang, 16
"Ko tao shan" (Mount of the Taoist Ko), 243
Kublai Khan, 145
Kuling, stern-wheeler, 285
Kung, Prince, 214
Kung lung Rapid, 126, 289
Kung t'an Hŏ, River, 126, 127
Kushan monastery in Foochow, 40
Kwangsi province, population of, 12
Kwangtung province, population of, 12
Kw..n-yin hsia (Gorge), 197
Kwei chow-fu city, 65, 68, 83,
84, 290, 291, 293; manufacture of salt at, 85; the Customs at, 87-89; revenue of, 88; drought at, 90, 91; streets and harbour of, 91-93; singing girls at, 93, 94; ponies of, 176, 177, 196, 197, 200
Kwei-chow province, 159; population of, 12
Kwei-fu, 112.. *See* Kwei-chow-fu
Kwei-hwan. *See* Kwei-chow-fu
Kwei-kwan barrier, 4, 237
Kwei-yang-Fu, city, 159

"LADDER of Mêng-liang" (Cliff), 84, 85
"Lamp-shine" Gorge, 53
"Lao-chün Tung" (Cave of the Sage Lao-tse), 159-161
Lao-lung-Tung (Cavern), 81
Lao-ma (Old Horse Rapid), 96.
Lao-tse the Sage, 159, 160
Leechuen, s.s., voyage of, to Chung-king, 277, 287-300
Letters' Water River, 140
"Liang-toh," channel called, 219, 220
"Li chêng yuen" (Garden of undeflected gain), 233, 234
Life-boats on the Yang-tse, 82, 243, 245, 246, 288, 291
Li Hung Chang, 281, 284, 285, 287
Likin office at Kwei-chow-fu, 87
Likin stations. *See* Tax stations
"Likwei Tan" (rapid), 82
Limestone mountains, 263
Limestone quarries, near Ichang, 53
Li-min fu, walled city of, 133
Lin chia kou, farmstead of, 192, 193

Lin-chiang, river of, 197
Lin-sze, village of, 128
Li-tu, town of, 127
Loch of the Tang Family, 132
Lo-chi, village of, 131; mat-making at, 229
London Mission at Chung-king, 172
"Longevity" city, 129, 229
Lu-chow, salt guild of, 276
Lukan Gorge, 60
Lung ching Wan, rapid at, 273
Lung-ma-chi, stream called, 61
Lung-mên Hao, 171
Lung Wang Tung (Dragon King Cavern), 42-44
Lu-tsz' T'o, expanse of the, 131
Lu-tze To, village of, 132

MACDONALD, Sir Claude, xii., 287
Mai-sze-yeh (Mr. Mai), 139
Manchus, the, in China, 208-210
Man-tze ("savages"), caves of the, 147, 198
Margary, murder of, in Yünnan, 4, 138
Maritime Customs of China, 9, 10
Matung Chi, 34
Mat industry at Lochi, 131, 229
Matting from Chang-sho, 129
"Mêng-liang ti" (Ladder of Mêng-liang), 84, 85
"Men Pai" (Door Shields), 109
Mesney, General, on snake and tortoise friendship, 148, 149
Messengers, official, 130
Miao chi-tse (Temple Stairs Rapid), 97, 293
Miao-Ho, village of, 60
Miao-tse saddle, 176
Mien-hoa pu, village of, 154
Min River, 261

Mineral baths near Warm Spring Gorge, 197
Mineral wealth of Szechuan, 268
Missions and missionaries in Chung-king, 154-156, 158, 172-174
Monsoons, 207
Mooring-ground for junks, 227, 228
Morra, game of, 142
Mount Omi, 262
Mount of the Taoist Ko, 243
Mu-chu tan (rapid), 75
Mutung, reach of, 229
Myers, Mr., 278
"Myriad" city (Wan hsien), 103

NANKING, 258; burning of, 214
Nan Mu yu'rh, village of, 75, 76
Nan-To, place called, 54
Narrow Barrier, place named, 83
Neumann, Mr., 29
"Ngai-teh Tang" (Hall of the Lovers of Virtue), 170
Ngan-hui, province of, 253
Nganking, city of, 16
Ning Kiang Hui-kwan (Kiangsi Guildhall), 153
"Niu-Kan ma-fei hsia" (Ox-liver, Horse-lungs Gorge), 59, 60, 123, 260, 289
Niu-kou-tan (Oxhead rapid), 67, 70, 292

OFFICIAL convoys in China, 112, 113, 130
Old Dragon Cave, 81
Old Horse Rapid, 96
Old Lady of Shen, boat named, 135
Omi, Mount, 262

Opera company from Wan hsien, 116
Opium cultivation in Western provinces, 193
Opium smoking, 74, 194, 195, 212
Opossum Point, 34
Ornithology of Szechuan, 266
Otter fisheries at Ichang, 39
Otter's Cave rapid, 56, 289
Oxhead rapid, 67, 70, 292
Ox-liver, Horse-lungs Gorge, 59, 60, 123, 260, 289

PA-CHOW, city of, 140; island of, 32
Pagodas; at Shasze, 27, 28; at Fu-chow, 125; in Eastern China, 71, 72; near the city of Wan, 103
Pai ai Shan (White Cliff Mountains), 41, 42
"Pai-Chien" (rocky ledge), 124
"Pai-Fang" (triumphal arches), 102, 128, 141
Pai-ti Chêng, old city of, 86
Pa ngai hsia (Gorge of the Eight Cliffs), 101, 102
Pao-Chao, General, 59
Pao-ning-fu, city of, 140; burned, 277
Pastimes of the Chinese, 157
Patung, district city of, 71, 72, 291
Peh-hsiang Kai, street in Chungking, 175
Pei-lo (back-baskets), 236
Pei-shih, village of, 76
Pei tsz, baskets called, 119
Photographer, a, in Chung-king, 211, 212
Pien Hō, channel called, 24
Pierced Mountain Gorge, 58, 59

Pillar of Heaven (limestone pinnacle), 54
"P'ing-fen" (grave-levelling law), 145
Ping-shan, 242
"Ping-shu Pao-chien" hsia (Gorge of the Military Code), 61, 62, 64, 290
Pliny, account of China, 250-252
Polo, Marco, on the "Great River Kian," 258
Ponies, Kwei-chow, 176-178, 196, 197, 200
Popoff, Mr., estimate of the population of China, 11, 12
Poppy cultivation in Szechuan, 118, 124, 193; at Wan hsien, 104
Population of China, 11, 12
Porpoises, 34
Post couriers, 159
Poyang Lake, 257
Proclamation re the Earth-pulse, 150-152
Pure Stream temple, 60
P'u-tan, place called, 20

RAILROAD from Shanghai to Woosung, 248, 249
Railway construction in China, 6, 7, 248
Red Sand Point, 103
Reeds in the Yang-tse River, 21, 22
Religion of China, 145. *See also* Fêng-shui
Richthofen; on Szechuan coalfields, 192, 250; and the red basin of Szechuan, 261
Roberts, Mr. P., 76
Roman Catholic missionaries in Chung-king, 165, 166, 172

Sai Feng tu, hamlet of, 232
Salt, from Szechuan, 10; at Ta-ling city, 79
Salt-boilers at Kwei-chow, 85
Salt depôts at Fu-chow, 234, 235
Salt junks of Szechuan, 217, 218, 222; stranded, 230
Sampans of the Upper Yang-tse, 237
Sam-shu (distilled spirit), 157
Sandstones of Szechuan, 268
San kiang tsao (Race of the three rivers), 229
San yeu tung, glen named, 48
Scholar's rapid, 232
Scinyang, district of, 273
"Scissors" Gorge, 129, 232, 297
Seaweed, imported from the Japan Islands, 235
Séng Ho. *See* Yang-tse River
Shanghai, 15, 24, 25; trade of, 4; price of salt in, 234; railroad from, to Woosung, 248, 249; waterworks at, 249
"Shan-hu Pa" (Coral Strand), 163
"Shan-pei To" (Fan Loch), 131, 229
Shansi Banks, 161, 162
Shansi Guildhall, 201-203
Shansi province, population of, 11; wildfowl in, 22; droughts in, 269
Shansi merchant, autobiography of a, 23
Shantung province, population of, 11
Sha-ping Pa, mansion of, 179-181
Shasze, port of, 18, 23-29, 254; the most important mart in China, 24, 25; embankment in, 26, 28; pagoda at, 27, 28; riot at, in 1898, 29
Sheng-chi Chang, market town of, 123
Shen Potse, boat called, 29-31, 215
Shensi province, population of, 11
Shih chia-lung, coal depôt of, 189, 192, 196
Shih chia te (reach), 232
Shih ma ho (stone horse temple), 199
Shih-ma Tsao (Stone-Horse Crib), 178
Shih men (stone gate), 199
Shih Pao chai, rock called, 109, 110
Shih Tao Tse (Stone Headland), place called, 32
Shin-tan pilots, 66
Shin-tan rapid, 68, 69, 290
Shin T'an, village of, 61, 63
Shu, graduate named, 72
"Shui fu san wan," josses called, 102
Shui-tu (Water-earth), climate named, 33
Siao Hŏ (Lesser River), 91, 140, 171, 181, 183, 204, 215; valley of the, 79, 149
Siao-ho-kou, 19
"Siao mao-rh" (Kitten rapid), 81
Sikawei, near Shanghai, 254
Silk cultivation in Western China, 11, 180
Silkworm Back Rapid, 241
Simonoseki, Treaty of, 286
Singing girls at Kwei-chow-fu, 93, 94

Smoke-towers, 59
Snake and tortoise friendship, 244; General Mesney on, 148, 149
Soap-trees, 265
Sow Rapid, 75
Spence, Mr. Donald, 40, 78, 139
Split Hill (cliff), 253
Spring Island, 32
Steam communication on the Yang-tse River, 5
Stone family pool, 232
"Stone Precious Castle" (rock), 109
Stone quarry, Mr. Tung's, 146, 147, 150-152
Streets in Chinese cities, 25
Su-chow, city of, 25, 261
Suilin, city of, 140
Szechuan, province of, 4; coal-mines in, 5, 6, 186-192; trade of, xi., 8, 9; population of, 12; river of, 27; boatmen from, 31; junks from, on Yang-tse River, 52; boundary of, 74; area of, 134, 135; rebellions in, 77; term "foreign devil" unknown in, 79; climate of, 138; junks of, built at Wan hsien, 106, 111, 112; scenery of, 108; caves in sandstone cliffs of, 147; tobacco of, 195; rivers of, 197, 199; depopulated by Chang-Hsien-chung, 199; native guilds in, 202; salt wells of, 10, 234, 235; the red basin of, 261; flora and fauna of, 264-266; fish in, 267; area of, 268; mineral wealth of, 268; famine in, 273

"TA-CHANG," mishap known as, 101, 102

Ta chi kou, village of, 82
"Ta Fo Sze" (Great Buddha's Hall, 133
Tai-Hu (Great Lake), 258
Tai-ping ho (River of Peace), 31
Tai-ping Rebellion, the, 2, 3, 75, 76, 180
Tai-Wo, steamer, 15
Ta-Kiang (Great River). *See* Yang-tse kiang.
Ta-ling, city of, 79
Tan chia t'o (Loch of the Tang Family), 132
Taoist monastery, on the top of Yun wu Shan, 47, 48
Taoist religion, 160
Taoist show, a, 206
Taoist temple, of Miao-Ho, 60; at Pei-shih, 76
"Ta-Tung" (Otter's Cave Rapid), 56
Tax stations in China, 4, 12, 13
Taylor Mission, the, in China, 213
Tea-house, Chinese, 62, 63
Temples, near Ichang, 40-44; of Literature (Wen-feng shan), 80; at Kwei-chow, 86; of the Eastern Ocean, 98; in Clouded Sun City, 99; called Chung-ku lo, 103; at Fêng-tu, 119, 120; at Fu-chow, 127; at Chang-sho, 129; called "Ta Fo Sze," 133; round Chung-king, 159-161, 183, 184
Temple Stairs Rapid, 97, 293
"Teng ying tse" hsia (Gorge of the Lamp-shine), 53
Three kingdoms, wars of the, 83, 84
T'ich Kwan tsai hsia (Iron Coffin Gorge), 75
T'ich men ka'rh (rapid), 117

Index   313

"Tien tze Shan" (Mountain of the Son of Heaven), 118–123
Tiger's Beard (rapid), 82
Tiger Teeth Gorge, 34, 35
Ting, Mr., walk through Chungking with, 169–175
Ti-shan Tang, benevolent institution at Chung-king, 169, 170
Tobacco in Szechuan, 195, 267, 268
"Tortoise Gate" (narrows), 232
Tortoises, friendship with snakes, 148, 149, 244
"T'o tu tze" (rapid), 82
Tower called Hoa Hoa Lo, 245
Towing-path at Chung-chow, 113
Tow-lines, made of bamboo, 115
Trackers on the Upper Yang-tse, 57, 94, 95, 110–112, 115
Trade in China, 3, 4, 7–10, 13, 14
Tranquil rock, 232
Transit passes, 87
Tsan pei tan (Silkworm Back Rapid), 241
Tsao mèn hsia (Furnace Gate Gorge), 240
"Tsei ka tse" (Narrow Barrier), 83
Tseng, Marquis, 248
Tseng Kwo-Fan, 248
Tsz' shui Ho (river), 140
Tung, Mr., residence of, 178–181; coal-mine belonging to, 186–192
Tung, official of Chung-king, 199
T'ung oil manufacture, 104, 115, 124, 189, 265
T'ung-Ling rapid, 59
"T'ung ling hsia" (Pierced Mountain Gorge), 55, 58, 59

Tung-Loa-yeh (Mr. Tung), 139; visit to country seat of, 140–152
"Tung-lo hsia" (Brass Gong Gorge), 132, 224, 225
Tung-ting Lake, 27, 32, 233, 254
Tung tsz' yu'rh (Dryanda Garden), 107
Tung yang tse' (cataract), 97, 294
"Twisted stern" junks, 233
Tyler, Mr., 278, 279

VARNISH-TREE, 58, 104, 115. *See also* T'ung
Vinçot, Père, 154

WADE, Sir Thomas, 248, 281, 284
"Wai pi-ku'rh," boats called, 126, 127, 236
Walsham, Sir John, 5, 285
Wang, Mr., 170, 171
Wang-chia tan, rapid of, 230
Wang sze Ta Jen (Wang, the Fourth Excellency) of Kweichow-fu, 92
Wan Hien, 296
Wan hsien (city), 102–106, 112 vale of, 105
Wang sho kung (Temple of Longevity), 99, 100
Warm Spring Gorge, 197, 229
Water-trackers, 57, 58. *See also* Trackers
Well, a dry, at Fêng-tu, 121
Wen-feng shan (Temple of Literature), 80
Wên Fo Shan, peak called, 43

Wen-tang hsia (Warmpool Gorge), 197, 229
Western China, British imports into, 7; exports from, 8-10; silk cultivation in, 11; population of, 12
Wheat plantations, 33
Wheeler, Dr., 139, 140
White Cliff Mountains, near Ichang, 41, 42
White Elephant Street, Chungking, 175
Wildfowl, the Chinese and, 22
Wild-goose Gate Barrier (city), 22
Wild Mule Gorge, 227, 298; rapid, 132
Witches' Mountain Great Gorge, 72, 73, 78
Woosung, railroad to Shanghai from, 248, 249
Wuchang, city of, 18, 244; hill in, 248
Wu-ling chi (point called), 108, 113
"Wupans" (sampans), 237, 238
Wu-sankwei, rebellion suppressed by, 77, 208
Wu-shan, city of, 73, 78, 80, 81, 292
Wu-shan Gorge, 80, 292
Wu-shan-ta-hsia (Witches' Mountain Great Gorge), 72, 73, 78

"YA-MEN runners," 130
Yang-tse River, the only road of intercommunication between the east and west of China, ix., x., 4; steamers on, 15, 16; an affluent of, 19; rests on banks of, 21, 22; different names of the, 27, 253; entry into the upper region of, 32, 33; width of, above Ichang, 51, 52; summer rise of, 53; stretch of, known as "Yao-tsa ho," 55; trackers on the, 57, 58, 94, 95, 110–112, 115; at Wu-shan, 80; gold-washing in the Upper, 102; known as the Chuan Ho and the Sêng Ho, 132; affluent of, known as the Siao Hŏ, 140; ferries across, at Chung-king, 159, 166; course of, between Ichang and Chung-king, 225; Blakiston and the *voyageurs* of the, 231; life-boats on the, 243, 245, 246; increase of junk traffic on, 247; volume of water, 255, 256; sediment in, 256, 257; Marco Polo on the, 258; sources of the, 259; fish in the, 267; first ascent of the Upper, by s.s. *Leechuen*, 287–300
Yang-tse valley, physiography of the, 253–271
Yang tu chi, village of, 116
"Yao-tsa-ho," stretch of the Yang-tse River, known as, 55, 261, 289
"Yeh-lo tze" (Wild Mule Rapid), 132, 227, 298
Yeh-tan rapid, 66, 69, 70, 291
"Yellow cat" Gorge, 53
Yellow River, the, 269
Yen men Kwan (city), wildfowl in, 22
"Yen-tun" (smoke-towers), 59
Yen-wei shih (rock), 83
"Yin" (Dead), temple dedicated to Emperor of the, 119, 120
Y-ling, twin screw boat, 36

"Yo sha Chi" (rapid), 82
Yule, Colonel, 258
Yü Mantse (anti-missionary rebel), 217 n.
Yung-tse, town called, 32
Yünnan province, population of, 12

Yun wu Shan (Cloud-mist Mountain), 44–48
Yun-yang hsien (city), 98–100, 294; rapid at, 246 n., 272–282, 294, 295; iron of, 108
Yung Yang Tse (Temple of the Eastern Ocean), 98

LONDON:
PRINTED BY WILLIAM CLOWES AND SONS, LIMITED,
STAMFORD STREET AND CHARING CROSS.

www.ingramcontent.com/pod-product-compliance
Lightning Source LLC
Chambersburg PA
CBHW020105020526
44112CB00033B/924